Westside

Disappearance at Devil's Rock

Center Point
Large Print

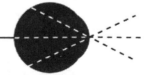

**This Large Print Book carries the
Seal of Approval of N.A.V.H.**

Disappearance at Devil's Rock

Paul Tremblay

CENTER POINT LARGE PRINT
THORNDIKE, MAINE

This Center Point Large Print edition is published
in the year 2017 by arrangement with William Morrow,
an imprint of HarperCollins Publishers.

Art on page 239 by Nick "The Hat" Gucker.

The text of this Large Print edition is unabridged.
In other aspects, this book may vary
from the original edition.
Printed in the United States of America
on permanent paper.
Set in 16-point Times New Roman type.

ISBN: 978-1-68324-235-2

Library of Congress Cataloging-in-Publication Data

Names: Tremblay, Paul, author.
Title: Disappearance at Devil's Rock / Paul Tremblay.
Description: Center Point Large Print edition. | Thorndike, Maine :
Center Point Large Print, 2017.
Identifiers: LCCN 2016044979 | ISBN 9781683242352
    (hardcover : alk. paper)
Subjects: LCSH: Large type books. | Psychological fiction.
Classification: LCC PS3620.R445 D57 2017 | DDC 813/.6—dc23
LC record available at https://lccn.loc.gov/2016044979

for Cole, Emma, and Lisa;
the ones who keep me found

Yet at no point is the work of the seer associated with the diabolical . . . She is the mouthpiece of God.

—GERALD MESSADIÉ,
  A History of the Devil

You will feel the way I do.
You'll hurt the way I do.
He's easily abused.
The devil in his youth.

—PROTOMARTYR,
  "The Devil in His Youth"

Elizabeth and the Call

Elizabeth is not dreaming. There's a ringing sound coming from far away, from elsewhere in the house, not the ringing of actual bells but the digital trill of the landline phone. The phone is cordless, cheap, neglected, often left uncharged and to be found, more times than not, wedged beneath the couch cushions alongside pistachio shells, pens, and hair elastics. Elizabeth actively despises the landline's inefficiency in regard to their everyday lives. The only calls the phone receives are credit card offers, scam vacation prizes, charities and fringe political groups looking for money, and the occasional mass recorded message from the town of Ames broadcasting the closing of school during snowstorms.

When the kids were little, Elizabeth wanted to keep the landline so that they'd be able to dial 911 should "anything bad happen." That was the phrase she used with her moon-eyed munchkins as she flailed at describing the nebulous and exciting emergency protocol of the Sanderson household. Fast-forward past those early years, which were harder than she would ever admit, and all three Sandersons have smartphones. There's really no need for the landline anymore. It survives because it is inexplicably cheaper for her to keep the phone bundled with her cable and Internet. It's maddening.

There's a ringing sound coming from far away, from elsewhere in the house, and not from the cell phone under her pillow. Elizabeth fell asleep waiting for the *Star Trek* phaser tone that announces a text from her thirteen-going-on-fourteen-year-old son Tommy. A simple text is a nonnegotiable part of the deal when sleeping over at someone else's house, even Josh's. She has already seen an evolution, or devolution, of communication from Tommy over the course of the summer reflected in his sleepover texts: In mid-June it was *I'm going to bed now mom,* which a few weeks later became *night mom,* then became *night,* and then *gn,* and if Tommy could've texted an irritated grunt (his subverbal communication method of the moment, particularly whenever Elizabeth or his eleven-going-on-twelve-year-old sister, Kate, asked him to do something), he would've. And now in mid-August, the exact date having changed to August 16 only a collection of minutes ago, there's no text at all.

One twenty-eight a.m. The landline stops ringing. The silence that replaces it is loaded with the dread of possibility. Elizabeth sits up and double- and triple-checks her cell phone, and there are no new texts. Tommy and his friend Luis are sleeping over at Josh's house. They've been on a sleepover rotation for a month now. Tommy, Josh, and Luis: the three amigos. She called them that earlier in the summer when the boys were over and watching all three movies of the Batman trilogy. Tommy groaned at her. Luis said, "Hey, is that a Mexican joke?" and Tommy's face turned redder than a stop sign while the rest of them laughed their asses off.

Elizabeth is out of bed. She is forty-two and has large, dark brown eyes that always look a little heavy with sleep, and straight, shoulder-length brown hair going gray on the sides. She wears thin shorts and a tank top, and the pale skin of her arms and legs is chilled now that she's out from under her blanket. The noisy air-conditioning ticks into life, swirling winds of cold, stale air. Kate must've sneakily turned the thermostat down below seventy degrees, which is totally ridiculous given she sleeps in a sweatshirt and covered with two comforters. You have to pick your battles.

No good news ever calls after midnight. Elizabeth knows this from personal experience. Instead of wading into the swelling sea of the blackest of what-ifs, she dares to think that maybe the call is a wrong number, or a prank, and Tommy just forgot to text her, and she'll yell at him tomorrow about his selfish forgetfulness. Getting mad is better than the alternative. There are other maybes, of course. There will be thousands more.

The phone rings again. Elizabeth rushes into the hallway and past the kids' rooms. Tommy's door is closed, sealed. Kate's is open halfway, and she's still asleep. The ringing phone doesn't wake her, doesn't even make her twitch.

Maybe Tommy's phone ran out of juice, lost its charge, and he's being a good boy, calling home on the landline to say goodnight. But if his phone died, then wouldn't he text her from Josh's or Luis's cell phone and not wake her so late with a call? She wonders if Tommy even remembers his own home phone number anymore. He's been so absent-minded and self-consumed in that new teen world he has just begun exploring, there's no telling what he's thinking anymore.

She's in the living room, hardwood floor cold and grainy under her feet. Kate was supposed to vacuum up the sand she and her friend Sam tracked all over the house after they'd come home from the pond. Elizabeth finally reaches the end table and extends a hand out to the phone. Its small display screen glows a sickly green. Caller ID reads *Griffin, Harold*. It's a call from Josh's house. So it's not the hospital or the police or—

Elizabeth says, quickly, "Yes, hi, hello?"

"Ms. Sanderson? Hi. This is Josh." Having read Josh's father's name on the display screen, Elizabeth was expecting Harry's cheerful baritone. It's like the phone itself is breaking a promise. She wasn't expecting Josh and the way his voice sounds: so light, careful.

"What is it, Josh? What's wrong?"

"Is, um, is Tommy there? Did he go back home?"

"What do you mean? Why isn't he with you?" Elizabeth hurries back into the hallway and to Tommy's room.

"I don't know, don't know where he went. We went out to Borderland tonight. Just to hang out. And he took off into the woods . . . Is he there? There with you? I was hoping maybe he went home . . ." Josh is talking fast now, reckless with words spilling over each other, overlapping.

"Josh, slow down. I can't understand you. I'm checking his room now." Elizabeth opens Tommy's door without knocking, which is something she hasn't done all summer, and she's thinking *Please be home please be home please be home* and clumsily slaps at the wall switch. She squints into the obnoxious light, and Tommy's bed is unmade and empty. "He's not in his room." Elizabeth quickly walks back out into the hallway, turning on lights wherever she goes, looking to see if Tommy is randomly somewhere else in the house, like a misplaced pair of sneakers. He's not in Kate's room. He's not in her room or the kitchen or the living room. She turns on the floodlights to the back porch, and there's no one there.

"No. No. He's not here."

"He's not? You sure?"

"He's not here, Josh." She's not quite yelling, but there's that same undercurrent of *You're a dumbass* Tommy's been using with his sister too often lately. Elizabeth runs downstairs into the musty basement, calls out to her son, but he's not there, either. Why would he be there, anyway? *Because.* He has to be somewhere.

"Oh, I'm sorry, Ms. Sanderson. Oh my God . . ." Josh says and then breathes heavily into the phone, sending sharp blasts of static. He's crying or working up to it. Elizabeth clings desperately to annoyance and anger at Tommy's clever, gregarious, best friend who has inexplicably morphed into a mewling child, a child who has stupidly lost her son.

She says, "Okay, wait. Quickly, tell me again. Let's figure this out. You were at Borderland? What were you doing?"

Josh spins through his quick and sloppy story of their hiking through the woods behind his backyard and into Borderland State Park, and then Tommy going off into the woods by himself and they haven't seen him since. Elizabeth hears Josh's parents talking in the background.

"When was the last time Tommy was with you?"

"More than an hour. Maybe two."

"Jesus Christ. And you're only calling me now?" Elizabeth is still walking around her one-level, ranch-style home, fighting the urge to open closets and cabinets, to look under the beds.

The landline is pressed against her cheek, and she watches her cell phone screen for a text, for anything from Tommy.

"We tried to find him. I swear. And we called for him, waited, looked around, but he didn't come back and we didn't know what to do, so then we walked back thinking he doubled back on us, but he wasn't here and he's not answering his phone or anything."

"Did you try calling anyone else? Where's your mom and dad?"

"Mom is right here." Josh is crying for real now. "She wanted me to call you. Hoping he was there. I'm sorry he's not there. Oh God, oh God—"

"Okay, shh. We can't panic. Listen. It'll be okay, Josh." She regrets saying that, even if it's only to placate Josh. She can't help but feel like she's jinxing her son by saying that out loud when clearly there is nothing okay about any of this.

She asks, "Did Luis try calling his parents?"

"No, not—"

"Tell him to call his parents. Then call Tommy's other friends, see if he went over to one of their houses." Elizabeth is not sure who those other friends would be, whose house he would go to instead of Josh's, Luis's, or home.

"I will, Ms. Sanderson."

There's a pause. Elizabeth needs to hang up but is afraid to. Once she does, then the rest of this, whatever this ends up being, will have to continue.

She says, "Call me back as soon as you find out anything."

"Okay."

"Tell your parents—never mind, I'll call back soon."

Elizabeth hangs up and drops the landline headset to the couch, and just like that, the call is over. The air conditioner clicks and whirs to life again. It's so loud, like a plane taking off. She's alone in the living room, shivering and cupping her glowing cell phone in her hands. She doesn't know what to do and thinks about waking up Kate to tell her what's happening even though she doesn't know what it is exactly that's happening. Elizabeth calls Tommy's cell phone, and it goes right to voice mail. Tommy's voice says, "Beep, beep-beep, beep, beeeep-beep-beep, beep, beep-a-dee-beep." Then a pause. Then he shouts a long and protracted "Beep!" And then the electronic beep sounds off and there's the hiss of you-are-now-being-recorded silence, and she hesitates to leave a message, hesitates to say anything, because somehow she might say the wrong thing and make all this even more wrong than it already is.

She says, "Tommy, we don't know where you are and we're all worried, call me as soon as you get this. Love you, bye," then hangs up.

That's not enough. There has to be something else she can do to summon Tommy back home from wherever he is, short of running up and down the street screaming his name. There must be something she can do *before* she calls the police. Elizabeth feels that call-the-police clock ticking out on her already, even though Tommy's friends haven't called everyone else yet. Everything is already moving so fast and yet so slow at the same time.

First, she goes back to her text screen and the thread of messages she exchanged with Tommy. She resists the urge to scroll back and read and reread the old texts with the crazy hope that she'll find him there hidden within his messages from the very recent past.

Elizabeth is still shivering, and her hands are shaking and heavy; her texting fingers and thumbs the equivalent of a desperate, pleading voice.

She types: *Please call home. Please come home.* Send.

She covers her eyes and says to herself and the quiet house, "This can't be happening. Not again."

Then she calls the police.

Josh at Home and with the Boys at Split Rock

It's 2:35 a.m., and Ames police officers Ed Baker and Steve Barbara interview Josh and Luis in the Griffin home. Josh has never felt so childlike, as though the two rigidly uniformed men are representatives of the unknowable and indifferent adult universe that will soon engulf him. The officers are monolithic, even sitting as they are with the boys huddled around the granite-topped kitchen island. Josh is lost inside of his own head; the questions the officers ask and the answers he gives them don't lead to anywhere recognizable.

Both sets of the boys' parents are at the break-fast table a few feet away. They halfheartedly sip their coffees and avoid looking at each other or their sons. They listen quietly, stirring when the boys admit that they were drinking earlier, that they took beer out of Josh's dad's always-stocked fridge in the garage and out into the park with them. The parents shake their heads and adjust their sitting positions. Perhaps, under much different circumstances, one or more of the parents would try to play it cool, wink, and wistfully say, "Boys will be boys."

Josh's mom is the only one to speak after the beer revelation. She whispers "We're sorry" to Luis's parents. Josh hears Mom even as Officer Baker launches into follow-up questions asking if they used pot or other drugs (the answer is no, and Luis practically screams it). Mom's apology strikes Josh as such a weird thing to offer to Luis's parents, because Luis is right there in their kitchen and he's okay.

As the interview continues, the boys map out their route and destination on a large map of the state park. The officers do not offer any assurances or promises that Tommy will be found and that he will be okay. They want one of the boys and a parent to accompany them into the state park now, to show them the exact location of where they spent most of the night before Tommy disappeared. Luis volunteers. Josh is ashamed at how relieved he is. He doesn't want to go.

Luis and his father leave with the two police officers to go to the state park. Luis's mother follows them out of the house to drive home by herself and call his college-aged sisters. Luis forgets his DC shoes sweatshirt, leaving it hanging on the back of the barstool chair in which Josh is sitting.

It's now 3:35 a.m. Josh is alone in the house with his parents. Dad rearranges the suddenly empty chairs around the kitchen island.

Mom goes out to the floodlit back deck and

17

returns a few minutes later, just off the phone with Ms. Sanderson. No word on Tommy yet. She shuts the slider and locks it, then yanks hard on the handle to double-check that the slider is locked. She says, "Oh, maybe I should leave it unlocked. Just in case Tommy comes back here." She shrugs.

Then she tells Josh to go upstairs and get ready for bed. He doesn't argue. He needs her on his side. After they came home from the park to find Mom waiting for them on the back porch, Josh knew she could smell the beer on them because of the way she narrowed her eyes and abruptly leaned away as they tried to explain what they were doing and what happened. He only had a couple of sips (he dumped most of it out like he usually did when no one was looking), but the taste and smell is still there, trapped and stinging the back of his throat.

Josh goes upstairs, closes the bathroom door behind him, and locks it. Fighting the rising urge to vomit, he washes his face in cold water.

Dad stays in the kitchen. He washes dishes by hand that don't really need to be washed right this second, including a small collection of plastic superhero cups he and his friends drank water and soda from earlier. Josh can hear Dad talking to himself even with the bathroom door closed. He's really talking to Josh, or talking to the Josh from two hours ago. Josh nods along to his father's spiel while brushing his teeth: Yes, of course, Josh is supposed to be the responsible one, the level-headed one, the one who should know better, the one who was supposed to do the right thing, not the one to be sneaking out of his own house and drinking beer and then participating in whatever idiocy it was they were up to in the park, and now, now something has happened, likely something terrible, and they will never be able to change that or take it back.

Josh brushes his teeth for an extra long time, the mint starting to burn his gums and tongue, and waits for his father to stop talking.

Mom is already in Josh's bedroom. She yawns and wipes her eyes as he walks in. Mom is loving, loyal, and intensely serious and has become more so as Josh has gotten older. The lamp with the long, adjustable neck clipped to his headboard is on. In its spotlight, she looks pale and too skinny. Her thin lips are pressed together, hiding inside her mouth. Gray roots are starting to show at the top of her head at the point where her hair parts. The gray practically glows in stark contrast to her thick, straightened, jet-black hair. Josh usually points out when it's time for the dye job with his self-proclaimed comedian's wit and charm. He's been told more than once that he'll be a politician someday. It's supposed to be a compliment, even though all the adults he knows do nothing but bash politicians.

"Did you wash your face?" Mom won't meet his eyes. She talks down to the pillows. "You need to shower first thing tomorrow."

Josh says, "Yes. Okay, I will, Mom." He changes into a clean T-shirt and shorts, turning away from Mom as he does so, embarrassed by the baby fat that softens his chest and stomach. He shimmies past her and climbs into bed. The wooden frame creaks as he adjusts his position, turning away, lying on his side, facing the wall. He's exhausted from trying to read silent adult faces and keep eye contact. "You'll wake me if anyone calls about Tommy, right?"

"Yes. Of course. Try to get some sleep."

Her saying that and the way she says it, to his back or into his back, threatens to make him cry again. He says, "Can you stay in here with me for a little while?"

"Just a little while." She rubs his back. Her hand is light but distracted.

There's no way he's going to fall asleep. He's never felt more awake in his life. He'll pretend he's asleep eventually.

Mom turns off the lamp and continues rubbing his back. Black clouds form and dance in his vision as he stares at the wall a foot or so from his face. She says, "Oh, Josh, what happened out there?"

"I don't know, Mom. I really don't." He blinks hard, balls the blanket up next to his mouth. Josh has been friends with Tommy since the summer before first grade. They met at the Ash Street playground, the one with a play area covered in wood chips that found a way to worm inside your sneakers. Josh's mom and the other moms whispered about a boy shyly going about the serious business of climbing the play structure shaped like a pirate ship. He still remembers how carefully the boy turned the pirate wheel and swept errant wood chips off the captain's deck with his feet. The moms called this boy the *Boy Without a Father,* and Josh wanted to know his story, wanted to know how that could possibly happen, because everyone had a mom and dad, right? Mom said she didn't know how that had happened, but it sure was sad. She encouraged Josh to go play with the *Boy Without a Father* because he really needed a good friend, a good friend like Josh.

Josh doesn't dare imagine where the *Boy Without a Father* is now.

Mom says, matter-of-factly, that if no one hears from or finds Tommy by early morning they'll all help search the park.

Josh doesn't want to go back to the park ever again. He wants to close his eyes and make everything like it was earlier in the summer.

It was late June. The day after the day after their last day of seventh grade. Josh and Luis rode their bikes up and down the Griffins' long driveway, jousting with Josh's replica sword and pickax from the video game Minecraft as they passed each other. That got boring fast, and it was too hot to shoot hoops. They sat on a shady patch of grass that outlined the driveway and checked for messages in Snapchat and Instagram.

Tommy pulled into Josh's driveway riding his black, dinged up mountain bike one-handed. He kept the bike seat as low as it would go, so his knees practically knocked into his chin as he pedaled. Tufts of dark brown hair stuck out of the ear holes of his helmet, and his bangs hung over his eyes. Tommy hopped off the bike without stopping and stuck the landing between Luis and Josh with a gangly, on-the-verge-of-disaster-at-all-times athleticism that only he seemed to possess. He put his long, skinny arms around their shoulders and said, "What's up?" His bike continued on a wobbly ghost ride and crashed into the front bushes.

Josh said, "My mom will stab you in the eye if she saw that." He was half-joking, and he checked to see if Mom was watching them through the bay window.

Luis: "Stabby stab stab!"

Tommy said, "Catchphrase," and tried to twist Luis's arm into a chicken wing, which then became a wrestling match on the front lawn.

Tommy was taller, stronger, more physically mature. Of the three boys, he was the only one with a dusting of teen acne and a voice that had fully dropped into a voice-crack-free lower register. Luis was hunger-strike thin, the shortest kid in their grade, and so he still looked and, with his high-pitched voice, sounded like a fifth grader. The usual jokes and taunts from the boys at Ames Middle School were a daily trial, and he was instantly labeled "adorable" by the older girls, and the meaner of that crew would pinch his cheeks and muss up his black hair as though they were patting a puppy.

Outsized as he was by Tommy, Luis was tenacious and didn't quit, didn't ever quit. He weaved himself between Tommy's legs and timbered him to the ground.

Tommy laughed and shouted, "Bruh! Bruh! Get off! You're twisting my knee!" Tommy's "bruh" was an affected accent on *bro*.

Luis shouted, "Get some!" stood up, and thumped his robin-sized chest with both hands.

Tommy groaned and complained about the pain as he overexaggerated a ruinous limp toward his bike, its front tire stuck in the bushes like the sword in the stone.

Josh pulled out a map of Borderland State Park from his back pocket. He said, "Yo, shit-stains, I got the map."

Luis and Tommy started singing the "I'm the map" song from *Dora the Explorer*. Josh pointed to a dark green blob labeled Split Rock and told them that was where they were going to hang out. On the way they would use previously unexplored trails, which was a bonus because they wouldn't be as crowded as the main walkways.

Luis said that Split Rock was too far away, and one of the trails they'd have to take was called Granite Hills Trail, which meant it was superrocky, which meant they'd have to walk their bikes half the time, which would take forever and result in general suckage and ass-pain for all involved. Tommy and Josh ignored his protests. Luis was a contrarian if a proposed activity or idea wasn't his originally, and he'd complain long and loud to be on record as having complained. To Luis's credit, he was never a told-you-so guy and he wouldn't revisit his earlier objections even if he did turn out to be on the right side of history. Not to his credit: After the fact, Luis often enthusiastically co-opted the ideas he'd initially rejected.

Josh grabbed his blue backpack full of Gatorades and granola bars from the base of the basketball stanchion. The boys walked their bikes through Josh's backyard and into the thick woods abutting the Griffin property. Last summer the boys had worked hard cutting a skinny path through the brush that led into the southwest section of Borderland State Park and to its Western Trail. Normally, they'd follow the Western Trail back toward the main entrance and ride to the Pond

Walk, which circled the Upper and Lower Leech Ponds, and from there take other well-worn paths designated as easier hiking or mountain bike trails. Today, they followed the Western Trail deeper into the northern, more rugged, and less traveled section of the park in search of Split Rock.

As the Western Trail gave way to the French Trail, Luis's prophecy was realized. The terrain became hilly and craggy, full of knotty, python-thick tree roots, jagged rocks, and boulders the size of small cars. They had to walk their bikes. They weren't good enough or strong enough riders, and with the exception of Josh's bike, they didn't have high-end mountain bikes built for such expert-level terrain. Tommy's bike was a beater his mom bought on Craigslist; only the rear brakes worked correctly. Luis's bike was a cheap knockoff from a generic sporting goods box store.

French Trail became the Northwest Trail, and the going was even rougher. Walking their bikes over minimountains was tiring, time consuming, and at times near impossible, and they had to carry their bikes over the steepest and rockiest sections. They briefly considered ditching their bikes and continuing on to Split Rock by foot, but they were afraid that even out here, deep in the middle of the woods, their bikes could still be messed with or stolen. As middle schoolers they lived in fear of being bullied and harassed by high schoolers who could be lurking around any bend in the trail.

They pressed onward. They had to backtrack on the Northwest Trail when they missed the not-very-well-marked right turn onto the lower loop of the Granite Hills Trail. Announcing that he was sweating his balls off and sick of walking his bike, Tommy tried riding for a stretch in the lowest gear he had, and he crashed almost instantly. His rear tire got pinched between two rocks, and he was tossed from his bike, skidding hands and knees first at the bottom of a small slope. He popped up quickly and said, "I'm good. No brain damage." He had a couple of raspberries on his knees. He wiped and checked his palms repeatedly as he breathed harshly through clenched teeth.

Luis laughed, said, "Dude. You okay?"

Tommy nodded as he walked his bike next to Josh. Josh could tell that Tommy was really hurting. His face was red and he blinked quickly like he did when he was trying not to cry.

Finally, they came upon the Split Rock trail sign. Two feet tall, planted in the middle of the path like a wayward garden gnome, the wooden sign was painted brown with carved, white lettering. A short walk later, they arrived at a wooden plank bridge that lay on top of a swampy patch, and it emptied them at the base of Split Rock.

Tommy: "This has got to be it, right?"

Josh said, "Yeah. This is it," and if his words lacked enthusiasm it wasn't because Split Rock was disappointing, but to acknowledge how hard their journey had been.

They sloughed off their helmets and dumped their bikes on the pine-needle-covered ground. Tommy set his bike loose on another ghost ride that ended as they usually did, with a metal-scraping and tire-spinning crash.

Split Rock was an impressive, glacial boulder; twenty feet tall, sixty feet at its widest. Calved neatly in half on its north side, there was a three-foot-wide crevasse through to the boulder's center. The boulder was a giant cake that had a thin piece cut out of it. The boys rushed inside the split and took turns taking pictures and videos of each other shouting, "Hardcore parkour!" and "American Ninja Warrior" while trying to spider-climb up to the top. Josh and Luis weren't strong enough, and they couldn't get leverage with one foot pressed flat against each wall, and they barely got a few feet off the ground before sliding back down. Tommy must've still been sore from his bike crash, because his legs started to shake, and he gave up climbing after getting maybe six feet up.

They walked around to the south side of Split Rock, where some of the boulder had collapsed and crumbled away. They quickly found a path over those broken and moss-covered rocks and scrambled to the top of the boulder, which was flat enough to walk around on without any worries of sliding or falling off. They were high above the forest floor, no doubt, but not up enough to see over the trees of the thick, surrounding woods.

Josh said, "Think anyone can hear us up here?" They hadn't passed any other bikers or hikers along the way.

"Don't know." Then Luis yelled, "Seven!"

Tommy said, "Catchphrase."

Luis: "All set. No one can hear us."

A thin crack in the rock led away from the big split to an eight-foot-tall tree that had somehow sprouted up through the middle of the boulder. It was dead now; sun-bleached gray, petrified, its surface stone-like in appearance. The trunk was sinewy, twisted, and pocked with knots and the stubby, sharpened bases of long-ago broken branches. The tree tapered and thinned to a spear-like point.

Tommy: "Whoa. Sick tree."

Josh: "Looks like a weird statue."

Tommy: "Like something out of the Nether." The Nether was the underworld or Hell of Minecraft, a shared-world video game the boys had been playing together, off and on, since fifth grade. Tommy wasn't the best player of the three but he watched the most YouTube Minecraft tutorials and Let's Play videos. Tommy had even set up and run his own white-listed (which meant private) server for the three of them to use.

They walked the perimeter edge of Split Rock, faked pushing each other off the impressive sheer drops to the jagged rocks below, reached out to the still-living trees that had grown around the contours of the boulder, and leaped back and forth over the split. Josh's stomach tightened every time he jumped over the crevasse and he felt that empty space opening up below him.

Josh hung his backpack on one of the weird tree's jagged branch stubs. He passed out the drinks and granola bars. His first sip was too greedy, and he spilled the red drink all over his white Ames Basketball shirt from two winters ago. When Josh had first played town ball as a fourth grader, he had been the quickest kid out there and easily made the town's travel team. Three years later he was cut. He was by no means fat, but he had gained weight in his middle and hadn't gotten much taller, not like Tommy had, and he certainly had not gotten any faster or any better at basketball. Too many other kids had passed him by athletically and skill-wise. Josh couldn't keep his dribble anymore and couldn't stop anyone else from scoring. Although he'd experienced plenty of other indignities as part of the daily horror of middle school, getting cut from the travel team was the most devastating.

Josh said, "Shit, shit, shit," and stood up, trying to keep the spilled red drink from dripping down onto his shorts and legs.

Luis: "You need a straw or a sippy cup?"

Tommy: "Chirps!"

Josh: "I'm gonna be all sticky. Bugs will be all over me now."

Tommy: "Just like Alyssa, right?" A smile flickered, aimed at his sneakers. It was so Tommy, typically unsure of himself, like he was testing out the put-down.

Josh said, doing his best Tommy-speak impersonation, "Whoa, chirps, bruh!"

Luis: "He wishes." He checked his phone. "Only one bar out here."

Josh: "No porn for you then."

Tommy: "Fap, fap, fap."

Luis: "I can still Snapchat your mom." He mimed taking a picture of his crotch.

Josh: "She wouldn't see anything."

Tommy downed his bottle and put the empty back in Josh's pack. He said, "This is it. This is the perfect spot, boys." He dragged out the *z* sound at the end of *boys*. "I'm claiming it. Could totally survive the zombie apocalypse right here."

Luis: "Too late. Josh was already attacked by the zombie tree."

Josh gargled and fell back against the dead tree.

Tommy: "Okay. Zombie contingency plans. Let's hear 'em."

Tommy and his zombies. Tommy freely admitted that he was a total scaredy-cat, refusing to watch zombie/horror movies and television shows or read the comics or play the gruesome video games. Still, all he wanted to talk about lately was zombies: how they could really happen and then how to survive the coming zombie apocalypse. He'd even made Josh and Luis read some blog articles and watch a video about some weird fungus in the South American jungle that takes over an ant's brain and how it could potentially spread to humans. In the spring, during a depressing discussion of environmental issues and overpopulation of humans and the challenge of feeding everyone on earth, their science teacher, Mrs. Ryan, had said that bugs would likely become our largest food source. Tommy— who usually didn't speak much in school, stayed hidden under his bangs—had stammered through a question: what would happen to someone if they ate a zombie ant infected with the brain fungus? He'd slunk deep into his chair after, embarrassed at the room full of giggles. Mrs. Ryan had said that while she didn't know much about that particular fungus, she was sure eating the ant wasn't a vector for the fungal infection, at least not in humans. Later that night, while online with Josh and doing battle with the sillier subspecies of Minecraft zombies (the zombie pigmen), he'd said Mrs. Ryan didn't really know

31

and he was still convinced that human zombies could happen via the ant brain fungus.

Luis: "Keep it simple. Fortify my house. Move all supplies up to the second floor and knock out the staircase. Then use a ladder and pull it up behind me when I was up on the second floor. Boom, zombie proof."

Tommy: "I like it, but what about emergency escape routes? And if you have to bolt, carrying supplies down a ladder would suck."

Luis: "Could chuck stuff out the window and jump down after them."

Tommy: "You're such a hardo." A hardo was someone who tried too hard to act tough or smart or cool. "No way, you jump and hurt your ankle and you might as well be a bucket of chum."

Luis: "Chum this."

Tommy: "I'd use Split Rock."

Luis: "You can't live on this rock."

Tommy: "No, but it could be, like, an extra holdout, or a—a safety station. Build a shelter or even set up a little tent here or something so you can come here in case your house or whatever gets overrun, or you need to hide from the non-infected for a few days."

Josh: "I'd be at the mall."

Luis: "Nah. No good. First place zombies go is the mall. Good for supplies, but you have to get in and get out, quick. See *Dawn of the Dead*." Luis, unlike Tommy and Josh, had watched every horror movie they'd ever heard of with his older sisters. "Tommy, you seen it yet?"

Tommy shakes his head no.

Luis groans. "Jesus, you're such a movie wuss. Just watch it. There's a zombie that looks totally like you in it. I mean, it's the seventies version of you. So weird. You have to see it. Even if you don't see the whole movie, YouTube that zombie."

Tommy: "YouTube search what? *Tommy zombie? Luis is a dick?*"

Luis: "That's a different movie."

Josh: "Hey. A school would be a good place to hide, fight off zombies. Lots of supplies there."

Tommy: "It's okay. But you can't stay there all the time. You keep a bunch of small bases, right? Spread out the supplies. Don't rely too much on one place. Living inside a fortress, that's a mistake. You need more than one place. I'd make this rock one of my bases. Definitely. It's up high like your stairless house, and you could hear and see the zombies coming from like a mile away."

Luis: "So where's your emergency escape route from the rock?"

Tommy: "Just slide down that tree over there like a fireman's pole. It's better than jumping out a window. And the rock would be easy to defend. We could lure them into the split, yeah? Stab them in the head with long spears."

Luis: "If there's a big herd, they'd fill up the split and they'd keep coming right up against the rock, crush into each other, and wash over this thing like a tsunami, man. Just like in *World War Z* and *Walking Dead*—"

Tommy: "That wouldn't happen in real life. They can't herd through these thick woods. It'd slow them down big-time."

Luis: "Yeah they can. They wouldn't have to stick to the trails, either. They'd stumble into the easiest way out here."

Tommy gingerly probed his scabbing leg wounds. "Nah. We're high enough that we'd see them coming, hear them coming, too. We'd be all right . . ."

Josh didn't like horror movies like Luis did, and he wasn't newly obsessed with zombies like Tommy. Those two had totally ignored his school suggestion for the apocalypse, and he felt dangerously out of their conversation loop. Which pair of the three friends was best friends and which one was the third wheel was always the unspoken fear, the unspoken competition. Tommy and Luis kept going back and forth, rapid-fire, like they'd rehearsed this zombie give-and-take without Josh. Maybe they had. Josh scrambled to stay relevant, to come up with something clever to add.

Josh said, "It'd be too cold out here at night."

Tommy: "We could keep a fire going—"

Luis: "Outdoor fire. Might as well ring a bell, send invitations to the zombie barbeque."

Josh: "Mmm. McRibs."

Luis laughed. Josh exhaled.

Tommy: "The cold would help, actually. Cold is good."

Luis: "Fuck that. Living out here in the cold would blow donkey balls."

Josh: "Zombie donkeys?"

Tommy: "I'm talking about the zombies. They'd totally freeze up. They're not alive. No body heat, right?"

Josh: "So you're saying they're what—like lizards? Cold-blooded? They need to sun themselves on rocks or something?"

Luis laughed again. "Zombies getting a tan. Hot."

Tommy: "Winter hits and it'd be zomb-cicles everywhere. Wait them out until everything freezes, then you could take them out so easy."

Luis frowned and furrowed like he was considering a great wisdom. "They didn't freeze up in *Dead Snow*—"

Josh: "What the fuck is *Dead Snow*?"

Luis: "Nazi zombie movie in—Finland. I think. I don't know. Some icy-ass country. The Nazi zombies didn't freeze and ran through the snow and everything. But they came back to life because of a shitty curse or something stupid."

Tommy: "No supernatural zombies. Those aren't like *real-life* zombies that can happen. Real-life zombies would freeze up."

Luis: "Yeah, maybe. Seems fucking stupid if

they all froze that easy and assholes like us could walk around cutting off their heads."

Josh: "We'd need a chisel or something if they were frozen."

Luis: "Whatever. You'd still probably have to survive at least a few warm months before the big freeze with the things herding around and eating the shit out of everyone."

Tommy: "I'm not afraid of the herd."

Josh: "Hardo!"

Luis: "You can't even watch Scooby Doo without getting nightmares."

Tommy shrugged and had a smaller version of his goofy I-got-nothing-to-say smile on his face, before it snuffed itself out. "I'd be all right, if it happened."

Luis: "Yeah, right. What about the one zombie that locks onto you. You afraid of that? It follows you wherever you go, never gives up because it picked you, likes your smell, thinks you're cute. Probably is someone you know, too—Zombie Josh. He'd follow you everywhere, but he'd be slower than shit—"

Josh: "Ha ha, go fuck yourself, shorty." He said it without malice. Normally Luis and Josh were the only ones who could comment on each other's physical limitations without either getting upset at the other, but Luis looked over at Josh quickly, as though trying to triangulate from where the lobbed stone came.

Tommy: "Bruh. Herd, rogue zombie; it don't matter." Tommy leaped over the split in the rock, triumphantly raised his arms up in the air, and shouted with mock authority and in his best stentorian voice, "It has been decided!"

Josh and Luis shrugged at him.

Tommy walked back over between them, pushed on the dead tree's trunk like he wanted to knock it over and see what was inside, and he said, "When it happens. I'm making my last stand here."

Elizabeth at the Park, at Home with Janice, Kate, and a Ghost

E ight a.m. Although Borderland State Park is officially closed to the public, the main entrance and the visitor's parking lot is overrun by SUVs, patrol cars (local and state police), and vans. Local news crews are staging their live feeds and reporter-on-the-scene shots.

Something like this doesn't happen in the affluent suburb of Ames, this happy little town twenty-five miles southwest of Boston, often listed in money and lifestyle magazines as one of the top places to live in the country. People certainly don't go missing within the boundaries of their beloved and well-kept state park. And given that Elizabeth Sanderson is a clerk for the town public works and is friendly, if not friends, with every last town employee, it's all hands on deck.

The police have taken over the Visitors Center, a one-level cabin, painted forest green, the tar shingles sun-bleached gray and spotted with lichen. Park rangers, Ames Police officers, and State Police pour in and out of the Center, which is situated on the edge of the main parking lot and the surrounding forest, and is adjacent to the beginning curl of the Pond Walk trail.

To the right of the Visitors Center and main parking lot is a large, open field that leads to the Eastman mansion—built in 1910, made of stone, three levels, twenty rooms, sitting like an ancient tortoise sunning itself on the green. Groups of search volunteers and park rangers are gathered there and begin to splinter and set off on foot with walking sticks, two-way radios, and park maps in tow.

Elizabeth remains at the mansion to wait for the detective. She paces behind a fold-up table, positioned at the foot of the front stairs, as though it were some invisible barrier. She fusses with the fliers and folders, and she has her cell phone clutched tightly in her left hand.

Detective Allison Murtagh makes the long walk from the Visitors Center down a dirt-and-gravel path to the mansion. The detective is in her late forties. Her graying, light brown hair is kept in a neat, straight bob cut. She's tall, angular, all arms and legs, and built like a scarecrow that's low on straw. Her skin is more Mediterranean than Irish, thanks to her mom. She wears a blue pantsuit, a single button above the waist.

Elizabeth knows Allison more than well enough to greet her by her first name. They've met and exchanged pleasantries on numerous occasions at

Town Hall, but it was this past spring when they had their longest conversation. They were at a graduation party of a mutual family friend. Allison talked about how hard it was deciding to move her father to a nursing home. Elizabeth discussed the rigors and challenges of being a single mom. They both talked about dealing with teens in general; Elizabeth as a mom of a new one, and Allison having dealt with teens her whole professional life. All the heavy, personal stuff eventually morphed into a casual conversation about town gossip and politics and then about nothing much at all. They both laughed and drank too-warm glasses of wine, and they made noises about getting together and hanging out later that summer, which never came to pass. That party seemed like it happened yesterday. Elizabeth wonders if Allison remembers meeting or seeing Tommy there.

Allison says, "Hello, Elizabeth," and she holds out her hand for the rigid formality of the handshake.

Elizabeth puts her hand inside of Allison's. Her fingers are cold and do not react to the handshake. "Hi, um, Allison. Or, sorry, Detective Murtagh?"

"No, please. Allison is fine."

They exchange weak and sad smiles.

Allison's dark blue pantsuit looks sticky and clingy in the heat. The local forecast has the temperature lurching into the nineties and to be weighed down with a typical summer-in–New England humidity that's as oppressive as the Puritans.

"Okay." Elizabeth sighs, emptying of all her air as though to build herself up to this conversation she must first deflate herself. Elizabeth wears baggy blue shorts and a billowy, fraying white T-shirt, its once-clever graphic long gone, eroded by years of callous spin cycles and tumble dries. "So what do we know so far?"

Allison says that according to the statements given by Tommy's two friends, the three of them were sleeping over at the Griffin house when they snuck out to drink beer and hang out at the Borderland landmark called Split Rock. Luis Fernandez had referred to the landmark as Devil's Rock, which initially confused the interviewing officers who were familiar with the park and had never heard the rock referred to by that name. The two boys claim Tommy drank half of the six-pack they brought, and then he ran off into the woods by himself. They claim his running off was sudden and without explanation. The boys were adamant that they hadn't been making fun of Tommy, hadn't been doing anything that would've angered, embarrassed, or dismayed him. They presumed Tommy was playing a prank, hiding somewhere in the woods to jump out and scare them. Tommy didn't respond to their shouting, and he wouldn't answer their texts. They claim to have searched the area around Split Rock for almost an hour before deciding to go back to the Griffin residence with the hope that Tommy had doubled back to the house to scare them or laugh at them when they arrived. They didn't call anyone's parents while they were on their way out of the park as their phones were dead, having spent the batteries while using the phones as flashlights. Tommy was not at the Griffin residence upon their return at approximately 1:25 a.m.

Minutes after Elizabeth called the Ames Police department, Tommy's name and information were entered into the statewide system created for missing children and teens. Officers began their search of the park around 3:30 a.m., including a pair of officers who had Luis and his father accompany them. A State Police helicopter equipped with infrared surveyed the park during the predawn hours but was unable to spot Tommy. The K9 unit thus far has come up empty. Officers from the Metro LEC (Metropolitan Law Enforce-ment Council; a consortium of over forty local police departments) are due to arrive at 9 a.m. for their own briefing.

Elizabeth says, "Jesus," checks her phone for a message that isn't there, and begins pacing behind the table again. "I don't understand why or how. Any of it."

Allison asks, "How well do you know Josh and Luis?"

"Very well. They're over at the house all the time. They've been Tommy's best friends for years—the only friends, really, that come over."

"Have you known them to be truthful?"

"Yeah. Always." Is there something—great or small—that's off in Luis's and Josh's stories of what happened last night? *Off* either by omission or addition? Despite her answer, Elizabeth knows all teens lie. Even hers. It's not necessarily that teens are being malicious or devious, but lying is an ingrained part of their makeup, of who they are; it's how they attempt to survive and navigate their incomprehensible day-to-day. Adults are big, fat liars too, of course, and they're usually better at it than teens. It's not because adults know more. It's because adults have decided that living with themselves is more palatable when they fully believe in their own lies.

Elizabeth: "Do you think they're lying?"

"No, not necessarily. I wanted to hear what you think of them, what kind of kids they are."

"They're the best, as far as I'm concerned." She feels strangely protective of Luis and Josh, and by proxy, Tommy, as though she's always believed the three friends would never do wrong, never have wrong befall them. "So, are you going to, I don't know, close down the park to help find him?"

Allison tells her that closing the park to the public remains easier said than done given the many paths and trail entrances (both marked and unmarked) along the borders and given the large number of homes in the towns of Ames and Sharon that abut the state park. The police are encouraging local residents to volunteer to be a part of larger search teams to systematically walk the trails. There are over twenty miles of marked and mapped trails, each with varying levels of difficulty. Borderland is almost two thousand acres large. That number doesn't include the neighboring wooded areas that are not technically within the park's boundaries, nor does it include the entirety of the Moyles granite quarry toward the treacherous and very much lesser-traveled northern end of the park.

Elizabeth knows the park and surrounding environs are large enough that someone, a teen, a kid, her kid, could become disoriented, particularly at night, and if he was drinking, too (*Jesus, Tommy, drinking? already?*) . . . he could get lost, hurt. Worse.

Allison: "Elizabeth, is it all right if I ask you a few more questions?" She pulls out a small notebook and gives Elizabeth what is supposed to be a commiserative look: a tight-lipped smile that isn't a smile, slightly arched eyebrows.

This observed detail is accompanied by what Elizabeth believes is her first glimpse into the truth: nothing good will come of any of this.

• • •

It's almost 11 p.m. and Elizabeth is in her kitchen, leaning against the sink, a cup of lukewarm tea cradled in her twitchy hands. In the last twenty-four hours she has mainlined a week's worth of caffeine, and it hums in her blood and gallops her heart. Her mother, Janice, sits at the small kitchen table with her own ignored cup of tea. Since Elizabeth returned home from the state park in the late afternoon, and returned home without any answers (never mind with Tommy), she's become stuck in silence. She couldn't say anything to her daughter, Kate, or her mother for fear of saying the wrong thing, something that would inadvertently keep Tommy hidden away from them. Elizabeth needs Mom to say something, anything; otherwise, Elizabeth will remain trapped inside her own head and silently praying to and talking with her dead ex-husband, William.

Please, William. Help us find Tommy safe. Please, William.

Her nebbishly handsome ex was indeed a William; never Will, Bill, or Billy. God, she couldn't imagine anyone ever having called him Billy. When they weren't getting along, during those inexorable, final days of their marriage, she called him *Billy* inside her head. She'd rehash all their arguments, and in those replays, he was inconsiderate-distant-selfish-neglectful-stupid-fucking-jackass *Billy*.

Elizabeth sighs, then puts her cup of tea in the sink and says, "Mom?" Her throat is scratchy, catching on itself. Speaking is a risk; it means she might start crying again and never stop.

"Yes, dear?"

"So Allison thinks Tommy—"

"I'm sorry, who's Allison, now?"

"Detective Allison Murtagh. She interviewed me at the park. She thinks Tommy is a runaway. Just like his dad, right?"

Janice says, "Did she actually say that? Did she say something about William?" Janice is sixty-six years old, tall, and broad shouldered. Her facial features are more forged than weathered. She still hikes to the top of Mount Monadnock in New Hampshire three times a week as long as there isn't a foot of snow on the ground. She split with Dad when Elizabeth was a senior in high school. Elizabeth is their only child. Her father has since remarried and moved to Virginia. He's been calling and texting, asking for updates on Tommy. Mom doesn't like to text or talk on the phone. She stuffed some clothes into her hiker's pack and drove down to Ames, arriving before lunchtime.

Elizabeth says, "She didn't say William's name or anything like that. But the questions she was asking, I could tell. She thinks Tommy ran away. Had Tommy been acting strangely? Did he seem sullen or moody? Was there any change in his behavior? Did we have any arguments recently? She kept coming back to that one. Asking if we'd all been getting along okay. Like she was blaming me or something. Not that I care what anyone thinks about me." She stomps her foot on the ground and shakes her head. "Goddamn it, I'm already blaming me, okay, and—all I want is Tommy safe and home."

Janice gets up slowly and walks over to Elizabeth and puts an arm around her shoulders. "Honey, this isn't your fault. She's not blaming you. No one's blaming you. She's trying to help. Like everyone else who was at the park today, trying to help find Tommy, right?"

Mom is her hero and thank God she's here, because Elizabeth would be a total puddle without her, but Elizabeth doesn't want Mom to be so damn reasonable and logical, not right now. Elizabeth wants her to be emotional, irrational, to tear through walls and run the streets like a town crier screaming at everyone to *fucking do something to find our Tommy!*

Elizabeth rests her head on Mom's shoulder. Tears come again and have been as autonomic as blinking since Josh's late-night call. "I know. But—I don't understand any of it. Why haven't they found him yet? Why hasn't anyone seen him? Where did he go? Why would he run away from—from home? Why is any of this happening?"

Tell him to come home, William. Tell him he won't be in trouble. No one will be mad. I won't be mad.

She's so worn out and tired and panicked that her thoughts are like water cupped in her hands and leaking out between her fingers. The fact of the matter is that his being a runaway is statistically likely. And his being a runaway is certainly preferable to many other possible scenarios, the ones that end with his being seriously injured, kidnapped, taken away, dead.

Janice says, "Elizabeth, listen to me, I want you to stay off the computer and phone and try to get some sleep."

"I can't—"

"Just a couple of hours." Janice gently grabs her arm and leads her out of the kitchen and into the hallway.

"Fine. Stop pulling me. What about—"

"Quit your fussing."

"I should really go talk to Kate. I haven't been able to talk to her. I've been barely able to look at her without falling apart, you know, when I should be telling her to think positive, to hope. I should be doing better, Kate needs me, but I can't. I can't—"

"You're doing amazing, really, Elizabeth. I couldn't be more proud. But if you don't get some sleep soon you'll be no good for Kate or anybody else. Least of all yourself. I'll sit up with Kate. You go."

"You sure? She's in Tommy's room. I think she fell asleep. In his bed."

"I won't wake her. I'll just check on her."

"Okay. Okay. I'm going. But I need my phone." Elizabeth pulls her arm away and shimmies past her mother in the narrow hallway of the 1960s-style ranch that she can't afford to update. She has always wanted to knock out a wall, make everything more *open concept* like they do in those home-renovation TV shows she watches. They always make that kind of change look so easy and pain free with the bright colors on the walls and golden sunlight shining on everything like the renovations won't ever go out of style or become obsolete again.

Elizabeth ducks back into the kitchen, fills a glass with tap water, and then fills her shorts pockets with the cell phone and house phone. She walks into the dark, cave-like hallway, the one that Tommy filled just yesterday with his cute and awkward lankiness.

Tell him to call home, William. I need to know he's okay.

Elizabeth doesn't hear the muffled voice of Janice talking to Kate anymore. Maybe they both fell asleep together. She should get up and go to them. She shouldn't be alone. Being alone is a mistake.

Elizabeth's glass of water is empty on her nightstand. The light is off. She sits at the edge of her bed in the dark. Her conversations with William are one-sided. He doesn't answer back.

You make a lousy ghost, William.

After William was eventually found dead, Elizabeth imagined his ghost haunting their house in Ames. She was self-aware enough to realize that she wanted to believe in ghosts, which wasn't the same as actual believing. To her shame, she even once told Kate when she was struggling in third grade (and being bullied by some piece-of-shit boy who no longer lived in Ames) that her ghost-dad was there, watching and secretly loving and caring for her, which was more than the live one ever did.

You have to find Tommy. You have to.

Elizabeth and William divorced when Kate and Tommy were two and four years old. Elizabeth knows there were serious trust and compatibility issues they ignored from the onset, and she was far from blameless when it came to the end of their marriage, but William radically changed after the kids were born. The one man who could always make her laugh became distant, cold, and he acted like their new family was the biggest mistake of his life, one he'd bear with stoic grit and a stiff upper lip. When he came home from work he disappeared to the little office nook to check his e-mail and do whatever else he was doing on the computer. She was working full time, too, and having to pick up their kids and cook dinner and get them in the tub and get them ready for bed. He came home from work an hour or so before the kids' bedtime, and all they'd get was a lame and perfunctory *Hi,* like his being with them was an unpleasant but necessary task to be performed, like taking out the garbage on Monday morning. Elizabeth and William argued often about his daily reentry into the house. It got to the point where he'd be with the kids, pouting and looking at his watch, counting down some pre-determined amount of time (fifteen minutes? twenty?) that was reasonable before ditching honey-I'm-home-family-fun time.

Elizabeth takes out her cell phone and stares at the string of messages she's sent Tommy since last night. Her thumbs hover over the digital keyboard, but even if he could answer his phone now, he'd likely have no battery life left. After getting back from the park this afternoon she'd quickly checked his room and the rest of the house for signs of his having packed up or prepared to run away. There wasn't anything out of the ordinary missing from the house besides him. At Josh's house, he left behind the overnight bag he'd packed for the sleepover. It was an *Adventure Time* cartoon backpack he'd bought at the grocery store for two bucks. Tommy had thought the very idea of him carrying around the cheap, plastic cartoon pack was the funniest thing ever. Inside that backpack: his cell phone charger; black Minecraft T-shirt and shorts (no underwear); toothbrush and deodorant inside a plastic ziplock bag, gooey on the inside with toothpaste that had leaked from an uncapped and smooshed tube; his wallet with twenty-five dollars in cash and a GameStop gift card he hadn't used yet. At home they weren't missing any phone chargers, and he still had a wad of money on top of his disaster of a bureau. Would Tommy have run away without taking all his money or taking anything of his with him?

No. She thinks Tommy is hurt and lost and they just haven't found him yet but he'll be okay. She's then shouted down by a mob of worst-case scenarios, the ones that more and more have the terrible ring of probability.

Jesus, what are we going to do? I can't lose Tommy. I can't.

Elizabeth is rocking in place without realizing it. In an attempt to distract herself, she gets up and goes to the bathroom to brush her teeth for a second time. She squints in the bright light, and her left eye, the one with the lid that hangs a little lower than the right, is shut all the way. She tilts her face up toward the vanity bulbs to let the light bleach clean everything in her head.

William disappeared four months after their divorce. It was a Thursday. Before going to some new sports bar with his coworkers, William emptied out his checking and savings accounts and managed significant cash advances from two credit cards. His coworkers said they didn't notice him acting strangely or drinking more heavily than usual. He left alone, and there was no sign or trace of him until he turned up dead eight months later. The details of how the onetime software designer accomplished his off-the-grid existence for as long as he did were still a little sketchy, but he spent the bulk of that time living out of a motel and busing tables at a dive pub on the outskirts of Worcester, only an hour or so away from where the Sanderson family lived. The night he died he was drunk and drove his shitty pickup truck back toward Canton; the town he'd lived in before pulling his disappearing act. No one knows why or where he was ultimately going. His truck rocketed down Neponset Street, and when he attempted to make the tight left curl underneath one of the arches of the massive, over-150-year-old Canton Viaduct, he skidded through the turn, ran over a cement traffic island, and smashed headfirst into the thick and unforgiving granite of the viaduct. He was airlifted to Mass General Hospital. His brain had swelled to three times its size before his body gave out. By the time Elizabeth got the phone call a little after 3 a.m., William had already been dead for three hours. Her contempt for William was something she had cultivated with the passion of someone starting a new hobby, so she felt an odd mix of told-you-so vindication and utter devastation now that he was permanently, irrevocably gone. The kids handled William's disappearance and death as well as could be expected. They were too young, especially Kate, to understand what had happened. With the divorce and limited visitation, William was already being phased out of their lives, and when he was gone and then gone-gone, it seemed a natural part of some sort of horrible progression; the disappearing father.

During the first few months of his absence Kate would occasionally trot from room to room and call out, "Daddy?" Tommy refused to talk about his father and would avoid his sister when she called to him or asked questions about where he was. But that phase of their grief passed in a blink. The days spent in the company of their father were soon outnumbered by their days without him. When Tommy turned ten he took up coin collecting like his father had, and he was obsessed with it initially, but he eventually gave it up for video games and general pre-teenager-dom. As the kids got older, the idea that they once knew their father became less a real thing and more like a folktale; he was this guy they barely remembered and only heard about in stories, saw in pictures. The kids never had that full sense of grief and loss, as they didn't really understand what they were missing. So it was Elizabeth and Elizabeth alone who still quietly grieved for the failure of their marriage, the disappearance, and the sudden death of a man she had once loved madly.

Elizabeth gargles and spits twice, then shuts off the light with the water still running. The darkness in the bathroom is complete. She leans on the sink, her palms flush against the cold granite, drops her head, chin into her chest, and listens to the trickle of running water in the sink until it sounds like murmuring voices; no voices in particular, certainly not her own. Maybe the water could talk her into sleeping if she left it running, running long enough to carve out a canyon in her sink. She turns the faucet off and darts quickly to her left and out of the bathroom, her hands and mouth still dripping wet.

Weak streetlight filters through the partially shaded windows, giving the larger shapes in her bedroom outlines to be filled in. She trips on her flip-flops and clothes she left in the middle of the floor. Earlier, when sloughing off the skin of the day, she didn't make it to the green plush chair that dots the far corner of the room, her usual dumping ground.

Elizabeth swears, bends over, Brailles her hands along the floor and gathers the flip-flops, a pair of sneakers, and a small pile of clothes. From her knees, she twists to her right, aiming to throw everything on or at the green chair, and throw it as hard and as dangerously as she can, like she's throwing rocks at a hornet's nest. If she misses and the sneakers crash into the window or her shorts fly behind the chair to never be seen again, then fuck it, that's fine by her.

As she twists and tosses her armload of stuff at the dark lump of the chair in the corner, she sees something further to the right, on the floor between the chair and the little white end table on which Kate painted purple flowers. That some-thing is up against the wall, taking up that dark space and filling it with more dark. The shape of a person crouched, or sitting, tightly wrapped into a ball, knees folded into his chest and arms wrapped around those knees, sitting there waiting patiently to be seen or to be found, or he's so cold and is trying to keep warm, or he's hiding from some-thing terrible.

And it's Tommy. It's him. It's Tommy sitting there folded up in that suddenly expansive space between the chair and her TV and the wall, and it's him because of the way, even only as a shape in the dark, he tilts his head while looking at her as if to say, *Don't you see me, Mom?* Then something happens to his face, and it happens in a flash, in less than a blink, it becomes visible, or part of it does, and it looks lumpy, misshapen, and where the eyes are, there are two dots.

The vision ends as her sneakers wildly tumble

into the plush chair and a white T-shirt flutters on top of the end table and then slides lifelessly to the floor. The noise that comes out of her throat is some ancient and awful involuntary precursor to language and then she says, "Tommy," repeatedly, and as desperately as an incantation. She scrambles on her hands and knees toward where she saw him a moment ago. She reaches her hand into the space, still saying his name. There's nothing there. She stands and looks behind the chair and all around the room, saying his name attached to a question mark. She runs her hands along the chair and the end table, and his smell is there. She gasps and greedily inhales, reprise breaths after drowning. She smells Tommy; he's still there, and he is sweaty.

She giggles despite herself. It's as though he's been out running around with his friends all summer afternoon and came home with slightly sunburned, pink cheeks and his brown hair gone black with sweat. His smell is a sharp, not wholly unpleasant tang of the inside of wet sneakers, that same smell that the day before would've had her asking him if he'd remembered to put on deodorant or if he'd showered that day, and he'd be embar-rassed but smile that frustrating but handsome I-know-something-you-only-say-you-know smile, too, like that body of his was some newfound power that he didn't fully know how to use or control. Elizabeth breathes in more, laughing and crying, and that new, more adult Tommy smell is still there, and she's inhaling so fast and so deeply her head goes dizzy and white stars pinprick her vision and she tries to blink them away. The smell changes, gradually, and becomes less recognizably Tommy and more earthy; like grass and soil that has been run on all afternoon, then wet pine needles and moss. And then there isn't any smell at all.

Elizabeth steps between the chair and end table and crouches down, careful not to disturb anything. She sits like he was sitting, with her back against the wall and her arms around her knees. The two phones in her pockets press up against her thighs, and Tommy's smell has faded, already becoming a memory, an imperfect one, one that she'll never be able to fully describe. She leans her head against the chair and cries great, wracking sobs that disappear into a gaping, interior void, a void into which her bones and whatever flagging spirit that filled them collapses, because she truly believes Tommy has somehow visited her, and that means her son is not lost or a runaway or is anything else but dead.

Kate Eavesdropping
and Finding Coins

Kate sits at the kitchen table with earbuds in her ears but with no music playing. Her friends have been texting her all morning with messages like *news?* and *u ok girl* and *I'm part of the Mountain Rd. search party, will keep u posted* and *stay strong!!!* and *they'll find him.*

Her friend Carly has started a Twitter hashtag: #FindTommy. Carly sends her screencaps of tweets from people all over Ames. Kate clicks on the hashtag and there are other tweets that Carly didn't send her. There's a bunch of high schoolers (she has no idea who most of them are, might as well be members of an unknowable and unfathomable secret society) tweeting that people who live near or on the edges of the park saw a dark shape walking through their yards and into Borderland last night.

Kate's classmate Sarah has an older sister (she forgets her name, and it's not in her annoying Twitter handle) in ninth grade who tweeted that she woke up in the middle of the night and someone or something was looking in her bedroom window. In response a bunch of Ames kids tweeted a picture of Bigfoot at her, and of course there were boys claiming it was them and asking her what she was wearing and some raging asshole (with a profile pic of his so-awesome flexed bicep) made a joke about a peeping Tommy. Kate wonders if any of these tweets about weird/random late-night sightings are legit, and if so are the police looking into it. She wants to ask Mom about it but is afraid to do or say anything to upset her and send her deeper into the scary shutdown mode she's been in for the previous two days.

Kate continues to monitor the live feed, and another guy tweets about a party at Split Rock tonight. Kate responds to that tweet and asks if she can go too and if they would help her search the park for her brother. He doesn't respond, and he takes down the tweet a few minutes later.

It's 2:30 p.m. and their neighbors, Frank and Mary Gaudet, have been in the living room since lunch. The morning was a steady stream of family friends and well-wishers at their doorstep, most dropping off premade meals and awkward hugs and promises to post fliers and continue to help searching the areas and neighborhoods surrounding the state park. Kate's best friend, Sam, and her mom came, and they were so nice. Sam, looking like she hadn't slept at all last night with her hair all matted and knotted up, stood as tall, thin, and still as a flagpole, and her not knowing what do with her eyes, that was okay by Kate. Sam and her mom being there was all it had to be, even though it made everyone cry and made Kate's chest hurt.

But unlike everyone else, the Gaudets have stayed. Nana Janice is totally ducking them, and like Kate, she sequestered herself in the kitchen. Nana is reorganizing the food in cabinets that don't need to be reorganized.

Mom would rather be out helping the search parties again, so why can't the Gaudets see that having to entertain them, to abide by their clinginess and rubbernecking, is sucking out what little energy they have left? Kate wants anyone and everyone to go away unless they've found Tommy.

Kate Sanderson will be twelve years old in two months. She's two years younger than Tommy. She's only a few weeks away from being a middle school student. She recently gave up gymnastics after four years of semienthusiastic participation and now plays lacrosse. She's aware that she isn't very good; she's not exactly fast when running, and catching and throwing the ball is kind of an issue. She not-so-secretly makes fun of the girls in her grade who are cheerleaders for Pop Warner football, but knows that worm will turn sooner rather than later. She hates pop music, really hates pop-country, and mostly listens to 1990s alt rock and hip-hop like Mom does. Kate has purple streaks in her brown hair, but she'll make sure to wash out all the color before school starts. It's easier to be herself in the summer. Kate is short and cherubic to Tommy's long and lanky court jester. Nana often referred to the two of them as Mutt and Jeff. Kate has no idea what that means, what the reference is from, and whether Mutt or Jeff is the short one. Kate hates having to literally look up to everyone and envies Tommy's wiry length. She has cultivated extensive and elaborate daydreams about being built like Tommy, but at the same time she knows it's easier to go into survival stealth mode and not be seen or noticed at her current size. Despite their obvious physical differences, and even with his features in the process of being distorted and exaggerated by puberty, one look at their faces and you can tell she and Tommy are brother and sister. They are fair-skinned, have the same walnut-shaped brown eyes and thin eyebrows, and each has a long nose that isn't exactly big, but always seems heavy enough to point their gaze away from other people.

Nana shuts the cabinets and says "Okay. I think we've all had enough of this" under her breath, but loud enough for Kate to hear it. Nana winks. Kate smiles and covers her mouth, even though there's no real danger of any kind of laugh escaping.

Then Nana walks out into the living room like an action hero before the epic ass kicking and says, "I'm sorry to be the mother hen here, but it's been a long morning after a long night after a long day . . ." and yes, she is stepping in and stepping up to ask the Gaudets to leave, finally.

Kate pumps a fist from her seat in the kitchen and whispers, "Go, Nana." She is sure that Mom will make her come out from the kitchen to join in on the rounds of *we're there for you*s and *thank you*s and *hang in there*s and then the uncomfortable hugs, but she doesn't. Kate listens to the Gaudets finally leave from the relative safety of the kitchen.

As soon as the front door is closed Mom says, "Oh, thank Christ. That was nice of them but— Jesus. How long were they here?"

Kate laughs to herself, and it almost morphs into a crying fit. She's actually relieved. This Mom sounds like her real mom, not the scary broken one from the last day plus. Kate doesn't know why or how Mom has rallied, but it gives her more hope for Tommy.

Nana says, "Too long. Let me answer the door from now on."

"Maybe. Let's set up a velvet rope and I'll give you an approved guest list." It's supposed to be a joke, but it sounds like Mom is serious.

Nana says, "I can be a bouncer if you need me to. Come on. Come sit down on the couch."

"I'm fine. I've been sitting and doing nothing all day." Mom sits on the couch anyway.

"Do you want a drink or anything to eat?"

"No. Actually, yeah. Just some water. And couple of ibuprofen. My head is pounding."

Nana comes back into the kitchen and fills Mom's order. Nana stops in front of Kate, waves a come-with-me hand, and motions toward the living room with her head.

Kate shrugs, shakes her head no, and doesn't get up. She'd rather stay and listen to them talk from here in the kitchen.

Mom and Nana fall into a quick, just-the-facts conversation about the updates, or lack of updates. The latest being the police have pulled the family cellphone records for calls and texts but have yet to find anything out of the norm.

Kate's stomach fills with mutant butterflies at the thought of the detective or anyone else reading the texts she sent out last night. She spent most of yesterday dropping sporadic messages to Tommy's phone like *I miss you, I hope ur ok, please come home,* like her texts were a trail of breadcrumbs he could follow. Then last night, as Nana talked Mom into finally going to bed, Kate was in her brother's room, in his bed, his blanket pulled up and over her head. Her phone phosphorescent white in the darkness, she typed, very carefully, *Tommy? Hi. Did you run away? Did someone make you run away? Is it my fault? Did I do something? I'm sorry for whatever it is.* And then she started crying and got so mad at herself and everything in the world and she fired off: *Are you trying to be like Dad? If you really ran away from us then you're a asshole like him and I hate you.* After she hit Send she cried harder and ran back to her room. She then sent him about one thousand *I'm sorry*s and *we miss you tommy*s, and she texted those messages until her thumbs ached, and Nana came in and gently took her phone away.

Nana is in the middle of a rant about the police and how she doesn't think they're doing a good job, and she punctuates with "I'm sorry," as though she's apologizing to Mom on the police's behalf. "But your friend, there, Detective Allison, and the rest of them, are treating this like some everyday ho-hum procedural thing when it isn't. This isn't an everyday thing."

Mom says, "She's not my friend. I mean, we're friendly—whatever." Mom grunts like she's frustrated with her own words. She adds, "She's working hard, Mom. They're all working hard." In a lower voice, not quite a whisper, she says, "Is Kate still in the kitchen? Is she listening to her music?"

Kate can't see her mother from where she is sitting.

Nana says, "What? Yes, I think so. Her earphones are in."

Kate loves that Nana calls the buds *earphones*.

She takes them out of her ears and rolls them between her fingers.

Mom asks, "Can she hear me?" Then she calls out "Kate? Kate!"

Kate doesn't answer. She hangs the buds over her shoulders, close enough to her head that she can stuff them back in her ears or pretend they fell out should either one walk into the kitchen. Kate calls up her *Beautiful Noise* playlist that begins with the only Sonic Youth song she likes. It's the one with Chuck D in the middle.

Nana says, "Do you want me to get her?"

"No. No, I—I don't want her to hear the rest of this."

"All right. Should I send her to her room?"

"Um. No, it's fine." She pauses to yell Kate's name twice more. "I don't want her to think I'm keeping anything from her. No matter what happens, I want her to trust me."

"What's this about?"

Everyone is quiet for a few beats. The tinny screech of guitars and a steady drumbeat pulse out of Kate's earbud speakers. Mom starts talking. She tells Nana she saw something in her bedroom late last night. She says there was a shadow or something between her chair and end table, like a ghost, but it was a dark shape, something made of more dark. Mom stops talking, and Kate turns that odd phrase around in her head, inspecting it for imperfections, like a jeweler, but finding none. It makes perfect sense to Kate. What else would a ghost be made of but more dark? Kate quickly calls up the tweets about the dark shape running through yards and looking into windows, and she wants to say something to Mom, show her what other people are saying about dark shapes, but she also doesn't want to be caught eavesdropping.

Nana says, "Okay, wait. What are you saying?"

Mom then says that what she saw was Tommy, all huddled up, and then at the very end, something was wrong with his face, and she knows that means Tommy is dead and that he's never coming back home. She says it so plainly, Kate almost drops her phone. It doesn't sound like Mom at all, but a narrator to one of those boring documentaries she watches sometimes.

Nana clucks her tongue, and although she doesn't raise the volume of her voice, she uses an argument-in-a-restaurant tone that's downright poisonous. Kate sinks deeper into the hard, wooden chair, having never heard Nana sound this cold and angry; it's terrifying. Nana asks how she could even think of saying such a thing about Tommy, and she says that Mom has to be stronger than this, that she thought she raised a tougher daughter, one that wouldn't give up so easily.

Kate says "Stop it," out loud to Nana, but she says it too weakly to be heard. Nana should let

Mom talk. Mom needs to talk, no matter what it is she says.

Mom says she isn't giving up and won't ever give up, but she saw what she saw. She says, "I saw him, Mom. I saw Tommy. It was him. It wasn't—it wasn't anything else and I wasn't dreaming and it wasn't a breakdown or a hallucination and I wasn't seeing things. I saw Tommy. I've never been so sure of anything in my life, Mom. Tommy was there in my room last night."

Nana says, "What we're going through, what you're going through, it's impossible, Elizabeth. It is. But you didn't see Tommy. You—"

"Mom. He was there. It wasn't just seeing him. I—I smelled him. His smell was there. I swear to God I could smell him, too."

And that's too much for Kate. She stands up, loudly knocking the kitchen chair back into the wall. She stuffs her earbuds back in, as deep as they can go so that the drone of Ministry's "N.W.O." jackhammers inside her head. She walks out of the kitchen and into the living room on the way to her bedroom. The living room really isn't on the way. Kate feels Mom and Nana call out to her, their words bouncing off her back. She doesn't stop. She doesn't end up going to her bedroom, either. She goes into Tommy's room.

His bed is made, which is just wrong. It makes Tommy's room look like a hotel room or a movie set. Mom must've come in and made it this morning before Kate got up. Tommy's bed is never made. It isn't that Tommy is a total slob; far from it. His room is always more clean and tidy than Kate's disaster area. Tommy never dumps his clothes (clean or dirty) on the floor. All of his books and comics are neatly stacked in the big bookcase along the wall and in the smaller one built into his bed frame. His desk is clear of clutter. His pens, pencils, and markers sit like floral arrangements in plastic cups of various colors, the color scheme hinting to some design and reason. Even his posters (Iron Man, the Avengers, a Minecraft Creeper, and a life-sized wall decal of the Legend of Zelda hero Link) are positioned in an orderly fashion; one on each wall, each hung from the same height. So Tommy isn't opposed to keeping his room neat; he only thought that making his bed was unnecessary. As he once eloquently explained to Kate and an annoyed Mom, making the bed was purely cosmetic. What was the point if no one was going into his room to see his bed anyway, and if he was going to turn down and sleep in the same blanket and sheets again? Kate agrees in principle, and she's adopted a more extreme version of Tommy's philosophy with her own room.

Kate turns off her music and listens for footsteps coming down the hall. There are none. She can't even hear Mom and Nana talking anymore.

It's dark in Tommy's room. She doesn't turn on a light. Instead, she pulls up the blinds on the two windows on either side of his bed and inwardly braces at the thought of finding someone (a dark shape, *the* dark shape, Tommy?) staring back through the glass. There's no one there. His windows are east-facing and look out into the green, rectangular backyard. It's sunny out, but the sun has already begun its descent on the other side of the house.

Tommy's desk is a sturdy hunk of lacquered wood that is probably older than their house. Mom picked it up at a yard sale a few years ago, and it took the three of them to lug it past the front door and then drag it (with towels underneath the desk legs) into Tommy's room. Tommy refers to his desk as Stonehenge, and it's as clean and kept as it was on the day they brought it into the house. It has none of the graffiti or gouge marks that splotch Kate's tiny, elementary-school-reject desk.

Kate sits at his desk, willing herself to not dwell on what Mom said about believing Tommy was dead and the shadow image of Tommy's ghost and how it oddly dovetailed with what kids were saying online. Of course not not-thinking about something like that is impossible, and she imagines his ghost all scrunched up below her, reaching out for her feet. She takes multiple quick looks under the desk and around the room, trying but not hoping to see Tommy.

The desk chair is hard molded plastic and is cold on the backs of her thighs. Adrift on the vast expanse of the desktop is his laptop. It's closed and unplugged. Stickers of cartoon characters are all over it, and the mostly ironic characters (like SpongeBob and Finn, Jake, and Lumpy Space Princess from *Adventure Time*) have mustaches and other black Sharpie alterations. There is one little square of duct tape in the middle, covering up the laptop's brand symbol, with a Tommy sketch: a puffy monster-cloud with angry eyebrows and a big, open mouth with two sharp fangs ready to devour a small flock of panicked birds. The sketch isn't very detailed and the birds aren't really more than rounded off Vs, yet the scene is clear and vivid, and funny as hell. Kate smirks at it, like it's too clever for its own good. She can hear Mom saying to Tommy, *No one likes a wise ass,* in a way that clearly means the opposite.

Kate opens the laptop and turns it on, but the log-in screen is password protected. She gives up guessing at the password after four tries, even though she thinks she's close. She doesn't want to guess wrong again and have the computer locked up. She closes the laptop and again looks at the monster-cloud sketch, which looks a bit more sinister with repeated viewings.

On the floor and adjacent to the desk is a milk

crate neatly filled with his many sketchbooks and notebooks. Tommy has been doodling and drawing ever since he could hold a crayon, and he's always been amazing at it. Tommy's attitude toward his talent oscillates between bouts of painful modesty and cocky showmanship. Kate pulls out a sketchbook from the middle. It's green and is filled with drawings of Minecraft characters, maps of houses and areas he's created, and brief scripts for his YouTube videos where he's describing the game play and his designs.

She takes out another notebook, one with a yellow cover. This one has outlines of giant waves braking over and around a jagged rock formation. A drenched boy about to be swept away clings to the rocks. His long bangs cover one eye, and the other looks up at Kate, pleading with her for help. Inside the cover, on the first page, in heartbreakingly small, careful script is the sentence "School is like drowning."

Kate, unlike her brother, has always got along with her elementary school teachers, and getting top grades has been easy. But the prospect of going to the middle school has left Kate utterly terrified. She thinks she can handle the workload; it's more the stories she's heard about what goes on in the lunchroom and hallways and bathrooms that has her anxiety level red-lining. Stories about girls getting their bra straps snapped or girls goosed in the hallways, and this year she heard there were some seventh-grade boys caught taking up-skirt pictures and sharing them online, and then there's all the stuff about the older girls beating up the sixth-grade girls in the bathrooms and making them do gross stuff. Nothing like that happens at the elementary school, and she doesn't understand what happened to everyone to make them so mean and awful. Her and Sam have been talking about nothing else this summer and doing their best to dismiss the stories as not true, as the older kids trying to scare them. But she doesn't know for sure, and there's no way she can go to middle school without Tommy being there. She's counting on him to look out for her.

Kate flips quickly past "School is like drowning." The subjects of the notebook's early pages are scattershot and seemingly unrelated: a giant, intricately detailed foot in the middle of a busy intersection; a cartoonish bear that's simultaneously cuddly and menacing wearing a wristwatch; a jagged cliff that has a sad-faced boulder sitting on top; open fields and rivers as viewed from up in the clouds, the view framed between two hands, a broken string looped between the right hand's finger and thumb.

She skips ahead and toward the middle of the book is a page full of cartoonish naked people, their eyes bulging and tongues wagging as they point and leer at each other. From there are pages and pages of huge breasts and asses, giant erect penises and scrotums, and dark triangular patches of hair, and all manner and derivation of frenzied coupling. Kate's face fills with blood and heat. She shuts the notebook and quickly throws it at the milk crate. She misses and it whooshes and claps against the floor. She looks around the room, wishing that Tommy would walk in and catch her, and yell at her, and she'd make fun of the pervy pictures and threaten to tell Mom. She waits, her breathing so heavy, but he doesn't walk into his room. She picks up the notebook and looks at the naked pictures again, quickly, before filing the yellow notebook in its Tommy-designated place.

Kate leaves his desk and walks over to his bureau. Even though she wants to, going through his drawers feels like she'd really be crossing a line that can't be uncrossed. And given the pictures in his notebook, she's a little afraid of what she might find, though she can't say what it is exactly she's afraid of finding. The top of his bureau is fair game, though, as it's all out in the open. One corner is stacked with baseball hats, in the middle is an assortment of superhero figurines and mini-Minecraft axes and swords, and there's a circular metal tin that once held holiday tea bags that's a catch-all for pocket-sized stuff; movie stubs he's saved (who knows why), key chains he's never used, a compass with the needle stuck in one place, loose change, small bills. She sifts through the tin and finds a plastic sandwich bag. Inside the sealed bag are two coins.

Tommy went through a coin collecting phase. One summer Mom had inexplicably given both of them a shoebox full of old coins their father had collected. The two of them reverently picked through the box and made a ledger detailing coin types together. Kate lost interest soon after the initial, found-buried-treasure rush. Tommy kept it going and added to the collection on his own, but Kate could've sworn he'd stopped collecting a few years ago, certainly before he went to middle school.

Kate opens the bag and slides the coins out onto her palm. One is a penny that's old (1956) but isn't a wheat back. What makes the penny remarkable is a large crack in Lincoln's head that runs horizontally; starting above his eyebrow and going clean through the back of his head. Or maybe it's a matter of perspective and the crack starts in the back of his head and runs through to the front, and it's a weird penny version of the Lincoln getting shot in the head (Kate learned about his assassina-tion in third grade). She runs her thumb over the crack and doesn't feel any raised edges.

The second coin is the size of a nickel, and its tails side features Jefferson's stately Monticello. There's no Thomas Jefferson profile on the heads side of the coin. Instead, there's a blank profile, a silhouette of a face: no features, everything perfectly smoothed over except the profile's outline. Hovering above this profile is a single eye, like the one on the back of a dollar bill. Kate digs through Tommy's tin for a regular nickel and compares the two. "In God We Trust" and "Liberty" and the year the nickel was pressed is gone, wiped away. The profile of the man on the coin is different from Jefferson as well; it's not just Jefferson's face with the details removed. It's someone else's silhouetted profile. The sharp nose and chin has been replaced with rounder versions and his long ponytail swapped out for a short, tight haircut. It's definitely a profile of someone more modern. She imagines Tommy using the coin as a joke and trying to convince people that the new nickel features Justin Timberlake or someone equally random. Kate thinks she should know to whom this mysterious profile belongs. Whoever it is, the floating eye above makes it weird and creepy, and she doesn't like looking at the coin or holding it.

Mom calls out Kate's name. Kate doesn't want to yell back from inside her brother's room. Mom hasn't come out and said she shouldn't be in here but the made bed might as well be a KEEP OUT sign.

Kate reseals the coin bag and places it back in the tin. She walks on her toes toward the door and the hallway. To her right is Tommy's closet, and that white door is open a crack. She allows herself to imagine Tommy—the real one, not ghost or shadow-Tommy—simply hiding in his closet, and when she opens the door he shrugs and says, "Sorry," and then he pulls the door shut.

Kate stares at the thin, dark opening between the door and the frame, and then she opens the closet enough to see two lonely button-down shirts hanging on a rack that's mostly empty hangers and belts he never wears. At the bottom of the closet are his dirty clothes piled up in the hamper. The dank, sweaty, stale smell is over-powering and seems somehow amplified. Does his closet always smell this bad? Is this the same smell that Mom claimed she smelled last night?

Kate believes in ghosts. She believes ghosts are everywhere and anywhere. They are always watching and they are always coming for you. They can be in any room, in any closet, under any bed or desk, behind the door, in any dark corner, more dark or less dark it doesn't really matter.

But Tommy isn't a ghost. He can't be, because right now Tommy is the opposite of a ghost. He is nowhere.

Kate leaves the closet door open a crack. Just in case.

Elizabeth Finds Notes
from Tommy

T he next morning Elizabeth is up and awake
before Kate and Janice. Outside the sun
peers over the backyard but it's still dark in the
house. She checks her phone for a morning-update
email from Detective Allison. There is one.

The search has expanded beyond the neighborhoods surrounding the park, and today they'll
canvass convenience stores, local malls, and other
places that are local teen hangouts. They are
monitoring local transit stations and bus stops.
They are working their way through the list of
acquaintances the other two boys and Elizabeth
provided. They continue to monitor Tommy's
cell phone number and records, and they are
monitoring various social media platforms for
messages about and/or directed at Tommy.
Overnight they received calls from three different
residents whose properties abut Borderland,
complaining of a person who cut through their
yards and then into the state park. The Ames
police responded and just after 10 p.m., they
found a group of high-school-aged teens gathered
at Split Rock. (Ill-advised vigil or mind-

numbingly tasteless party, Allison didn't specify). The SPLIT ROCK sign was vandalized to read "Devils Rock." The teens were escorted out of the park, questioned about Tommy, and were released to their parents.

Elizabeth responds with a thanks, I'll call soon, and a question: Have you ever heard of Devil's Rock before?

Elizabeth leaves her bedroom and doesn't turn on any lights on her way into the kitchen. She intently stares under the kitchen table and into dark corners and nooks. Last night, she didn't sleep much and spent most of the evening exploring dark spaces, looking under her bed and in her closet and staring at the emptiness between the chair and end table, desperate to see what she saw the previous night. Desperate to see Tommy again.

She pours herself a glass of orange juice instead of making coffee, and she slowly shuffles out into the living room, still with the lights off, looking nowhere and everywhere at once. She slumps to the couch with her glass huddled against her and finds the TV remote wedged between the back of the couch and the cushion to her left. She'll be careful to not tune the TV to any of the local news stations, most of which have been calling the house asking for statements and interviews. To any news source looking for information or a comment, she's given one, and she's e-mailed digital copies of Tommy's seventh-grade school photo and a cropped candid of him taken at the Griffins' Memorial Day barbeque. Tommy has on a red Iron Man T-shirt and baggy black shorts that hang down below his knees, and he's almost smiling.

She points the remote at the TV, and she notices something on the floor. In the middle of the throw rug, like a small pile of leaves, are pages torn from a magazine or book.

Elizabeth leans to her right, reaches over the arm of the couch and sets down her glass hard on the end table, sending juice as sticky as tree sap spilling over the rim. She then fumbles to turn on the lamp.

The pages are yellowish and covered in black scribble, covered in handwriting, not the neat type of something that was printed by a machine. She falls forward and to the floor, to the pages, and there are three of them. She flips the pages front to back and back to front. She sees the words without really reading them at first, registering that this is something that belongs to Tommy, this is something that he wrote. Her eyes fill with tears and she blinks madly to clear them.

The pages, jagged along the left margins, must have been torn out of one of his sketchbooks. Accompanying the text are strange little drawings and doodles, each ranging from quick scribbles to one intricately detailed drawing of a zombie with both loose flesh and icicles hanging off his arms, nose, and hollowed-out cheeks. Some of the scribbles look like Minecraft characters. She doesn't know their names but knows enough to know that the blocky little beasties belong to that video game universe. There's a skeleton with three heads, a pig-faced human, and this one thing with creepy tentacles dripping off the front of its face. She remains there, on her knees and on the floor, reading the pages. The first page is a title page. It has a 3-D block-lettering title of **MENTAL DROPPINGS 2.0**, made to look as though it was carved from solid rock, and it takes up almost the whole page. Below the title, writ almost indecipherably small:

*check the fine print

*seriously . . .

*<u>THE FINE PRINT!!!</u> keep out of my ROOM and NOTEBOOKS Kate and if you are reading this now I'll flick your ears SO hard the lobes will stretch out like bubble gum and stick to the wall then I'll take pictures and sell them on the net to people who like that freakshow

The notes on the next page are written as bullet points:

—Mental dropping it here like da bass like ant brain fungus (wait that don't make sense)

—Wonder if there's any girl out there in the WORLD who looks at my instragram pictures like I look at theirs and that sounds creepy but don't mean it in a creepy way

—EYES OF ENDER would be a badass band name

—My shins still huuuuurt. Stupid biking in nature! Back tire got caught between two towers of obsidian. Bike stayed. I kept going, Shins jammed so hard into the pedals surprised they didn't shhhnap.

—Split Rock ruuuullllllzzzzz!!! That tree up top is sick, looks like twisted up taffy. Totally Nether. Wonder what its roots look like, how far they go down between cracks in the rock. Freaky!

—Movie idea. FROZEN, WITH ZOMBIES. When ICY Princess loses it and freezes everything zombies freeze too. No words or singing to the songs, all grunts and moans. Movie ends withe the BIG melt and zombies free again and they eat the

snowman's face off. Chew crunch
BRAIN FREEZE!
—I am a genius!
—*note to genius* Hey, genius, make
bike totally out of soft squishy bouncy
rubber and not ouchy metal. Then
you take picture of rubber bike and
post on the gram. Then girls will
follow you. Girls like rubber bikes?
—I'm not so genius. Still want a
rubber bike tho.
—ZCP (zombie contingency plans)
wish list items: lacrosse helmet,
spiked elbow pads, waders, steal toe
boots, wind-up flashlight, girlfriend,
bungee cords, machetes, cross bow,
lighters/matches, canteen, rubber
bike

The last page doesn't have any drawings and
is written in a big block paragraph and the
sentences all smooshed together, as though the
text is a written equivalent of a whisper.

The other guys weren't into zombie
contingency plans. Josh was extra
pissy with hot sauce when we talked
about it today and Luis said
everything I said was wrong. Don't
know why. ZCP is fun and maybe

could be important. They laugh at me when I say the zombie ~~apocolypse~~ pocketclips could really happen but I think they know it could and are pretending they're not scared. They're scared. I know because I'm a scardy cat too. Its weird, zombie movies give me nightmares and I can't watch anything scarier than the orcs in the Lord of the Rings so Hollywood zombies scare me but I'm not scared by real ones. Really, I'm not. If you can plan for something like the zombie pocketclips, it takes that fear away, I think. Takes it away at least a little. Plenty of other things scare me. Like there's this show that I haven't watched yet but its about people disappearing and no one knows why or where they went. I'm totally afraid of that. Just disappearing. Like Dad did before he died. I think about why he left sometimes. Did he really plan it out for like weeks and months or did something suddenly snap in his head and made him go? I was barely there when all of it happened and to me it was like he was there one day and then gone the next. Poof! Gone!

Or pop? Like those bubbles that you make by sticking the plastic wand thingy into the soapy bubble-stuff (what do you call that? bubble juice? sphereoid compound liquid formula number 7?) and you blow on the wand and make bubbles, and those bubbles float there, they exist and they're fun to look at I guess and everyone laughs and kids and dogs chase the bubbles around and then they pop and are gone forever with no sign of them ever being there. Unless you pop a big one over cement and it leaves a wet ring, but still, it popped and its gone. Yeah. Anyway disappearing, popping out like a bubble, that's scarier than zombies to me. Sometimes I think that I'm more than halfway disappeared already. I'm invisible to so many kids at school. Don't say anything in class. Don't say anything to anyone in the halls or at lunch and its like you're not there until someone like bumps into you and that look they give you like they didn't know you were even there and they don't like you being there taking up their space and that's the worst look ever and I'm sorry if I've ever given anyone that look, or if Todd or Mike or that total dick Mac thinks you look funny that day for some reason then you're all there and they make sure everyone else knows it and then you want to be a bubble that can pop yourself and disappear for real. Its not so bad now in summer but when I'm in school I think about fadeing away and disappearing like Dad did and when I think about it long enough it feels like its happening already and there are no contingency plans that I can make to stop it from happening.

On the kitchen table the pages are carefully laid out, one next to the other, like tarot cards. Elizabeth sits with her chair pushed back, her hands folded on the table, and her chin resting on top of her hands. At this awkward and extreme angle, the pages are blurry and the text cannot be read. The pages feel safer that way. Maybe if she keeps them all blurry like this, they'll disappear and she'll forget she ever found them or read their messages.

Janice enters the kitchen yawning, and walks directly to the coffeemaker. She says, "Good morning." She has on a blue, long-sleeved T-shirt with NANTUCKET printed across the chest, though as far as Elizabeth knows, Janice has never been to that island. Certainly not recently.

Elizabeth bolts upright in her chair, like she's a kid again, guilty of hiding something. " 'Morning, Mom." She is about to say something about the pages but doesn't. Maybe she won't say anything until Janice walks over to the kitchen table and discovers them for herself.

Janice says, "Any news? Did the detective call or send a message?"

"I got an e-mail but nothing really new. I'll give her a call at eight if she doesn't call first. But Mom, you need to come look at this."

Janice says, "What is it? Do I need my glasses?"

"Yes, you do."

"What is it?" She pats the pockets of her pajama pants and pulls out her pharmacy-bought readers. The frames are rainbow striped and totally not her, but at the same time they are her.

Elizabeth doesn't say anything and rearranges the pages on the table, playing the shell game, until they are in their proper order from left to right. She gets up so Janice can take her seat. She avoids physical contact with her mother as they pass each other. Janice sits and holds up the first page close to her face and her hands tremor a little. Elizabeth turns away and finishes making the cup of coffee her mother started.

"Oh my goodness, where did you get these?"

"When I got up this morning, I found them in the middle of the living room floor."

"What do you mean in the middle of the floor?"

"They were there." Elizabeth makes a circular motion with her right hand. "In a pile on the throw rug. No book or anything to go along with them, just these three pages."

"How did they get there?"

"No idea. I'm guessing you didn't put them there."

"No, of course not. Why would I do that?"

"I'm not saying you would do anything, Mom. You want your coffee?" Elizabeth places the steaming cup on the kitchen table, then backs away and leans against the kitchen counter.

Janice carefully puts the pages down in a neat stack, safely away from the coffee. She says, "I don't understand."

"Hi." Kate pokes her head into the kitchen but leaves the rest of her body out in the hallway like she's ready to bolt, a prairie dog nervously surveying the plains for hawks. She tucks her purple-streaked hair behind her left ear and half-smiles.

Neither Elizabeth nor Janice responds right away. The way Elizabeth feels right now, she would be content to never have to say anything to anyone ever again.

Janice finally says, "Hi, Katie, my dear. Come sit next to me, honey."

Kate shuffles into the kitchen and looks at Elizabeth with her head slightly turned in a way that silently asks if she's in trouble. She's so easy to read sometimes. Kate says, "What's going on? Oh my God, do you know where Tommy is?" She dashes across the kitchen and sits at the table and leans against her grandmother.

Janice says, "No, dear, no. We haven't heard anything new about Tommy from the police, but we want to share something your mother found this morning. Right, Elizabeth?"

Elizabeth remains at her post, leaning against the kitchen counter, arms folded across her chest. She quickly runs through for Kate the what and the how of her finding Tommy's pages this morning.

Kate goes monosyllabic with, "Huh. Wow."

And sometimes, she isn't so easy to read. Kate looks the pages over and her cheeks turn red right before she swaps the first page for the second. She must've read the "fine print" section that was directed at her.

Janice fidgets, waits for Kate to be done reading, and says, "Have you seen these before? You have been spending a lot of time in Tommy's room." She enunciates each syllable properly.

Kate says, "I've been in his room, I guess, yeah. No. I've never seen these. Not these ones."

Elizabeth repeats what Kate says as a question. "Not these ones?"

"Yeah. I mean, I went looking through some of his notebooks and stuff but they're all drawings and sketches." The first half of her sentence is quiet and then she gets really loud, almost to the point of yelling. Her cheeks go an even deeper shade of red, like when she gets a high fever.

Janice has one hand on the center of Kate's back and she rubs little circles. "Where'd you find his notebooks? Are they out in the open?"

"I know I shouldn't have been looking through—"

"It's all right, it's all right. Where'd you find them?"

"They're next to his desk. In the milk crate. But those notebooks aren't like this." Kate holds up the pages. "This—this looks like it's, um, from a diary, or something. I didn't even know he had a diary. Didn't see any in the milk crate. He makes fun of my diary, you know, says it's such a girl thing to do." Kate talks fast, spewing out words until she runs out of breath.

Janice says, "So you haven't seen these pages?"

"Right."

"You're sure you haven't seen these before, Kate?" Janice asks in that quiet I'm-on-your-side-but tone that drives and has always driven Elizabeth absolutely bonkers.

"What? Yes. I'm sure. Why do you keep asking

me? I haven't seen these, Nana. I haven't." Kate's voice rises in pitch, turning into a persecuted whine. She always gets like this when she's caught in a lie. But what if she isn't lying? Maybe Kate is simply flustered and upset by reading what Tommy wrote. How could she not be? While she believes Kate, or wants to believe Kate, Elizabeth doesn't mind that Janice is the one stepping up to ask from where the pages came. She doesn't want to take part in this interrogation, even though Elizabeth knows that Janice arguing with and openly not trusting Kate could permanently tarnish Kate's near-blind love and adoration of her grandmother. Add it to the terrible growing list of everything happening to her family that can't be fixed or taken back.

Janice says, "Okay, okay. Did you take one of his notebooks out of his room last night, and carry it out here—"

"No! No, I didn't take anything out of his room or do anything like that. I swear!" Kate volleys back and forth between looking at Janice and Elizabeth and the pages.

Janice throws up her hands and says, "I don't understand where the pages came from then."

Kate: "Well, it wasn't me. Don't blame me."

Janice: "No one is blaming you, sweetie. Did you, or you, Elizabeth, take a book—"

Kate: "I didn't do anything!"

Elizabeth says, "Mom," but stops there, not sure of what to say or how to proceed or how to stop any of this.

Janice lowers her volume and softens her tone and pitch. "Okay, take it easy. Let's not get upset. I know. I'm just asking. I'm not saying you or your mom took one of Tommy's notebooks, okay? Or did anything on purpose. But how about *any* book or magazine or . . . something? Could've come from your room or the bookshelves or anywhere in the house, and maybe Tommy hid the pages inside and they, I don't know, got loose and fell out without you knowing they were there."

Kate gets up and stomps out of the kitchen and runs down the hall.

"Kate, I'm sorry. Please, come back. Kate?" Janice looks at Elizabeth and holds out her hands, palms up. "Do something?"

Elizabeth is still leaning against the counter and she shrugs. They both wait to hear Kate's bedroom door slam shut. But that doesn't happen. Janice releases a series of sighs and readjusts the pages and coffee cup on the table.

A few moments later Kate stomps down the hallway and into the kitchen, and she throws a plastic sandwich bag on the table that lands with a hard clunk.

She says, "I didn't see or take or do anything with those pages, all right? I looked at a couple of his sketchbooks and then I found these weird coins on his bureau."

Neither Janice nor Elizabeth makes a move toward the bag.

Elizabeth says, "I believe you, Kate. I do, really."

Janice, for the first time since she arrived at the house and hugged and held her inconsolable daughter on the front stoop, starts to cry. Her reading glasses are still on and she sticks her hands under them to cover her eyes. The little tremor that was in her hands earlier now spreads through her body, most notably to her head, which shakes as though it's impossible to continue to hold up.

Kate folds her hands into little balls and holds them close to her mouth so that they block most of what she says. "Nana, please don't cry."

Janice says through her hands, "I'm sorry. I'm sorry. Kate, I believe you, too. Okay? I'm sorry. Look, I'm not blaming anyone. I'm not trying to blame anyone. I just don't get it. I don't get how this could happen. Any of this. You know? And I don't understand how the pages got to where Elizabeth says she found them."

"I'm not making that up either, Mom."

"Oh, Christ, I'm not saying you are." Janice finishes wiping her eyes, the skin around them now puffy, and splotchy red. She takes off the reading glasses, puts them on the table, and sits up straight. Her head still shakes a little and she looks down into her black coffee. "Look. We need to figure this part out. The three of us. At the very least, we can figure this out. Can't we? If it wasn't one of us, even if it was by accident and we didn't know that we'd somehow carried the pages out there and dropped them, then what? What's left? One of his friends snuck into the house in the middle of the night and left them on the floor? The doors were all locked, right?"

Elizabeth says, "I've been leaving the back open. Just in case." No one needed to ask what her *just in case* meant.

Kate: "Kids on Twitter are saying there's been someone running through people's yards and looking into houses and going into the park and stuff at night."

Elizabeth: "Really?"

Kate: "Yeah. I can show you."

Elizabeth: "Detective Allison told me they found high school kids sneaking into the park, going out to Split Rock."

Janice: "All right, I guess we should make sure to lock the doors. Still, who would come into the house in the middle of the night, and what, drop Tommy's diary pages on the middle of the floor? How would that person even have Tommy's diary? I don't think—I don't know. I think we're simply running out of explanations if it wasn't one of us."

Kate still has her hands all balled up, held up close to her face, ready to block a punch. "I don't know, maybe they were like under the couch or something, and they got blown out from under there by, um, wind?" Kate drops her hands, looks at Elizabeth and adds, " 'Cause the front door opened and closed like a million times yesterday. Right?"

Kate's explanation is weird and awkward and only makes sense in a dog-ate-my-homework way, as her scenario is technically possible, but not bloody likely.

Elizabeth wraps herself more tightly within the coils of her own arms. She says what she's been thinking (and secretly hoping) all along: "Maybe they came from Tommy."

Janice says, "Well, yeah, no one is disputing that he wrote them."

"No, I'm saying that maybe Tommy left the pages, and he wanted us to find them and read them."

Janice says, "What? No. Jesus H. Christ, no, Elizabeth, no. What are you saying? Are you saying Tommy's, what, in hiding? And he snuck back into his own house to drop those notes and then go away again? That doesn't make any sense. Why would he do that? He wouldn't do that to us. Even if he did in fact run away, do you think Tommy would do that to us?"

Elizabeth: "No, Mom, that's not what I'm saying at all."

Janice: "What are you saying, then?"

"It was him."

"Elizabeth—"

"It was him. Just like it was him I saw and smelled in my room the other night."

"You can't talk like this. I know what you're going through is—is impossible but—"

"You weren't there in my room the other night to see what I saw. You weren't there. I was."

"But you can't be like this, Elizabeth. You can't. It's not right and it's not true—"

"It was him, Mom. And last night Tommy came back and left those notes for us to find, to send us a message or something."

Janice is crying again and says, "Stop it, Elizabeth. We don't know. Nobody knows what happened to Tommy."

Elizabeth: "I hate myself for having to say it and I hate myself for believing it, but Tommy's gone. He's—"

"Stop it! You can't say that. We don't know that. And your son is not a goddamn ghost."

Elizabeth says, "I saw what I saw and I felt what I felt, and I've never been so sure—"

Janice shouts, "You didn't see or feel anything!"

No one else speaks. No one gets up to go to the other. They stay at their three points on a triangle. The kitchen is all quiet tears and quick breathing.

Kate drops her hands away from her face long enough to pull her gray sleeves up and over her hands, and then she hides her face behind her hidden hands. Elizabeth uncoils and walks over to Kate and pulls her into a hug. Kate allows herself to be hugged but doesn't lean into it like she usually does. She holds her ground.

Elizabeth believes what she believes but doesn't know what to say or what to do anymore, if she ever did. She's empty of hope and couldn't be more disappointed in herself that it simply isn't there inside her and seemingly can't be willed back. She's lost and broken and tired, and so terrified of the future: terrified of the yawning void of a life without Tommy, but also terrified of the microfuture, of the horrors of the truth about what happened to Tommy surely there waiting for them tomorrow, or in the next hour, or the next minute.

Elizabeth lets go of Kate, who loosens into a shaky orbital path toward the refrigerator. Elizabeth says, "What did you say was in that bag, again, Kate?"

Elizabeth, Out of the Corners of Her Eyes, and More Notes

Elizabeth calls the detective at 8 a.m. and tells her that she found pages from Tommy's diary. She doesn't specify how or where she found them and doesn't know what to say if Allison presses her on those details. She reads some of the passages over the phone, fills in the last names of students Tommy mentioned, and she e-mails her pictures of the pages. Allison doesn't ask where they were found and only asks if there are more. Elizabeth tells her she isn't sure, but Tommy kept a lot of notebooks, mostly for his sketches, so she will keep looking.

Allison details the itinerary for the day, including an expanded search of areas that stretch into Sharon and West Brockton. She again tells Elizabeth that multiple residents have reported seeing a person or persons at the edges of their properties sneaking into the state park late at night. The police have increased night surveillance, and thus far they've only come across that group of high schoolers at Split Rock. Otherwise, there are no new leads or information, or there's nothing new that Allison is willing to share. Perhaps it isn't fair to be mad at Allison for doing something that she hasn't necessarily done yet (keep information from her), but when Elizabeth hangs up she wishes irrationally that she kept Tommy's pages to herself and is nervous that she's breaking an unspoken promise to keep their secrets.

Elizabeth, Kate, and Janice spend the rest of the morning and afternoon dealing with more visits to the house. One of the visitors is Tommy's and Kate's second-grade teacher, Ms. Lothrop. Even though school hasn't started yet, she managed to collect a box full of letters of hope (that's what she calls them) from her incoming second graders.

Phone calls and texts and tweets of support continue, many of which are flooding in from people they don't know. Elizabeth and Kate get separate invitations to join the *Find Tommy Sanderson* Facebook page. His picture and a plea for anyone with information to come forward are liked and passed around cyberspace, his face to be forgotten by most, like yesterday's cat meme. A local church is holding a vigil tonight to pray for Tommy's safe return, and Elizabeth politely declines their invitation to attend. She spends over an hour on the phone with her dad, who insists that he's flying up there at the end of the week if Tommy isn't found. She tells him that's so nice and he doesn't have to, but if he does, she could set him up at a local bed-and-breakfast. Dad says that he doesn't care and that he can sleep on the couch or in the basement or in his car and he promises that he won't get in anyone's hair (which is one of his favorite sayings, and a nod to the still-strained relationship between him and Janice) and he wants to be there to help and support.

During the lulls between visitors, Elizabeth, Janice, and Kate stay in their own separate corners of the house. What rooms they individually occupy changes throughout the afternoon, but no matter the room-swap permutations, the result is the three of them remain isolated from one another.

The afternoon fades into early evening, and with Kate in her room and Janice watching TV in the living room, Elizabeth announces from the kitchen, "We should probably think about dinner." She stands indecisively in front of the open fridge and freezer, each overstocked with premade meals from friends and neighbors. She can't bear the thought of eating one of those meals tonight, not tonight, and almost cries tears of relief when Janice appears over her shoulder to suggest that she go out and pick up some Chinese food. Janice brings back two large brown bags full of fried rice and appetizers and a big plastic container of hot and sour soup, and the three of them sit together and eat at the kitchen table. They don't talk. Their silence isn't the awkward eggshell of a group afraid to say the wrong thing. Their silence is commiserative, as though they are factory workers having earned each other's company after completing their most recent, endless shift. The small hot mustard packs and fortune cookies go untouched, and Elizabeth throws them away.

They wordlessly relocate to the living room couch and watch a minimarathon of home improvement shows. Kate falls asleep on the couch, leaning up against her grandmother. Janice eventually wakes her and says, "I wish I could still carry you to bed, honey, but I can't." She leads a groggy Kate to the bathroom with one arm hooked through hers. Elizabeth is a few steps behind, making sure they get to where they're supposed to go, and in a way, eager to start the rest of her night. Janice waits in the hallway for Kate to pee and brush her teeth. She tells Elizabeth to try to get some real sleep, as though she knows what Elizabeth has planned. The bathroom door opens before Elizabeth says an unconvincing "I will," and Janice follows Kate into her bedroom.

Elizabeth plans to spend the overnight awake, in her room, and with the door open. A one-woman vigil, she will watch and listen to the sleeping house, dream its dreams, while simultaneously hoping for and dreading a reoccurrence of the experience she had the other night. She lifts the comforter from her bed and pushes the plush green chair deeper into the corner. She sits and pulls her feet up off the floor, wedging them against the cushion and armrest. But instead of being more in tune, more open, more ready for such a reoccurrence, as she planned, her mind sprints in the opposite direction.

Her memory of seeing and sensing Tommy's presence only two nights ago is already receding, becoming hazy and incomplete, as is the clarity, the surety, of what she thought she saw. Despite everything she said earlier to Janice, she's newly hesitant to call what she saw a ghost, superstitious that doing so would somehow guarantee she'd never see or hear from Tommy again. Now that the buzz of finding the notes and the rest of the day is over and she's here and alone in her own head, so alone that she may as well be the last person on earth, she worries at the details of Tommy's sighting. And she keeps coming back to what exactly did she smell. She hasn't been in Tommy's room since the night he went missing, which means she hasn't collected his dirty laundry piled in his closet, and if she were to go into his room now and grab a T-shirt and hold it to her face, would it be his smell? What if that was gone, too? What if the details she still does remember (his crouch between the chair and end table, knees clutched to his chest, the tilt of his head, the quick image of a swollen face, of dots for eyes) are enhancements, embellishments to whatever it was she experienced? What is it exactly she believes happened that night? What does she believe happened to Tommy? Can someone forget how to believe?

Yes, she's sitting in the chair and waiting to find Tommy here again, but she also has an ear cocked toward the hallway, listening for the creak of the front door, or the back door, or Kate's door, or for something else entirely, and then a rustle of falling pages. The pages. She read them so many times she has memorized what Tommy said about how he felt like he was disappearing already. Is it some terrible coincidence? (Is there any other kind of coincidence?) Did he really run away like his dad? Because of his dad? Did she really believe a ghost-Tommy left those pages out on the floor?

And now Elizabeth thinks about waking up her mother and apologizing. Maybe tell her that she's right, tell her that she doesn't know what she saw or what's happening and she didn't mean to give up on Tommy still being alive. Tell her she hates herself for doing nothing, for not having left the house since the first day at Borderland and coordinating the search parties. Tomorrow morning, if he hasn't been found by tomorrow morning, she'll do something. Tomorrow might be her last chance. She'll leave the house and go door to door. She'll help search other neighborhoods, other towns. She has to do something, right? Fuck tomorrow. Why not start now? Elizabeth visualizes herself firing up the computer and scouring the Internet for clues and creating an overnight social media frenzy that can't be ignored. Or why not get up and leave the house right now and walk into the woods, paint every single tree and rock with that flashlight, and call his name and call his name and call his name. Then she imagines finally finding him at Split Rock, he's huddled deep inside in the crack between the boulders, and she has to go inside because the flashlight doesn't go that far, and she shimmies into the split, which seems to go on forever, into the core of a lost world, and there at the end, his shadowy shape, the shadow within the shadow, and he looks exactly as he looked when she saw him pinned between this chair and the end table, and he doesn't say anything to her and what she wouldn't sacrifice to hear him say something to her again, even if it is goodbye, and she goes cold and she smells the wet, damp earth, and when she finally remembers her flashlight and focuses the beam on him, Tommy's gone, he's gone and there's nothing there but the skinny trunk and twisted and gnarled gray roots of a dead tree, the leg and talons of a great bird as it calves the rock in two.

It's a little after 3 a.m. and Elizabeth twitches

awake, legs falling off the chair and dragging the comforter down to the floor. She's freezing and the room feels different now, not quite dangerous, but that doesn't mean she can't get hurt. Elizabeth looks straight ahead at her bed and wall and closet. She focuses on the darkness in the periphery, the outer edges of her vision, the corners of her eyes, and Tommy is there, standing next to the bathroom, and he's there again near the shaded window on the other side of her bed, and he's there, too, in front of the dresser, but whenever she snaps her head around to look directly at him, she sees nothing. She says his name and hears nothing. Tonight isn't about more dark, it's about more nothing.

She wipes her eyes and cannot see Tommy anymore. She climbs out of her chair. The muscles in her lower back groan and her knees are cranky at having been folded and scrunched up for so long. She stumbles into the hallway, stops, and stares down its length toward the front of the house. She opens Kate's door. Janice and Kate are both in the double bed, under the covers, sleeping on their sides and back-to-back. The covers are pulled up so high Elizabeth can't tell who is who. She watches them sleep, and even in here, she keeps thinking she sees Tommy out of the corner of her eyes (over there, but don't look over there, next to Kate's shelves, he's standing there, right there!), and maybe that's a comfort, because if she doesn't ever look perfectly straight ahead again, he'll always be there, in the periphery.

Elizabeth leaves the bedroom and walks down the hallway and to the living room, afraid of what she might find and afraid of what she might not find. There are two pieces of paper on the floor, grouped in the same area of the rug. The living room feels like her bedroom felt when she saw Tommy the other night. Already Elizabeth builds an argument against the idea of Kate getting out of bed, pulling these pages from a secret hiding place, sneaking out to the living room, and then back to her bed without her or Janice hearing any of it; arguing the possible is impossible and the impossible is what is true.

She picks up the pages, the torn edges make crinkling sounds at her touch, and she nearly sprints down the hallway. She is going to spend the rest of the night back in the chair and with the pages, but first she detours into Tommy's room. She throws open his closet, as though she'd lose her nerve if she didn't do this quickly, recklessly, and she plucks a T-shirt from the top of his laundry pile.

Back in her plush chair she turns on the reading lamp on the end table. Tommy's T-shirt is draped over her left shoulder, and she periodically holds the shirt's collar over her nose and mouth as she breathes in, once, twice. Whether it was the same as what she smelled the other night doesn't matter.

Trapped in the fabric, Tommy's smell is there and it's real. She fears she's absorbing it with each inhalation, and it'll have to be rationed out through the rest of the night.

Elizabeth hunches over the two pages; Ebenezer Scrooge pouring through his ledgers, the Scrooge from before the ghosts. She reads and rereads the diary entry, retracing every loop and crossed T, searching for hidden meanings beyond the obvious: there are more notes.

I watched these videos called Calculus and Zombies done by some college profesor and it was supposed to be about how math could really help you survive zombies. The vids were kind of dumb but fun, not scary or gory, and there wasn't much math to it, really, just some graphs with curvey lines, yeah, so the vids, not much help. Not to me. Nothing I didn't know already. Thinking of a better video idea, like a top 10 how to zombo demo, something more realistic, maybe. Now it seems kind of dumb and Josh and Luis probably wouldn't want to do it anyway. Before I work up to writing stuff here I have all these great ideas (Let's Play zombie vids!!!) and things to talk about and then they're not there when I pick up the pen. It's not like drawing where I can shut off my head and let it happen and my hand sort of takes over and does what it does, it's so easy. Writing is not like that. Writing kinda sucks. Why does anyone write in a diary? Who are they writing for? You write something down because you want someone to read it, right? Diary writers must imagine some sort of reader. Yeah? Why do it if no one is going to read it even though all diaries say that you're not supposed to read any of it. I think a diary is like a dare.

I dare ya to read this!! Kate,

I'm really not daring you to read this. So stop.

I'm not saying much anyway. I went back and read my first mental droppings book and torched it. Burnt it out back in the fire pit. That book was so embarrassing. Puke. I hated reading it. I sounded so

DUH stupid. Makes me wonder if I always sound stupid and only see that when its all written out. Will probably end up torching this too. It sucks because I usually sit here and stare at it and wonder about random things and then when I get nothing I go back to a drawing notebook. If I want to make my own comics I have to be able to write, you know, so I'm practicing. That's what this is. Too bad it is THE suck. The last few times I've tried writing stuff I end up thinking about my father. Isn't that weird? It's capital F Fweird. I barely remember anything about him and mom doesn't talk about him like ever but I've been thinking about him all the time lately, and not thinking about why he ran away. WEIRDNESS WARNING—if and WHEN the zombie pocketclips happens I know it won't be dead people rising up from their graves but alive people turned to zombies by a virus or the ant brain fungus, so I know dead people won't be coming up through the ground and stuff but sometimes I think about my father as ZOMBIE DAD, if

109

he did rise up from the grave would he come back for me. Yeah, dumb because there isn't much left of him by now and I wonder what he'd look like. What if he looked like he did when the ambulance showed up and what if instead of moaning groaning BRAIINNNSSS his zombie brain got stuck on the last words he ever said. Maybe he said those words to the ambulance people when they found him with his head all smashed up or maybe he said them when he was by himself and before they showed up, and so I guess his last words disappeared like he did. And when I think like this, I get stuck on it and wish I could somehow know what his last words were and then it wouldn't matter why he disappeared and I could write those words down here. Then this stupid diary would be worth saving.

Luis Goes to the Sandersons, Kate and All the Apologies, Luis Asks Questions

L uis doesn't want to do this. Sure it sounds weak, cowardly, particularly given what happened to his friend, but he's not sure he'll make it through. The odds of his throwing up in the backseat during the short ride over to the Sandersons are much greater than, say, an asteroid cratering into their car. He'd rather the asteroid.

It was only a half an hour ago that Mom shook him awake, yanked the bed covers off of him like an angry magician, and told him to take the world's fastest shower. Luis bolted upright, in a total panic thinking about the police, more police, and more and more interviews, and maybe this time they wanted to bring him into the station. Would Mom make him shower before they threw him into a cell? Or was she waking him because his parents gave in to a media request? When Luis asked, "Why?" Mom said they were visiting the Sandersons and yes they were doing it right now because Elizabeth was going to be out for most of the day. Luis's parents were in such a rush they didn't even get on him, like they usually did, when he turned down offers of cereal, Pop Tarts, and blueberry muffins, saying he didn't want any breakfast and he wasn't hungry.

Luis's short black hair is still damp from the rushed shower. Even though it's already humid and the temperature is pushing into the eighties, Luis wears a blue, logo-less hoodie sweatshirt at least one size too big. Most of his clothes (including his baggy camo shorts) fit like hand-me-downs from ogre-sized older brothers. Luis has no older brothers, but two older sisters who tower over him literally and figuratively. He does love them and he enjoys their company when they're around, which isn't often anymore. His sisters already left for school two weeks ago; they both attend colleges in the southwest. They called last night to ask him how he was doing and to say they were sorry his friend (they didn't say Tommy's name) was missing and hoped and prayed that he'd be found soon. His older sisters are smart, cool, and fun in their own way, but they have always seemed like adults to Luis; like younger, newer versions of his parents with motivations and decision-making processes alien and unknowable.

Luis has had no time to prepare for the impending visit to the Sandersons, and that's probably for the better. Luis would've been more of a basket case than he is already. Of course, now that they're minutes away, Luis is actually hungry. His stomach stings in little starbursts of pain that radiate throughout his midsection and up into his esophagus. He considers asking Mom if she has something to eat with her. When Luis was younger, she used to keep small sandwich bags of dried plantains and other fruits in her bag and offer them to him as surreptitiously as a drug dealer. More annoying than the OCD frequency with which she asked if he wanted a snack was her exaggerated look of pouty defeat when he invariably said no.

Luis's fingers twitch for his phone, and he wishes he could escape to its digital hideouts and numb himself with Minecraft or Madden football. On the way out the door his dad made him put his phone in his mother's purse. That they still treated him like a small child was an argument for another time, when or if this nightmare with Tommy ever ended. Tommy. Even thinking about where Tommy was and what might've happened to him stirs that hive of angry wasps in his stomach.

Tommy's house appears as they round the final corner, and it looks exactly the same, looking like it always has, which is a surprise to Luis. How in the world could it be the same place without Tommy around to be in it?

Josh and his parents beat them to the house. Their black, freshly washed SUV is parked next to the mailbox, and they are already standing on the front stoop and standing so that they face the closed front door.

Dad says, "They said they were going to wait for us." He sounds pissed. The Fernandezes and Griffins have done many of their official statements and interviews as a group. They've also been eating lunch and dinner together, spending the recent long summer afternoons and shrinking nights at each other's houses; the parents watching the boys while drinking all the wine, the boys quietly watching the same movies they've watched countless times before. They have become a reluctant team, a team Luis didn't think anyone rooted for.

Dad pulls up tight behind the Griffins' SUV. Mom's door is open before the car is fully stopped. She speed-walks across the front lawn, moving like a broken robot alternating short strides with big, uneven steps that threaten to topple her over. Luis climbs out of the car and he sinks into the grass, which is still damp from the morning dew. His feet and ankles are instantly wet. Tommy's only been missing for a handful of days but the long, snarly grass looks like it hasn't been mowed in weeks. Now that he's closer to the house, almost standing in its shadow, Luis thinks it does look different. He can see this place easily becoming the neighborhood haunted house, the one the kids tells stories about, and they'll tell them so often you'll have no choice but to believe them.

Dad edges Luis forward with a slight shove and

a "Come on" that has an exasperated edge to it. Luis's father is older than everyone else's dad; his late fifties is a decade and a half older than Mom. He and Mom are the same height, five foot seven, but physical opposites otherwise. Dad's hair has gone totally gray. He's thick through the chest, shoulders, and arms. His legs are as skinny as picket fence posts. Dad is generally kind, particularly to strangers, and loyal to a fault, but he craves confrontation like the morning's first cup of coffee.

Elizabeth Sanderson opens the front door. She is dressed for a jog: black yoga pants, sneakers, blue short-sleeved outer shell. Elizabeth offers Josh's mom a weak smile that instantly collapses like a long-neglected bridge, and they embrace. Josh and his dad stand to the side, their heads down and hands folded in front of them. Luis's mom climbs up the brick stairs, puts a hand on Josh's dad's shoulder before stepping in front of him. Elizabeth hugs Luis's mom next. Luis is still slowly walking across the front lawn.

Mom and Elizabeth continue to hold each other. She looks over Mom's shoulder and she locks eyes with Luis. It's not the hardness, the completeness of her stare that makes him feel so small, smaller than he always feels. It's how quickly she looks away from him. Luis imagines his smallness as a condition without a cure, and it's accelerating. He'll shrink so that the grass is over his waist and then over his head, and he'll continue shrinking until the grass stalks are as large as redwoods, until he's down in the dirt with the ants and the ticks and the spiders, and then he's even too small for them to bother with, and maybe it would be okay living down here alone in the secret roots of the world.

Kate hovers back at the borderline of the kitchen and living room, running her foot along the crack between the hardwood and tile. Luis, Josh, and both sets of their parents are inside her house, grouped together in the small entryway that spills into the living room. They shouldn't be here. Is it unfair of her to think that they're here to make themselves feel better? Nothing they can say or do will help make Tommy come back. Kate didn't quite articulate it in that way earlier when Mom announced who was coming over, but it was implied in her "Mom, you should've said no."

Kate hates the Griffins and Fernandezes right now. She blames them and hates them, all of them, even Luis, whom she's had an obvious crush on forever. Luis has always made her laugh, and whenever the three boys were together in the house, Luis was nicer to her than Tommy was. Tommy would snap at her, tell her to leave them alone and go play with her own friends, and he wouldn't even look at her when he'd say it. Luis would be the one to say, "Don't listen to him" and

"Let her watch us play Mario Kart." A week ago Luis and his big brown eyes, jet-black hair, and sneaky smile would've sent an embarrassed and exhilarated Kate and her just-got-up morning wear (baggy sweats, dingy T-shirt, no training bra) retreating to her bedroom. Look at Luis now, hiding behind a wall of parents, and slouching next to Josh, both boys with their heads down and their hands in their pockets, like cowed prisoners. Two stupid-ass little boys. The stupidest. That's all they are, and they lost Tommy. They took him and they lost him.

Everyone is standing and not quite sure what to do or where to look. Mom insists they sit on the living room couch and be comfortable. Mom sits first but no one follows her lead, so she stands back up.

Kate stares at the boys, daring them to look her way. Neither of them have yet.

Nana, taking over the hostess role, politely asks if anyone wants any coffee, water, something to eat.

Mrs. Fernandez says, "No, no thank you," and the other adults mumble similar sentiments.

Nana disappears into the kitchen and tends to the coffeemaker anyway.

Sighs and awkward smiles are passed back and forth until Mom breaks the Antarctic ice and says, "Thank you, guys. For—for coming over. It's good to see you."

Kate seethes. No, it's not good to see them standing like their presence in and of itself is some sort of apology or admission of guilt that's to be absolved by this weak-sauce act of contrition. And even worse, now they're making Mom do the talking.

The two dads blurt and bumble over each other's words and it amounts to nothing at all, the drowsy buzz of a couple of dying bees. Mrs. Griffin nods, folds and unfolds her hands, and smiles the watery smile of the fuck-up, of the coward who knows what should be said but won't or can't.

Mrs. Fernandez says, "It's so good to see you too, Elizabeth. And Kate. And please, thank you for having us. We won't keep you long. And—" She pauses, and sighs, and then talks again but the sentences don't quite work and the accents are in the wrong places and so are some of the words. "You must—you're so busy. We know. I mean. I can't imagine, what, you know, and all you have to do. We thought it important. The boys, the boys—" She pauses again after saying "the boys" twice, like it's a recognition that *the boys* no longer refers to the three friends. "They wanted to say that . . . they wanted to say something to you. To you both."

Kate stuffs earbuds into her ears. There's no music playing yet. She has "Heart Shaped Box" queued up in case of emergency and she needs to drown them all out.

The parents part, eager to offer up a sacrifice, and the two boys step forward, toward Mom. Josh's eyes are puffy and he's already crying, his lower lip caught in an earthquake, and it's clear he can't face her, that he won't be able to say anything.

Mom is stone-faced, unreadable, and stares at Josh, daring him to say something, anything. Josh covers his eyes with his hands and his head tilts toward the floor like Mom's stare has weight, forcing his head down to never look up at anyone again.

Kate's anger softens and now she's scared. What is Mom going to do or say? Is she going to start screaming at them all and blame them for Tommy's disappearance? Pre–summit meeting, it was what Kate wanted, but now she wants Mom to endure whatever it is they have to say and then let them leave without any fireworks so they can handlethis on their own. Is Mom going to tell them that she believes Tommy is dead and that she sees Tommy's ghost and he leaves her written messages?

Luis says, "I'm—I'm sorry, Ms. Sanderson."

Mom visibly twitches at the sound of her last name. Luis hasn't called her anything but Elizabeth in all the years he's been Tommy's friend. In recent months he has been greeting her with playful variants of *How the heck are you, Elizabeth?* Luis isn't a total mess like Josh is, but his voice is so off, or turned off. This is not Luis talking.

The real Luis's voice is a live wire; words crackling with energy, wit, and sometimes anger, always challenging you in some way. This Luis drones on in a toneless dirge like a talking head reading a teleprompter with news of an impending calamity that cannot be avoided or prepared for.

"I'm sorry we snuck out and took those beers with us. I don't know what we were thinking exactly. We're not drinkers, really we're not. We were trying them out, and we didn't drink that much. And I know that's not the important part, but I'm sorry we were so stupid. About everything. And then he left and we should've followed him right away, and I don't know why we didn't, and I'm sorry. I'm sorry we don't know where Tommy went and I'm sorry I don't know what happened. I wish I could take it all back. That's all I wish. Just take that night back."

Mom pulls Luis into a hug and she is crying, but it's an under-control crying. She says, "Thank you, Luis. Thank you. It's okay."

It's not okay, but that's not what she means, can't be what she means. Luis looks so small and Mom has him totally enveloped in her arms, squeezing his head against her chest, her long hair falling over him. Luis hesitantly puts his arms around her waist.

Kate turns on her music, the languid opening guitar notes lurch before the hesitant bass and drums keep the odd time loudly, and it looks like

Mom and Luis are slow dancing. They break the hug as the chorus is shouted over the fuzzed-out guitar, and Luis goes back to his side of the room with the other parents. Mom quickly hugs Josh, too, rubs the top of his head as he shuffles away from her, and then Mom is alone on her side of the living room again. Kate should probably go over and stand with her, but she doesn't.

Mom starts speaking and gesticulating with her hands. The hand gestures are indecipherable without the words. The other parents stare down at their sons, and Josh and Luis shake their heads no in sync, and they occasionally shrug and say something brief. Kate doesn't shut off the music, and she turns it up louder to ensure she doesn't hear anything they say. She focuses on the secret choreography of their collective nonmovement.

The two families eventually float toward the open door like lost balloons. They wave sheepishly at Kate and they squeeze Mom's hands and arms as though testing out how strong or durable she is. Mom watches them trek across the lawn from the open door. After their two cars drive away, she turns to Kate and pantomimes taking out the earbuds. Kate takes one out.

Mom says, "I'll be back later with lunch."

"Where are you going?"

"Out. Text if you want anything." Mom waves bye with her car keys cupped in her hand and she shuts the door behind her.

They're all gone before the last song of the album, "All Apologies," finishes.

Luis's parents decide they're not going into work for another day, and Team Griffin-Fernandez reconvenes at Luis's house. The adults sit at the kitchen table like weary delegates while his dad makes coffee and puts out a box of little powdered donuts. Josh takes a handful. Mrs. Griffin's look of you-don't-need-to-eat-all-those is as loud as a scream. Luis takes one donut to make his mom happy. He is not hungry anymore and the stomach pains from earlier have short-circuited out.

Mr. Griffin says, "I'm glad we went. I mean, we had to go, and we wanted to go. But that was hard. Nothing compared to what poor Elizabeth is going through, I know, but I'm just saying, that wasn't easy."

Luis wants to say something smart, something that stings and horrifies, something to make him stop talking.

Mr. Griffin ends with "Proud of you boys for stepping up."

Josh, the kid who always has something to say, doesn't say anything. Just like he didn't really say anything at the Sandersons. Josh stuffs two donuts in his mouth, and the white powder clumps on his lips. He wipes his mouth with the back of his hand, and little clouds of sugar float down to the table.

Luis's dad says, "Creamer, anyone?" and puts a bottle of Bailey's next to the donuts, like a dare. "You two can go down into the basement and watch a movie if you want."

Josh doesn't move from his spot. He likes hanging out with adults and listening to them talk. Even now, Luis knows Josh can't help himself and would prefer to stay. Luis can't leave this room fast enough.

Mrs. Griffin says, "Go ahead, Josh. We'll go home when you're done with the movie."

The boys leave the kitchen and walk down into the partially finished basement. Luis's dad did all the work himself, sacrificing almost a year's worth of weekends and a handful of off days. In the early stages, while framing the space, he kept trying to get Luis to help him. Luis didn't want any part of it. He wasn't handy, and to his shame didn't have that family DIY knack. Dad's false mantra of "You're doing great" and his manic see-how-patient-I'm-being-with-you vibe sent Luis retreating to his room and the computer.

The carpeted basement stairs curl around to the left and into the finished space, a common room. The drop ceilings are low, the walls a bright white, and the floor covered with a spongy, beige rug. A bar is on the far wall; a couch in the middle faces a long, rectangular entertainment center, its lower shelves spilling over with DVDs and video games. There's an Xbox, DVD player, too, and squatting on top like a large, black bird is the TV. All the random tennis balls, knee hockey equipment, and Nerf hoop stuff has been picked up and put away in crates pushed underneath the foosball table no one ever uses anymore. It smells musty down here, and Luis wonders if there's a leak near the window over by the bar again.

Luis asks, "What do you want to watch?"

Josh says, "Whatever. It doesn't matter to me."

Luis sifts through the DVD library that he's ordered according to preference; his action and horror movies are in the front and faced out. The movies his sisters didn't take to college with them (*Bring It On*, *Grease*, *Pitch Perfect*; he would never admit that he liked *Pitch Perfect* and had even watched it twice on his own) are stuffed way in the back of the shelving along with all the Disney and Pixar movies with which he used to be obsessed.

Luis says, "Come on, pick something. You know what I got." If Josh doesn't pick anything then he'll put in *Dead Snow* or maybe *Dawn of the Dead*, the original, the one with the insanely bright colors, that radioactive red of all the blood and guts, and in a weird way that makes the movie seem more real to him than all the CGI and dark shadows of the remake. His parents would be pissed if he put on a zombie/horror movie even though they didn't say not to. They don't understand how those movies are a comfort to him. In his favorite horror movies, he knows the rules by heart and the consequences of the rules being broken.

Luis pulls out *Dawn of the Dead* and shakes the movie at Josh. The loose DVD inside rattles in the plastic.

Josh, sitting on the couch behind him, says, "No zombies."

"Hey, you said whatever."

"Superhero or something funny. Seriously, no zombies."

Luis wants to be mean right now. He wants to call Josh a pussy and put the movie in anyway and then see what Josh does to stop him. But then Luis flashes on one of the iconic scenes in *Dawn* and it features the zombie who looks like Tommy. That Tommy zombie gets a machete stuck in his head and his brown eyes are huge and there's a diminishing intelligence leaking out that's utterly horrifying, but what's worse is his lower jaw drops like a trap door and it hangs open and there's all that darkness inside. Remembering that zombie, his favorite zombie, looks so much like Tommy makes his stomach hurt again.

"Fine." Luis throws the *Dawn of the Dead* DVD to the back of the shelf with the other banished movies. He pulls out *The Avengers* and pops it in.

They don't talk during the opening scene with Loki kicking S.H.I.E.L.D.'s collective ass. Luis can't watch his favorite zombie movie anymore, and he doesn't want to watch this, either. This won't shut his brain off.

Josh finds the TV remote on the couch cushion between them and mutes the movie. He says, "My parents search through my phone now, every night. Looking for, I don't know, something."

Luis's parents have always checked his phone periodically, so nothing new there. Luis unmutes the TV and the music and explosions are loud. He scoots closer to Josh so he can be heard without having to raise his voice, and asks, "Did you know anything about Tommy keeping a diary?"

After Luis's long hug with Ms. Sanderson, she asked the boys if Tommy had been acting depressed or preoccupied or strange in any way before that night in Borderland. They both shook their heads no. Then she told them she found a few pages from his diary and how Tommy wrote about zombies and other random stuff, and how he wrote about his dad. She asked them if they knew anything about that at all. Luis and Josh spliced two mumbling, sputtering sentences together into one answer. They weren't lying. At least, Luis wasn't. He honestly knows nothing of a diary.

Josh: "No. I mean, I know he has all kinds of drawing notebooks, but like, a diary, no. He never showed me anything like that."

Luis: "She made it sound like she only found, like what, pieces of it? A few pages and not the whole thing? I don't get that."

Josh: "Yeah, I don't know."

Luis: "What do you think is in it?"

Josh: "In what?"

Luis: "The diary."

Josh: "I have no idea."

An underground base collapses and explodes on the TV screen, and the bad guy, that agent of chaos, is free.

Luis: "Do you think Tommy wrote about . . . ?" He stops, afraid to say anything more.

Josh: "I—I don't know."

Luis is irrationally angry with Josh, sick of him saying *I don't know* to everything. He thinks about asking Josh if he knows how it felt when Tommy's mother was hugging him and holding him like that, like he was the one who needed to be comforted, not her. When he told her he was sorry he meant it like he's never meant anything in his life. The *sorry* saturated him down to the mitochondria, and there's no way Josh knows how close Luis came to telling her that he felt like the biggest fraud and phony in the history of the world and that he wished it was him instead of Tommy that was gone.

Josh says, "I saw him standing outside my window again last night."

Luis doesn't say anything. Doesn't look at his friend.

"That's three nights in a row."

Luis asks, "What are we going to do?"

Josh says again, "I don't know."

Elizabeth at Split Rock, Camera Set Up, Notes About a Man Named Arnold

Elizabeth hasn't been back to Borderland since the morning after Tommy disappeared, four days ago. The police presence there this morning seems to be minimal, with one cruiser parked in the nearly empty main lot. There are two news vans, but the doors are shut and its occupants are nowhere in sight. With the hours and now days ticking away on Tommy like a doomsday clock, no media coverage is bad coverage, and she will knock on the van doors before returning to her car, but what she's planning on doing now she wants to do alone and without distraction if at all possible. Elizabeth parks a few rows over from the vans and puts on one of Tommy's baseball hats, one he stopped wearing and she found hanging by itself on the coat rack next to the back door like a dead leaf that hasn't yet fallen. The hat is blue with some sort of blocky, video game symbol on the front panel, a broad-winged bird of prey with its thorax as a pyramid of triangles. A Legend of Zelda symbol maybe?

Between the rugged terrain and her having not

jogged in weeks, she gets painful shin splints on the Pond Walk trail. She stops once, leaning on a tree, and tries to stretch them out. It doesn't help. She's so tight she can't grab her toes without having to bend her knees. She jog-walks the rest of the way, the shin splints still barking, and she's a little light-headed and overheated. She regrets not bringing a bottle of water.

It takes her more than forty minutes to get to Split Rock. Elizabeth is alone. She expects police tape around the giant boulder, or maybe across the path leading to it, and a reporter or two circling the area—there was one reporting live from the rock on TV yesterday afternoon, or a policeman stationed at the rock to, what, guard it? To keep vigil at the one place they know for sure Tommy isn't? Elizabeth spent the last half of the walk in her head rehearsing what she might say to that oafish Officer Stanton, because he'd be the one to pull that kind of duty. Whenever he comes to the DPW office (which is way too often), he takes half the chocolate kisses from the bowls on their desks and he flirts with the women in an ugly and obnoxious you're-so-lucky-I'm-even-looking-at-you way.

The park's SPLIT ROCK sign has been vandalized, with *Devils* gouged roughly into the wood above the slashed and scratched-out SPLIT. She can't help but notice the improper punctuation, the lack of the possessive apostrophe-*s*, unless the vandal meant plural or multiple devils. No ownership implied but a place of congregation. The weed-/alcohol-fueled teen likely didn't think that deeply about *devils*.

Did Detective Murtagh tell her about the sign and she forgot or was it mentioned on the news report she watched yesterday? So many of the details of the preceding days are jumbled and mixed, an oral history suffering from too many or two few retellings. Is Devil's Rock what the kids in the area call the place or something Tommy and the boys called it? She still doesn't know.

Elizabeth limps around the rock's perimeter twice before entering the actual split, which is plenty wide enough to walk into. She runs her hands along the rough granite walls that stretch high above her head. The pine needles beneath her feet are matted into the hard packed dirt. Where the split ends in the middle of the calved boulder is a small collection of notes and trinkets mixed with dead leaves that have somehow managed to survive through the previous winter, spring, and now summer. Elizabeth kneels down (there isn't room to sit with her legs crossed), and tries to sit back on her feet, but with the shin splints still aching she's not flexible enough to do so.

There are two flowers on the top, laid so that their stems cross and make a prohibitive *x*. There are two small teddy bears. One is black. The other is brown and has a broken heart stitched onto its chest. There's someone's beat-up Ames baseball hat, its black sun-bleached into light purple. There are candles with hardened tentacles of wax clinging to notes and cards that read "We miss you, Tommy," "We believe you'll come home," and promises that God and Jesus will look out for him. Elizabeth sifts through the loose notes and a coin slides out, bounces off her thighs. It's a penny, weathered and stained almost black, making it difficult to read its minting year, but it's not a wheat back; there doesn't appear to be anything special about it. Elizabeth flashes to Tommy's coins Kate had shown her. The thought of bringing the penny home and adding it to Tommy's collection feels like a false step or a step too far, and hopelessly cabalistic. She drops the penny into her shell's front pouch pocket anyway. She picks through the rest of the notes, some of which are inside plastic bags. Other notes have gotten wet and then dried, the ink dissolving into clouds. She had a feeling this morning, a hunch, that she'd find another note from Tommy here at the rock. It's why she came.

She pulls out two *MISSING: HAVE YOU SEEN* fliers she and Janice made. Janice suggested using his school picture, which was a retake of an equally awkward photo because Tommy never smiled for real in a posed picture and was always uncomfortable in those staged surroundings, so

Why are you looking at me? She chose a picture of him from earlier in the summer. In it, he stands over his bike just back from one of his friends' houses, the lazy sun going down somewhere behind the trees, and he's caught in the middle of taking off his helmet, his hair all over the place, a thick-lined and joyous scribble, and his smile is a real one, as uncontrollable as the gasp right after jumping into cold water on a summer day. Janice didn't think the picture was a clear enough shot of him, but this picture is Tommy and Elizabeth is convinced that anyone would recognize him from this photo. She can't even look at the picture now, though, with that *MISSING* headline screaming on the paper below him. She places the fliers on either side of the pile of tokens and trinkets; it's what the bottom of a dried-up wishing well might look like.

Elizabeth climbs back to her feet unsteadily and with the help of the boulder. She pauses at the edge of the split, waiting to hear someone walking down the path. If she listens hard enough, maybe she can hear the reverberations of the mysterious steps Tommy took away from Split Rock that night, and she could follow them. She would, too, even if it meant her own disappearance.

Elizabeth doesn't come home for lunch. She spends the rest of the afternoon driving through neighboring towns. She moves mainly north and west of Ames, first going into neighboring Stoughton, then Canton, Norwood, Westwood, and Needham. She uses her Facebook page, which is drowning in well-wishes and messages, to check in with a picture of Tommy and update her geographic progress. She tags the local newspapers (if the town has one) or the town's Patch page. She stops in their downtowns and squares, and if there are people walking by, she hands them a flier. When there are no more people to give fliers to, she staples fliers to walls and telephone poles and posts pictures of the hanging fliers to her and Tommy's Facebook pages.

Her last stop is the big-box technology store on Route 1. It's as cavernous as an airplane hangar, and there couldn't possibly be enough buyers for all the shiny, hungry-for-electricity gadgets housed inside. She buys a wireless high-definition security camera that she'll be able to control and monitor with her smartphone. The young woman at the register offers her a 15 percent discount if she signs up for a new credit card with them. Elizabeth gets the card even though she has too many already, never mind spending this money she doesn't have on the camera.

When Elizabeth pulls back into her driveway it's after 5 p.m. She stays in her car to read and answer texts and e-mails. There are a slew of Facebook comment notification e-mails, most of the in-our-prayers / stay-positive variety, but there's one from some guy with a bald eagle head as his avatar. His message: *Maybe you shouldve watched him better then you did then he would'nt have sneaked out drinkin and doing whatever else he should'nt be doing.*

Elizabeth grunts, drops the phone, and yells, "Fuck you!" repeatedly, and pounds on the steering wheel with an open palm. She scrambles to pick up the phone down at her feet and writes responses in her head that threaten this jackass's life in great and terrible detail, to say in no uncertain terms that he deserves a humiliating, limb-ripping, skin-rending death. Her left palm is red and throbs, and the instant she stops indulging in her righteous wrath fantasy, she deflates. Knowing she can't risk any public backlash, Elizabeth writes back: *I don't care what you think of me, but please keep your ears and eyes out for Tommy. He's just a boy and he needs everyone's help.* She types, erases, types, erases, but finally leaves what amounts to a paper cut compared to his assault. *Oh, and nice grammar.*

Elizabeth reads the rest of her e-mails. She agrees to participate in a phone interview with a midmorning AM radio talk show, one she's never listened to before. The exchange with the show's producer is as matter-of-fact as the confirmation of a dentist appointment. There's an e-mail from a lawyer who wants to represent her family's "best interests." She has been getting those e-mails for days now. She laughed at the first ones. Now she wonders if there's any way she could afford one, or if she could find one to work pro bono. Lastly, Detective Murtagh has nothing new to report. Elizabeth sends Allison a link to the jackass's Facebook thread/comment and she asks how are the Devil's Rock and the-boys-were-out-drinking details getting out to the public. Her *What's going on here? Are you telling me all I need to know?* at the end of the e-mail nicely summarizes every-thing.

Elizabeth turns her almost dead phone off and leaves the car. Once inside the house she announces, "Hi, guys," aware of the crinkling sound the plastic bag makes as the camera sways and bounces off her leg.

Janice and Kate are in the kitchen, sitting on opposite sides of the table. Janice cooked one of the premade meals left by well-wishers. Chicken marsala. Kate hates mushrooms. Maybe that's why she sits before an untouched plate with her head down and arms folded across her chest. Janice looks upset, too, or maybe she's pissed off. Something happened. Did they see the Facebook comment, too? Kate made herself a coadministrator of Tommy's page.

Elizabeth says, "That smells good," and drops the bag on the counter.

Janice: "It is good. Delicious."

"Great. I'm starvin' like Marvin." Elizabeth sits

next to Kate and rubs her back and kisses the top of her head. That she has walked into the house like *Hey Mom is home and life is good* dizzies her head. She's trying. She's trying even if none of it is working.

By the looks of her almost empty plate, Janice is done eating. She says, "What did you buy?"

"It's a surveillance camera. I'm going to set it up tonight and monitor the living room and maybe, I don't know, the front door, too. Just in case."

"Yay." Kate says it like the *fuck you*s Elizabeth spewed in her car. "Then Nana will finally see that it's not me leaving the notes." She gets up and stomps out of the kitchen.

Elizabeth calls out after her. "Kate, you need to eat something, sweetie. How about I make you some eggs and toast? Breakfast for dinner? Your favorite, right? I'll make it as soon as I'm done eating, okay?" Elizabeth takes Kate's untouched plate and gives her mother a good stare.

Janice says, "Just in case what?"

"What?"

"You said you'll monitor the front door, too, just in case. Just in case what?"

"You know, on the off chance there's some-one—" Elizabeth pauses, as though to allow both of them to fill the blank with names or faces "—I don't know who, sneaking in the house at night, leaving the notes, as a message, as a what, an

136

elaborate, cruel fucking prank. I don't know, Mom. I'm trying—trying to cover the bases." She doesn't add that she's desperate to see what she saw in her room two nights ago. It's really why she bought the camera.

Janice shakes her head, as though she hears Elizabeth's unspoken thoughts, and says, "I guess we'll see what we see."

"If it works."

"How much did it cost?"

"Enough."

Janice softens and rubs her face with her hands. "Well, my day was stupid, because, well, I'm stupid. How about yours?"

Later that night Elizabeth and Kate are on the living room couch, sitting with legs pressed against each other, the camera box open on their laps. Janice with her book and cup of green tea sits ramrod straight on the love seat, her reading glasses sliding to the edge of her nose.

Elizabeth tells Kate that she didn't get a demonstration nor did she ask any of the sales associates about the camera. She assumed it would simply record and save everything at the touch of a button.

Kate, without even having looked at the box, scoffs, "Mom, there's no way that thing has that kind of memory, unless it's uploading to some cloud you probably didn't purchase."

Elizabeth says, "Cloud? I definitely did not purchase any fluffy clouds," trying to be obtuse enough to get a smile. Kate's grunt of disproval is close enough.

They read the instructions pamphlet. The camera does have a streaming component. Via the phone app you can watch live what the camera sees, but it doesn't record the stream. Through the app you're able to change the camera angle and zoom ratios. It's supposed to adjust from night vision to daylight settings automatically. There's also a motion sensor with sensitivity settings, and if triggered, the camera takes and saves snapshots or a five-second video clip and an alert message is sent to the phone.

Elizabeth: "Snapshots and clips? That's all? I thought it would record stuff."

Kate: "You can return it and get a better one."

Elizabeth says, "Nah," though she does briefly consider repackaging the camera and the twenty-five-plus minute drive back to the box store. "You mean a more expensive one? It's fine. It'll work. You can help make it work right. Right?"

"I guess," Kate says and then snatches Elizabeth's phone away from her.

They upload the app, pick a username and password. Its configuration and connection to the device is tricky and doesn't work at first. Kate goes to the family computer and calls up a slew of YouTube video tutorials for setting up the device. Kate shouts, "This is way more complicated than it needs to be."

"Tell me about it."

Janice gets up and says, "I'm going to bed early. Good luck with the camera, girls."

Elizabeth says, "Aw, we need you to be our test subject, and do that Bigfoot walk of yours."

Kate giggles from the computer desk. When the kids were young, Nana told stories about seeing Bigfoot in the woods and wilds of New Hampshire. The kids' favorite game involved Janice pretending to be Bigfoot and she'd stomp and chase after them in the backyard as they screamed. Even as the kids got older, Janice would occasionally and unexpectedly walk through a room like the arm-swinging Bigfoot in the infamous Patterson film for a laugh.

Janice says, "Well, maybe she'll make an appearance later. You never know. Bigfoot usually has to get up in the middle of the night to go pee now."

Kate whispers, " 'Night, Nana."

Janice walks by, gives her a hug and a long kiss on the top of her head.

Kate says, "Okay," and pushes the rolling chair away from the desk, and she spins onto her feet. "I think I got it. And hey, looks like you have thirty free days of cloud space to save snapshots and clips, too, if you want."

The phone and camera are synced. Elizabeth

messes around with the app, but it crashes after trying to switch from the live stream to the camera control screen.

"Grrr. What a hunk of junk. I guess I am taking it back."

Kate says, "Relax. Apps crash. It's what they do. Try rebooting your phone."

Elizabeth turns her phone off and then on. "Oh, okay. Looks—good, I guess. Let's test the sucker out."

Elizabeth places the camera on the TV stand next to the stereo receiver that doesn't work anymore. The body of the camera is small, rectangular, and white, with a cyclopean lens in the middle. Elizabeth thinks it looks like a mini HAL from the movie *2001: A Space Odyssey*. She adjusts the view so that the entire living room fills her phone's screen. The edge of the hallway that leads to their bedrooms is a shadow stage left.

"All right. I'm going in the kitchen. You stay out of sight until I'm ready."

"Yes, ma'am!"

Elizabeth shuffles out of the living room while watching the static video. She announces, "Okay."

"Okay, what?"

"Lights out. You get the desk lamp, please." Elizabeth kills the lights in the hallway, kitchen, and living room. She leans up against the fridge, her hands cupped around the glowing screen of the phone. The night vision is black-and-white, but it's a crisp, detailed shot. She can see the rug, the couch, the whole room, no problem. She brings the phone closer to her face, as though looking for small-scale flaws or cracks. "Wow. I can see everything fine."

"Weird. Your voice came through the camera. I forgot to tell you there's a speaker and a mic, too."

"Really?"

"Yeah. You can talk through it and record sound, too. Ready for me to walk in?"

Elizabeth drops her voice into her lowest register. "I'm sorry, Dave, I'm afraid I can't let you do that."

"Um, what was that supposed to be?"

"Nothing. Quoting an old movie. Go. Go ahead."

Kate hesitantly walks into the shot from behind the couch. That far away, she looks so small, like a toddler, and then she grows exponentially as she approaches the camera.

Elizabeth says, "So weird. Your eyes and teeth are glowing."

"Hit the Record button. I want to see it." A little hesitant wave, exaggerated wide eyes, a big-mouthed smile. Light leaks out of her.

Kate runs to the kitchen and watches the recording. She says, "This is so cool."

"Isn't it?"

Mother and daughter share a look that quickly crumbles as they remember the purpose and point of the camera.

Elizabeth says, "Okay. It works. But I want to test the motion detection part, and then we'll call it a night."

The app is glitchy again. The motion detection only seems to work when Kate makes exaggerated arms movements. If she walks through the room slowly, nothing is triggered. The same happens when Elizabeth tries. Kate turns the motion sensitivity settings lower, to five feet in front of the camera and they get better results, but still not perfect.

Kate asks, "What do you think?"

"We'll give it a shot tonight, I guess. Maybe I'll return it tomorrow. Go brush your teeth and get ready for bed. I'll meet you in your bedroom."

Elizabeth adjusts the camera so she gets a shot of the front door and the living room, and nothing of the hallway or kitchen. She meant what she said to Janice about ruling out someone sneaking into the house. She speaks into the phone: "Hello? Hello?" There's a second or two lag from the phone to the camera's speakers, and she hears herself distorted and tinny, like the treble on an old stereo turned all the way up. Would Kate even know what treble is? She wants to cry that she's already thinking of Kate as being singular and without Tommy.

Elizabeth says into the phone, "Is anyone there?"

Kate calls out from down the hallway: "Mom? Mom? Are you talking to someone?"

"No one. Myself. Testing the speaker."

"Okay. Come on, let's go. I'm ready."

Elizabeth follows Kate into her little yellow bedroom. Kate says, "Don't turn off the lights until I'm in bed." She's still so young sometimes. Middle school almost broke Tommy in sixth grade, as it almost breaks all of us, and Elizabeth can't think of Kate being in that place by herself. Elizabeth slides into wild contingencies and scenarios that don't make any practical sense: Janice moving in and homeschooling Kate for a year (never mind that Mom has no teaching experience), or paying (with what money?) a rotation of tutors to teach Kate what she needs to pass the sixth-grade state exams, or begging the town to let her repeat fifth grade for her own emotional health and well-being and to keep Kate in a safe place for one more year, just one more year.

"You can turn the light out now."

"Right. Sorry."

Kate curls up under the covers. She makes Elizabeth promise to wake her up if she sees anything. She also makes her promise not to stay up all night watching her phone. Elizabeth gives noncommittal okays to both.

Kate flips onto her stomach, and with her head

turned away from Elizabeth she says, "This is hard, Mom."

"The hardest."

Kate says, "I want Tommy to come back home."

"Me too." Her words are an exhale and a resignation to play the part, to see this through until the end, whenever that might be, even if it's never.

"Do you believe he will?"

"I'm trying, Kate."

"Or do you believe he's a ghost?" Kate whispers *ghost*.

"It's awful but—I think I do. I don't know, Kate. I don't."

"You don't know what you believe?"

"Yeah. Is that weird?"

"No. That's how I feel, too."

Elizabeth sits at the edge of the bed and rubs Kate's back until her breathing is deep, long, rhythmic. Kate doesn't move when Elizabeth finally lifts her hand away. Elizabeth turns on the camera app and inspects the empty living room and implacable front door, staring into the corners and crevices of the screen, looking for shapes, for shadows. How can she not watch this all night?

Elizabeth tiptoes out of Kate's room and into the hallway. She listens and only hears the hum of the refrigerator. She holds the phone up to her face and whispers, "Are you there? Tommy?" and her digitally transmogrified words echoes back down the hallway. "I'm so scared." Her pixilated voice limping back to her is the loneliest sound in the world. She can't bear to hear it again.

Elizabeth opens her bedroom door and remains standing in the doorway. She considers spending the night on the couch and having a staring contest with the camera's eye, to see who blinks first, when there's a knock, or bump, and a shuffle, or something rubbing, sliding on the floor, perhaps. The sounds are mixed up, doubled, an echo within an echo, and Elizabeth realizes the noises are coming from two places at once. Muffled, distant, a thunderstorm at least five-Mississippis away, the sounds originate from the living room, it has to be the living room, and those same sounds, compressed and static filled, filter out of the tiny speaker in her phone.

"Hey? Hello? Is someone there?"

Elizabeth runs down the hallway into the living room and finds it how she left it: dark and empty. She stands in front of the couch and listens, listens so hard, willing those sounds and its unknown source to regenerate, to show itself, or (as she hopes and fears) *him*self. She goes to the app's audio menu, finds that nothing was recorded, nothing was saved.

She falls backward, landing on the couch, and her phone vibrates with the motion detection alert, then a video clip opens of her sitting on the couch, light spilling out of her eyes.

• • •

"Elizabeth? Elizabeth? Are you up?"

Elizabeth pulls her head from between the pillows. It's painfully bright in the room. She cocks one open eye to her bedroom doorway. Janice is standing there, but Kate is there, too, peering out from behind as though her Nana is a hiding spot.

Janice says, "Sorry, honey. I'm glad you actually got some sleep, but there are more pages on the living room floor."

"Shit! What time is it?" Elizabeth sits up quickly and paws around the bed for her phone.

Janice: "A little after 8:30. I was the first one up. Found the pages there. Same spot. I haven't read them yet, but Kate just did."

"Phone's on the floor. There." Kate edges halfway into the room and points.

Elizabeth scoops up her phone and there are five motion-detection-triggered notifications on the home screen. "Dammit, I slept right through them." She sits back down on the bed. "The camera was set off a bunch of times!"

Janice: "It went off after Kate and I got up and went into the kitchen and living room."

"Oh, yeah, right. But hey, there's a couple notifications from when we were all sleep."

The first notification was at 2:11 a.m. and has an accompanying snapshot of the living room. There's nothing there in the still photo: no diary pages on the floor, no person walking through the door or into the room. Nothing out of the ordinary that she can tell.

Janice: "See anything?"

"The first one is just a picture. And nothing. Room's empty. So why did the camera go off. Something had to set if off, right?"

Janice: "Not necessarily. You were complaining last night that the camera wasn't working right."

Elizabeth checks the second notification, which was at 4:34 a.m. She says, "Hey, there's a video clip!"

Janice turns on the bedroom overhead light even though the room is plenty bright enough with the morning sunlight bullying through the windows, and then she sits in the plush chair. Kate slowly walks over to the bed, next to Elizabeth, and cranes her neck to watch the video on the small screen.

Elizabeth hits Play. A pile of pages are already there on the living room rug. The clip runs and she tenses up, waiting for something to happen but there's nothing. No movement, no sign of how the pages got there.

"Pages on the floor but that's it. How did they get there without the camera going off, right? Hold on, hold on . . ." She hits Play again.

Kate says, "Mom."

Elizabeth: "Wait. Okay, the pages are already there. Did I miss something? I had to have missed—holy shit! See that! See that shadow? There was a shadow right there next to the front door!"

Kate: "I saw it, too!"

Elizabeth looks up at Kate and then over to Janice. "Come on, you have to watch this."

Janice and Kate crowd closer around Elizabeth and the phone, and she replays the video. Five seconds in Elizabeth says, "There! Did you see it? Let me go back. Did you see that? There was a shadow of someone standing there, long and thin, and then shrunk down to nothing, like it winked out or went offscreen or something. Did you see it?"

Janice: "I'm not sure. Maybe?"

She plays it again. And a third and fourth time. No one says anything.

"Now I can't see it. Wait. I saw it. It was there. You said you saw it, Kate, right?"

"Yeah. But I don't know now."

Janice: "Maybe it was how you were holding or tilting your phone that first time, and you saw a weird reflection."

Kate says, "Mom," again, like she wants something from her.

"No, it was there. You saw it, too. It was there. And the pages are there and something had to set off the motion detector." She keeps hitting Play. She wants more. She wants to see more.

Kate: "Mom."

"What, Kate, what?"

"You really should go read the pages, like now," Kate says. "They're on the kitchen table."

Elizabeth goes to the kitchen and sits at the table. She reads the pages and then she reads them again, and the possibility of what is and isn't on the camera footage gives way to the certainty of despair, that something unimaginably awful has indeed happened to Tommy, or maybe even worse, will happen to Tommy, and there's nothing she or anyone else can do. There's no overt or obviously stated threat within the pages. But the possibilities, the horror of possibilities. Then a manic third read. Each read happening faster, the words beginning to be memorized, categorized, but their meanings, their stories, their poor representations of what it was that actually happened are still out of reach. During a fourth read, Janice and Kate's distant rumble of recriminations and arguments and accusations explodes. Kate is all but screaming her denial that she is the source of the mysteriously appearing diary pages.

Elizabeth stands, and she yells, "Shut up! Both of you! Just shut the fuck up for once! Can you do that? Can you?" It isn't fair and she doesn't mean it. The outburst is not really directed at them, but at the avalanche of the what-ifs smothering her.

Elizabeth can't look at either her mother or her

daughter. There's a light sniffling coming from one of them. She says, "Look, I'm sorry. I shouldn't have said that. Please, we need each other. We can't do this or be like this, you know? And I'm—I need it quiet right now. Okay? I'm calling Detective Allison."

Allison answers after the second ring. Janice and Kate stand in their respective corners of the kitchen. Kate runs her fingers through her hair, pulling it over her face. The coffeemaker needs more water and it flashes a blue light on Janice's elbow. Elizabeth tells Allison she's found more of Tommy's diary pages, and she describes their content. When asked where the pages came from, Elizabeth says she has yet to find their source, and that Tommy had stuck them in different places in his room and the house. Elizabeth says she doesn't know why he would spread those pages out like that, but she will keep looking and digging around and let her know if she finds more. Allison asks if she can come pick up the newest pages now. Elizabeth says, "Yes. Come on over. We'll be here," and hangs up.

Janice says, "What are we going to say to the detective about the surveillance cam?"

"Nothing. Unless she asks."

"If she asks?"

"The truth. I'm watching our front door and our living room for—"

"For who, Elizabeth?"

"For whoever it might be." Elizabeth stares at Janice until she looks away.

Kate walks out of the kitchen and goes to the bathroom and turns on the fan. Janice tends to the coffeemaker. Elizabeth stays at the kitchen table and reads the pages once more. Then she turns them over, print side down. She goes back to her phone and studies last night's snapshot and video clip. She's convinced that when she first watched the video Tommy's shadow was there. Just like he was there that night in her room. He was there in the video, a shadow hiding in the dark, huddled in the kitchen. There. He was there even if he isn't there now. She compares the snapshot to paused stills in the video, searching for subtle variations in the tone, color, depth of the images. She's missing something, and maybe if she watches the video the right way at the right angle, he'll be there again.

WEIRD DAY Slee pee, Headache, and feelin kinda wizzy,. Not all bad. I guess. Wizzy because of my first beer ever. YOU READ THIS AND TELL MOM U R DEAD KATE! Papa sneaked me sips at bbq's when I was little and he laughed at my yuck face but today was the first time I ever drank all the can. Most of it.

Taste, still not great, especially near the end when it gets warm and flat. Josh and Luis were hardos + acted like they loved every drop. Yeah, right. I saw Josh sneak dumping his beer out when he climbed down to take a leak. I was NOT so sneaky about it, yeah, I poured the dregs out into a crack in the rock behind the devil tree and three big black ants were caught in the beer river. I tried flicking them out and I know Arnold saw me dump the beer but he was cool about it. Didn't care. RESTART! Soooo me + the boyz rode to five corners and the 7-11. Out front we were sitting on our bikes talking about zombies and Minecraft + Minecraft and zombies, and then Arnold came over and jumped right in, saying something about the first time he tried sleeping in Nether and he almost shit his pants when the bed exploded and his spawn point was so far away he lost like three hours of build. We all thought for like a second Arnold was some high schooler with buddies that would jump out and hassle us or some random creeper but he's not. He's a

good guy. Then we talked about
zombies too and I told him how I
wanted to use split rock as a base.
He knew where I was talking about
but he called it devil's rock. ??? is
what we all said without saying.
YOU DON'T KNOW WHY IT''S
CALLED DEVIL'SROCK? He told us
to meet him out there later and he
left and we weren't sure and we
went to the rock anyway. Luis
brought a backpack with his old
metal tee ball bat stuffed inside like
that would do anything to protect
us. We got there early + Arnold
showed up with a brown bag, inside
was a six pack. He started talking
more Minecraft stuff about his own
server and not using ice torches for
light when building with ice. Luis
said no suh, really? Like the dink he
is and I said Chirps! and Josh hardo
hand motioned Luis and we all
laughed. Arnold didn't even ask and
tossed us beers, didn't make a big
deal about it. He said, Drink it or
don't, its all good, yeah? White foam
gushed out my can and I tried to
suck it all up before it spilled all over
me. Then I looked around like a cop

or something would jump out from behind a tree. No one there. I took another sip, then kept the can hid behind my leg. Arnold told us the story of devil's rock, it was kinda long but it started with the devil, he called him old scratch, kinda cool + creepy, and how the devil stole souls in the woods that eventually became borderland and that dude Eastman bought the land and figured out how to trick old scratch into disappearing and that creepy tree grew up out of the devil's footprint on split rock. Luis loved the story (no duh) and asked 37 questions about the devil and if Arnold watched horror movies blah blah blah. Josh tried to make jokes and pretended to drink his beer. Kid needs to chill. I drew old scratch in my head. Arnold told us to meet him again in two days. The ride home was painful. Knees all hacked up, nasty bruises on my elbow and shoulder. Three of us crashed our bikes into stuff and each other on purpose pretending not-pretending we were drunk riding. Yeah, I know, right? Totally crazy and messed up given what happened to Dad, and I knew it when we were doing it. I don't know if Luis or Josh even thought about it, I couldn't stop myself and was going harder and harder into them until they complained and told me to take it easy and my last crash, the tree in Josh's front yard, I didn't even brake at all and went flying over the handlebars and then rolling through the grass. And sitting here now, I'm shaking a little bit, and it's all so fucked up ~~that I could cry about it.~~

Check this out!!! HEY Kate are you reading this? For reals? I'll wait. Really? You reading this? How bout . . . now? I pretend I'm talking to you when I write in here because you're probably reading it anyway. I keep saying that because it's true. I might go talk to you about this. It's too weird and amazing. We met Arnold out at Devil's Rock again. He brought more beer and he chirped Josh about needing to take a leak before he started drinking. It wasn't mean or nothing, Arnold isn't like that at all. Josh laughed + finally relaxed. Luis chirped kinda mean at Josh and Arnold gave Luis OUR hardo hand symbol! The three of us cracked up. How'd he know, right? We only used it once, maybe once, in front of him, and he was like perfect with it, used it like we'd use it. Then we talked zombies again and the brain fungus + outlined my full plan. And it was CRAZY! Arnold totally guessed that Luis wanted to fortify the second floor of a house and even threw in the knocked out staircase, and he guessed that Josh wanted to hole up in a mall or a school, some big place with supplies. So yeah. He. Was. Spot. On. We asked him how he guessed that? He said that he's a SEER, that he can see things, like no biggie. I laughed + was the only one who laughed. Arnold didn't get mad. He's a good guy, little weird, little off, but very cool, and smart in a way that isn't hardo, okay? he smiled and said no, it was true. Sometimes he can see things as they are, as they were, as they will be. Not all the time, but sometimes. He said he sees great things for us and toasted us. We toasted too, Josh even did it, and spilled and then choked like mad. Luis in full wiseass mode said You didn't see that coming, did ya? Then he wanted more from Arnold, to prove it. Arnold pointed at Luis and said that his father was a hardo (Josh and I looked at each other, how does he know our word, right???), and said some serious stuff about Luis's dad that's like scary true, and then he pointed at Josh and said it was his Mom that was the hardo and said SPOT ON stuff about her too. Luis tried to brush it all off and said that everyone's parents were hardos. Arnold looked at me and said not everyone's parents were hardos. Then he looked kinda sad, like he had something he didn't want to say, it was like he's been always looking at me. Freaky shit I know. THEN he said that someone important was gone from my life and then nobody said anything. I know I didn't say anything, and then he said Your father? He said it like a question but not really a question. Made it seem like it was a guess when there's no way it was a guess. He knew!!!

Somehow he knew! I told him yeah and then I started talking about Dad and how he ran away and then died for the first time ever out loud to anybody. I thought I was going to start crying but I didn't and after I felt so, I don't know. Good? Lame I know, but I'm having a hard time explaining how it felt, how I felt. That's why I might go talk to you about this with YOU, K8. After we hung out and drank the beers (I had two this time) and I know it sounds MORE lame but it was all just awesome.

Allison and Luis, Luis and the Devil at the Rock

D etective Allison Murtagh meets with Luis's parents at their house, sequestered just off the kitchen, sitting at the dining room table that likely isn't used for very many family meals. Their dining room table has no tablecloth. The tabletop is thick, darkly stained, and as weathered as a New England farmhouse with deep gouges and cup rings eating into the wood. Mrs. Fernandez apologizes for the dusty table and for the place being a mess. Allison stops herself from blurting out *If you want to see a mess, you have no idea.*

Three months ago Allison moved her eighty-four-year-old father (suffering with Alzheimer's) into a nursing home, and she has since moved out of her condo to live in her family's old house in Ames. She uses her parents' old dining room table as an open filing cabinet. With a single chair (the rest of the set is moldering in the basement) situated in the middle of the table lengthwise, the right side of the table is covered in legal documents, Medicare forms, communiqués from the lawyer and nursing home, tax records, each and all part of an ongoing legal evolution that began over six months ago after her father signed over power of attorney, allowing Allison to make decisions regarding his health care and finances. On the left side of the table are piles of Dad's bills and receipts arranged into stalagmites of varying heights. All of her waking off-hours (which, these days, aren't many, given how much time she's dedicated to the search for Tommy Sanderson) are spent visiting Dad or holed up in the old house trying to get her father's affairs in some sort of order. The only time she's ever been more exhausted, physically and emotionally, was when she broke up with her longtime girlfriend, Amy, three years ago.

Mr. and Mrs. Fernandez offer Allison a coffee or water. She refuses both and places a notebook on the table. A black pen bookmarks the bulging spine. The Fernandezes are polite if not grim, serious, difficult to read. More cooperative than most. She tells them about Tommy's diary pages that were found this morning, but not more than they need to know. And she tells them about a man named Arnold who spent time with the boys, and she would like to ask Luis about him.

Allison says, "I'm certainly a long way away from being able to say that Arnold is in any way related to the disappearance, but he is someone I'd like to know more about." She's careful with pronouns, to say that *she* wants this information and not use *we,* even if it would be a *royal we.*

Allison knows that at times a more personal approach in interviews is better than portraying herself as a mouthpiece of the State, as Amy so lovingly used to put it.

Mr. Fernandez says, "I'll go get him."

Luis walks in with his dad's heavy hand on his back—a gesture of comfort or a push, Allison cannot tell. Mrs. Fernandez moves her chair over and tells her husband to bring the other chair around so that the three of them are sitting on the same side of the table, with Luis the farthest away from Allison.

"Hi, Luis."

"Hello, Detective Murtagh."

Allison can't get over his size, or lack of size. Everything about him is small and young, especially his face; gaunt, all dark eyes, smooth skin without a hint of the transformation to come. That he's poised to be an eighth grader is, frankly, shocking. His middle school experience must be similar to the smallest gazelle on the Serengeti.

"Ms. Sanderson found some diary entries of Tommy's, and in them he writes about you guys hanging out with someone named Arnold." She stops there, knowing that she hasn't really asked a question. She wants his reaction.

"Okay, yeah. Arnold." He's sheepish, but a normal sheepish, the appropriate level of distrust within a room full of adults watching you being interviewed by an authority figure.

"He's older than you are, correct? Any idea how old?"

"Definitely out of high school. Early twenties maybe. Midtwenties? Don't know for sure."

"How long have you known him?"

"We met him earlier this summer. In June. Not too long after school got out."

"Where and how did you meet him?"

"We rode our bikes to the 7-Eleven at Five Corners. We did that a lot this summer. To buy soda, gum, candy." He pauses and looks at his parents. They both nod. "And me and Josh and Tommy, you know, the three of us, hanging out front. Arnold came by and he started talking, and . . ." Luis shrugged. "And we started hanging out together."

"Where did you hang out together that first day?"

"First just at the 7-Eleven, but then, we met him, later, in the afternoon, at Borderland."

"Any particular place inside the park?"

"Yeah, at Devil's Rock."

Allison could almost hear Mr. Fernandez's knuckles tighten into fists he's keeping hidden under the table. Mrs. Fernandez is turned away from Allison and watching her son.

Allison says, "What were you guys doing?"

That shrug again. "Hanging out. Talking."

"Anything else?" Allison sits up straight in her chair and pushes her notebook away, but not far enough away that she can't consult it or add to it.

"He, uh, he brought a six-pack?" Luis says it like a question, but it still comes off as confident and surprisingly composed, especially for a kid admitting he was drinking beer with some random older guy in the woods, the same woods and same spot from which one of his best friends has gone missing. It's a reminder that he is indeed older than he looks.

Mr. Fernandez sighs at this and then folds his arms across his chest.

Allison: "Did you drink?"

"Yeah. Just one, though. First one ever."

"Did the three of you ask him to buy for you when you were at Five Corners? Charlie's Liquors is right there."

"No. No." Luis turns to his parents and says, "None of us asked him to buy or bring anything. He just showed up with them, I swear."

"Do you know his last name?"

"No, he's just Arnold."

"What does he do?"

"I don't know. He mentioned something about being between jobs, taking the summer off."

"How much of him did you see this summer?"

Luis looks up and to the left. "Like . . . five times at Split Rock, I think. And we ran into him sometimes kinda randomly at the 7-Eleven, too."

"Randomly?"

163

"Yeah. We never really planned anything with him. We were there a lot with nothing to do and sometimes he'd show up and we'd go to Devil's Rock."

"You mean Split Rock."

"Yeah, same thing, I guess. Detective?"

"Yes."

"Are you asking me about Arnold because you think he has something to do with Tommy disappearing?"

"I'm asking to find out as much information as I possibly can. Why hasn't Arnold come up before today? You and Josh were very forthcoming in providing a list of Tommy's other friends' and classmates' names. Why not Arnold?"

"I—uh—I didn't think of him like that."

"Like what?"

"Like a friend."

"So he's not a friend? What is he then?"

"No, I guess he is. That's not what I mean . . ."

"How did you mean it then?"

"I don't know, it's hard for me to—to describe, I guess? I thought you were asking for kids our age, you know, for places Tommy might go to."

"Really, Luis?" Allison tries to muster the right amount of sarcasm to lighten the blow but at the same time make her point. Why didn't he and/or Josh give up this guy's name days ago?

"Yes, really," he says, and his voice goes high-pitched whiney and he's a little kid all over again.

"We hadn't seen him in a few weeks and we don't know where he lives or have his phone number or anything like that. Tommy wouldn't know where to find him even if he wanted to."

Mr. Fernandez blurts out, "I can't take this. This is bullshit. You and Josh didn't tell the police about this Arnold guy because you were covering your own asses, not wanting to get in more trouble for sneaking out and drinking and doing who knows *what* else with some goddamn loser. Probably, what, your drug dealer too, right? Is that it?"

"What? No! It's nothing like that, Dad!" and all three Fernandezes are yelling over one another.

Allison doesn't interrupt and waits for the storm to pass. It does only after Luis throws his cell phone on the table and dares his parents to check the phone numbers and text messages. The three of them stare at the phone and are breathing heavily. Luis lifts his feet onto the chair, wraps his arms around his knees, rolled up tight in a little ball of anger.

Allison locks eyes with Mr. Fernandez when he reaches out for his son's phone. She says, "Is it all right if I continue?"

He says, "Yes. Sorry about that." He has the phone in his hand but places it in front of Mrs. Fernandez. "Sorry. Go ahead."

"Thank you. I understand this isn't easy. Luis, to be clear, I'm not accusing Arnold, you, or your friends of doing anything wrong. I'm trying to get all the information I can. I appreciate you being so helpful. Okay?"

Luis nods and loosens back into his original posture.

She says, "Let's go back. I'd like you to tell me more about that first time with Arnold at Split Rock."

"Okay."

Now that Arnold was up on the rock with them, he seemed bigger than he did when they were sitting on their bikes at the 7-Eleven. He wasn't *huge,* there were some guys bigger than him at the middle school, but he was a shade taller than Tommy's five feet eleven and three quarters. Luis wouldn't let Tommy call himself six feet until he was actually six feet. It was only fair. Arnold was thicker and outweighed Tommy by a good forty pounds, which wasn't saying much given how stick-man thin Tommy was. Arnold had on jeans that weren't tight but not quite baggy, either, and were too long in the leg; the bottoms pooled around his feet and were all dirty and frayed from being dragged across the ground. He wore black Chuck Taylors on his feet, the logo scratched off, and a tight long-sleeved shirt, black with green stripes, the sleeves pushed up past his hairy forearms and over his elbows. He had one of those survival bracelets that you could unravel into ten feet of camo-colored emergency nylon rope. Luis had had his mom buy him one for his birthday in the spring, insisting she get a regular adult one, not kiddie-sized. He didn't wear it because it was like a hula hoop for his wrist and he could slide it up to his elbow. Arnold didn't have a beard but maybe what he had would be considered a full-blown beard if he didn't shave tomorrow. If not for the facial hair, he could pass for high school, or college, or whatever came right after college. Luis didn't know for sure as he categorized anyone more than a few years older than him into a nebulous, vast galaxy of adults younger than his parents and teachers. Arnold's dark brown hair was short on the sides and slightly longer at the top, pushed up into a faux hawk, a point at the top of his head. His chin came to a sharp point, too. His lips were pulled tightly over his sizable front teeth. He had thin but clearly delineated eye-brows, like borders on a map. His eyes were dark and always up, never down, and you knew when they were looking at you.

Arnold said, "Drink it or don't. No pressure. Not a big deal. It's all good." He plucked cans from the six-pack like he was choosing the ripest fruit from a tree.

Luis almost dropped the beer when Arnold tossed it to him underhand. Tommy caught his with one hand and then opened it right away in a show-off motion that was pretty cool until the foam volcanoed out. Tommy laughed and started drinking, trying to catch it all. After he pulled the can away he covered his mouth with the back of his hand and his eyes were big, blinking, and watery.

"Sorry about that. The long walk in here shook them all up." Arnold smiled and he looked at Luis and said, "Tap on the top of the can like this for a little bit before you open it. Helps calm down the suds." Luis did as instructed and tapped the can with his pointer finger, tapping hard enough that his woodpecker-like fingertip went pleasantly numb. He stopped when Arnold stopped. Josh did the same. Luis dug his fingernail underneath the tab and pried it up. The crack and fizz was loud, and there was no foam. The smell hit him right away, and it smelled like the recycle bucket his dad used to keep in the garage and now kept out by the shed. The first mouthful expanded and filled Luis's head, and it was too warm, too bitter and sharp. His throat, with some limbic mind of its own, constricted, and he struggled to swallow it all. He was abnormally aware as it slid down through him and then leached out from his middle. That people enjoyed drinking this seemed like a secret he'd never be privy to. But the second sip was a little better than the first. The same with the third. He could do this.

Arnold said, "Welcome to Devil's Rock, guys. Cheers!"

Tommy: "Cheers, sir!" He looked to Josh and Luis for a reaction. His goofy smile dimmed, and his sip was nowhere near as enthusiastic as his first.

"Yeah, let's hear it." Josh sat down on the rock, totally fish-lipped his beer and put it down, hiding it under his tented legs.

Luis was going to stay standing and make sure he would take bigger sips and be the first one to finish his beer. Maybe he'd even crush the can with his hand, or better yet, stomp it flat under his heel. His next sip was too big and hurt his chest going down.

Arnold stayed standing, too, and he stood in the middle of the triangle of the three boys, the split in the rock as a boundary to his left. "This is a good story. It gets a little long because I like to tell it, but we'll deal. It's a story about an old friend, of course: the devil. Or Old Scratch. He has lots of names but that one's the coolest. Old Scratch sounds sexier, meaner."

Josh said, "Old Scratch," in his deepest voice. "Hey, he's right."

Tommy laughed, but Luis cringed at the self-proclaimed future politician trying to be . . . what? Political? Luis couldn't really put into words how it was Josh acted around adults, but it annoyed him. Why couldn't Josh be normal, or at least normal around this guy? Luis dismissively threw "Hardo" at Josh from the side of his mouth and pointed an open, karate-chop hardo-hand at him, too.

Arnold says, "This story goes back to the Puritans, yeah? They were always screaming about the devil and blaming him for everything bad they did and everything that went wrong. Which was fine by him. The devil's in the coincidence? Right?"

Josh: "Isn't it 'the devil's in the details'?"

Arnold: "Same thing. And I like my saying better. It's more accurate. You'll see. Anyway, without the devil even doing anything, they could already see his hand in every action, hiding behind every tree, crouched in every shadow. No deer in the woods, bad year for crops, unfaithful husband, sick and dying kids, all his fault, right? Those Puritan dickheads were the perfect marks. And sometimes Old Scratch would make things more interesting, stir up a little chaos, you know. Tell them what he could see." Arnold arched his eyebrows and took a sip of beer.

Luis took a sip, too.

Josh, again: "Like what?"

"He'd tell 'em how their neighbor was the one who stole potatoes or a chicken, or that guy over there, he poisoned your crops and was saying stuff about your wife, too. He'd tell 'em what should be done about that cute minister's daughter, or that so-and-so's wife wanted to fuck you and if she wouldn't, no worries, you could accuse her of being a witch and stay in the Lord's good graces. He's good at pushing you into doing stuff that you only daydream or think about, yeah.

"There are stories about the devil everywhere you go in New England, but these woods in this area here were feared more than any other. Especially the old quarry. You guys been there yet?"

Luis answered for the group. "No."

"You should go. So cool. Almost two hundred years ago, when a local railroad company used the granite from the quarry to build a huge bridge, the workers told stories about seeing the devil hiding in the surrounding woods or down in the rocks, peeking out through the gaps. They said he had secret caves and he would whisper to them, telling them terrible things. Everyone was spooked. Except Oakes Eastman."

Josh: "Oakes? What kind of fucking name is Oakes?" He laughed that fake, little high-pitched laugh, a combo of voice crack and fake stoner.

Luis sighed. A little buzzed and too annoyed to feel guilty for wishing that they had left Josh at home.

Arnold: "One of the Eastmans, the famous Eastmans, you know, the same one who bought all this land and built the estate. He was a weird guy; a botanist or some shit like that—with a name like Oakes, guess he was destined for that bullshit, huh? No such thing as coincidence, boys. Like I said, coincidence is where the devil lives, man. And hey, his wife was an artist and into drawing freaky stuff, too. The perfect couple to buy up a bunch of creepy woods and call it *Borderland*.

"Before he built the mansion Oakes went for walks all up and around the ponds to do whatever a botanist does, and he saw the devil watching him. He could only see the devil out of the corners of his eyes. You know what I mean? You know how to look out of the corners of your eyes, right? You can only see him when you're not really looking at him." Arnold turned so that he wasn't looking directly at any of the boys. "But Old Scratch was there, dancing around in the edges, and getting closer. On one of Oakes's walks he found this boulder, the one with the split in it like it was a door to Nether, right." Arnold stopped and started coughing. "Dry throat. Anybody want another beer?"

Tommy and Josh said no. Luis could tell their cans were still practically full. He had maybe a quarter left. Luis said, "Almost ready." He took a deep breath to gird himself up for the big finish.

Arnold grabbed himself a second beer. "So, before they moved limestone one to start building his mansion and the natural pool and all the rest of it, Oakes decided he'd fix his devil problem, and he came up with a plan. He invited anyone and everyone who said they could help. Priest or rabbi or pagan or one of his folklore Harvard professor friends, didn't matter, and like I said, Oakes and his wife knew a lot of weird people. He took them all to Split Rock when the sun was bright and as high above their heads as possible and he had all of them bless or put spells, not on the rock, but on the ground, the dirt between the split, down there. You can't bless or un-devil—" Arnold laughed at his own made up word, and Luis did, too "—a rock. But you can bless dirt and clay, though."

Josh chimed in again. "Why not?"

"Ever heard of consecrated ground?"

"Yeah. I guess."

"Ever heard of consecrated rock?"

Josh shrugged and made a face. "No. I don't know, I have no idea. I—"

"Dude. It's just a story. Almost done."

Arnold walked over to the split, the four-foot-wide gap between the calved boulders, and pointed down. "No one really knows which one out of all the prayers or rituals or spells exactly worked. It doesn't matter, I guess. What does matter is that Oakes like napalmed the ground down there with all sorts of hocus pocus."

Luis said, "Hocus pocus? Was the guy Harry

Potter or a kid's birthday party magician?" and he gave Arnold a wiseass smirk. His chirp was cool, well timed, not annoying like Josh. Josh was like the auto-correct on his cell phone.

Arnold returned Luis's smirk. "Abracadabra?"

Luis groaned and shook his empty beer can at him.

Arnold didn't ask Luis if he was sure he wanted another or if he could handle another, and he didn't suggest that Luis slow down because he wasn't a *big* guy. Arnold laughed, slapped Luis on the back, and handed Luis a second can. Luis turned so that his back was to Arnold, puffed himself up, and flexed his arms for his friends. He said, "Come get some." Tommy and Josh rolled their eyes, but they were also visibly uncomfortable while looking at their own still-not-empty beer cans and not really doing anything with them. Luis had the wild urge to jump one of them, slip behind them and put them in a headlock, and then roll them off the rock and be king of the hill. He stayed close to Arnold, sitting a few feet away, then opened his beer and took a greedy sip, big enough that he felt a little dizzy after.

Arnold continued his story. "Later that night Oakes went for a hike in the woods. He carried a lantern"—Arnold held out his can in front of him, pantomiming *lantern*—"and a walking stick, and made his way to Split Rock. The whole way

174

there he felt Old Scratch nipping at his heels, and he heard him whispering into his ear, telling how he could make sure his family was rich forever, how he could make him governor like he made his father governor—that one freaked the hell out of Oakes—promising Oakes anything he wanted; make him stronger"—Arnold held his beer in front of his crotch—"or longer, all he had to do was say the word. Oakes was careful not to say anything, and he walked straight to Split Rock. He climbed up to the top and stopped right before the split. Old Scratch followed, and his feet sounded like they were scratching up the rock. Might be one of the reasons why they call him Old Scratch. I'll show you later, but there's a spot down there that looks like one of his footprints in the rock." Arnold paused and walked in a circle, then he put one foot over the split, straddling the gap. "Oakes turned around to face the devil, like this. He made sure to keep the split between his feet.

"He told the devil that before he agrees to anything, he wants to know if the offer is legit. Oakes said he's heard stories of the devil cheating folks. The devil heard that kind of stuff all the time, so that didn't bother him. He laughed and said that a deal was a deal, his word was his word. Then he said, 'I can show you.' Oakes asked him how he could show him. And the devil said, 'I'll come over there and make my eyes your eyes.

Oh, the things I can show you.' Oakes could *feel* Old Scratch say that, like the devil was already inside of him this whole time. Oakes was shaking scared but held his ground as the devil came closer and closer, and then the devil reached out for him, and right as those cold claws were about to touch him, Oakes shuffled his feet back quick—" Arnold moved backward, too, hovering his torso above the split "—and with the devil leaning forward, off balance, Oakes swiped the devil's feet out from under him with that walking stick and he fell down into the split. He landed hard but got right up and started scrabbling around down there like a trapped animal, and he was screaming and yowling, so loud, the worst sounds ever. The devil wasn't hurt, but he was stuck. Couldn't climb up the walls and he couldn't just walk out between the boulders into the forest. It worked. Whatever spell it was they put down there, or the combo of all of them together, it worked. The devil was trapped.

"That night everyone who lived in Ames could hear his howling and crying all night long. The next morning, Oakes went back and the devil was gone. There was nothing there." Arnold walked away from the split and sat down in the middle of the boulder, held his beer can up, and took a long sip.

Luis said, "That story is *the* awesome. Should be a movie."

Tommy: "Okay. Devil's Rock it is then."

Josh said, "That's it? The devil just went away?"

If Luis's can was empty, he would've thrown it at Josh.

Arnold said, "Sort of. Oakes built his mansion and cut the walking paths through Borderland and everything was fine for years, decades even. Then, later when they were both old, Oakes and his wife started seeing someone peeking into their windows at night, watching them sleep. They could see it out of the corner of their eyes, but when they went over to the window and really looked there was nobody there, and no footprints or nothing outside below their window or anywhere on the grounds. His wife even thought she saw someone standing actually inside their bedroom, standing there and watching. Oakes, when he was an old, old man, like a year or so before he died, went back to the rock for the first and only time since that night he tricked and trapped the devil, and he found this tree, right there, reaching up and out above the crack like a claw."

Josh: "Pfft. That tree isn't a hundred years old."

Luis: "Shut up."

Arnold held up his hands. "I'm telling you like I heard it. And legend has it that you need to keep away from the tree. If you touch it, it's like you're calling the devil, inviting him for a visit."

Luis said, "Josh loves to touch it."

Luis and Josh exchanged a volley of masturbation and small dick insults, each one with a little bit more of an edge to it than the previous.

Tommy said, "Who told you this story?"

"My uncle. The Rev. Well, he used to be a reverend. He was always filling my head with stories about the devil. When I was little, he had me convinced the devil was following me around, that he followed everyone around. I was scared shitless all that time. But now I know."

Tommy: "Now you know what?"

Arnold: "That it was all bullshit."

Luis was in the giddy grips of his first full-on buzz by this point. His head hummed pleasantly and his tongue was sluggish and imprecise. "I'll drink to that, yo."

" 'Yo'?" Tommy cracked up laughing. They all did.

Two days later the boys trekked back to Devil's Rock, as planned. The trip out was arduous, as they were still all nicked up and sore from their epic, drunken crash-and-ride out of the park. Tommy's front bike tire was a little warped. He'd tried to bend it back into shape before they left, but it still had a wobble, and the tire would intermittently rub up against the brake pads, slowing him down considerably. Luis led the way, driving them harder and deeper into the woods, until the boys got to Devil's Rock and got there early, before Arnold.

They inspected the spot down near the base of the rock. Arnold had claimed what they were looking at was the devil's footprint. There were two round spots, the heel and ball of the foot presumably, and then four long scratches, or gouges, above the spots.

Josh said, "That's not anything. Everyone knows the devil had hooves, not, what, claws?"

Luis: "Everyone knows the devil has your dick."

Tommy: "No idea what that means. But I like it."

Josh went on critiquing the anatomical validity of the footprint. Luis had to admit, it had looked more realistic, more possible, the other afternoon than it did now.

Tommy filled a pocket with small stones and twigs then climbed up to the top of the rock. Josh and Luis followed. Tommy grabbed Josh and pulled him toward the gnarly tree, trying to push him up against it.

Tommy said, "Go ahead. Touch it, touch it," in some unidentifiable accent.

When Luis tried to help Tommy double-team Josh, it was a trap. Tommy let Josh go, who spun away awkwardly, landing on his hip, one foot dangling into the split (Josh shouted from behind them: "Assholes! I could've fell in!"), and Tommy wrapped his arms around Luis and kept saying, "Touch it, touch it!" in that weird voice. Luis put up a good fight, but he had no leverage. Tommy was already up underneath Luis's arms, lifting him up. He couldn't keep his feet on the rock

and he lost, his chest and shoulder pinned up against the tree, and pinned hard.

Luis said, "Okay, okay. Goddamn it. Get off!"

Josh came to his rescue, jamming two hard fingers into Tommy's side ("Ow! Don't taze me, bruh!") and the two boys muscled Tommy's back into the tree. Then it was Josh's turn to be pushed against it, because fair was fair.

After wrestling, they sat with their legs dangling over the edge of the split, and they tossed the stones and twigs Tommy had brought up, trying to hit an assortment of targets, including ants that were climbing the rock face.

Arnold arrived a few minutes later with more beer hidden inside a brown paper bag. Despite the heat and humidity, Arnold still wore the same pair of jeans with the long, floppy cuffs. He had on a plain black T-shirt this time. It was too big for him, the sleeves drooping to his elbows and the bottom of the shirt sinking almost to the tops of his thighs. He had a green Boston Celtics hat, worn backward, the oversized bill sticking out behind his head like a ledge.

"Gentlemen! You look thirsty."

Josh and Tommy exchanged are-we-really-doing-this-again? looks. Luis laughed at them, his first hangover—a headache that felt like there was another, bigger head inside of his trying to push its way out—now forgotten, and said, "I know I am."

Arnold gave Luis a beer and a fist-pound to punctuate the exchange. Luis paced quick circles on the top of the rock, too excited to sit still.

They drank, joked around, and talked, and Arnold fit in so easily, to the point where he started anticipating what joke or friendly put-down was next. Arnold also picked up on their *hardo* lingo and the accompanying hand signal, using both perfectly, like he'd always done it. Luis marveled that Arnold had not once talked about what he did when he was their age, and that he had yet to place Luis and his friends in an arbitrary age hierarchy like high school kids and other adults would normally do. Everything Arnold said to them was about the present, their inclusive, shared present. He was and wanted to be a part of their group, and Luis couldn't have been happier.

The conversation shifted to zombie contingency plans, as it generally did when Tommy was around, and Arnold's prescience gained momentum, started getting strange. Josh was being annoying again, overreacting (or acting drunk because maybe he actually drank some of the beer this time and didn't dump it out), shouting a long, drawn-out "Whoa!" to everything Arnold said.

Tommy was more straightforward and asked how Arnold guessed that Luis wanted to knock out the stairs to the second floor of his house and that Josh wanted to hole up at a school when the zombies attacked.

Arnold said, "Well." He scratched the side of his face. "I can see things."

"Really. No, really?" Tommy laughed like it all was a joke.

"Yeah. Seriously. It's not there all the time, you know? But sometimes I can see things as—as they are, if that makes sense. Or as they were. Or as they will be. I know, it's weird, but it's true. I'm a, uh, seer." He tilted his beer can at Luis and added, "It's runs in the family. My uncle, the Rev, he was a seer, too. And good news. I see great things for you guys."

Josh said in a bad imitation of Luis's voice, "I'll drink to that, yo," and giggled.

Tommy: "Chirps!"

Luis: "Now I hate myself as much as I hate you."

Josh choked and coughed midsip, and beer dribbled all down his front. "Ah, man. Now I'm gonna smell like beer. I can't walk into my house like this."

Luis looked at Arnold and said, "Didn't see that coming did you, seer?"

Arnold: "Seer sees a drinking problem."

Tommy and Luis yelled "Ooooh!" and pointed and laughed at Josh.

The laughter gave way to an awkward lull. They nursed their beers, everyone unsure of what to say next with the odd seer revelation out there. Luis wondered if Arnold regretted saying anything about it. Was Arnold being serious, or was he setting them up for a big joke? Either way, it made Luis wonder who Arnold was and what did he want from them?

Luis asked for more proof of Arnold's "seership." It came out somewhere between accusatory and wiseass. He didn't mean it that way. He only wanted to keep the conversation or joke, whichever it was, going. Arnold looked at Luis with narrowed eyes and a titled head, like the quip stung, and Luis instantly wanted to apologize.

Arnold said, "Okay. It doesn't always work on command. It's kinda frustrating sometimes, you know." He walked around the interior of their circle, staring at each of the boys. Tommy covered his eyes, pretending to be embarrassed. Arnold laughed and punched Tommy in the shoulder. "Jackass."

"Hey, child abuse!"

Arnold suddenly turned and pointed at Luis, and said, "His father is a hardo."

Josh: "Ah, come on. That's too—"

Arnold kept talking, not so much to Luis, but at

183

him. "Your father is all over you about homework, right? Am I right? Like all over you? When you come home or when he comes home, he works late a lot?" Arnold spoke in questions that were actually statements, as though fishing for clues.

Luis didn't saying anything back. But not because Arnold wasn't correct.

Arnold: "Before your father says *hi* or *how was your day, son?* or *talk to any cute girls?* he asks if you've done your homework. And how much you have. He always asks how much, yeah? And you say"—the *you say* was long and drawn out—"*not much?* even if there's a shit ton to do. If you blow an assignment he gets so mad. It's like he takes it personally. Of all the things to get pissed about, right? Homework? And it's the worst when you have some big project or paper due, right? He dogs you about your plan and when you're gonna start and all that shit, yeah?"

In fourth grade Luis was assigned a land-forms project. He was supposed to build a diorama with a waterfall, forest, desert, and mountain all jammed into a cardboard shoe box. On the first day he legitimately forgot to bring the project notice home from school. He was so anxiety ridden about the imagined trouble he'd be in for failing to take something so important home, he vomited twice that night and missed the next day of school and the day after that. Then it was the weekend. When he finally went back to school on Monday the notice was there in his desk, and that was where it stayed. He left it there for the two-plus weeks given to complete the assignment. He remembered the page sitting there inside the dark of his desk, always right there, on top of everything; he was careful not to bury it under his journal or textbooks. He'd lift the lid during class periodically to look at it. He wasn't so young or so addled as to believe it would disappear by itself. He couldn't explain why, but the more days that passed, the more impossible it became for him to tell his parents about the project, never mind actually completing it. The night before the project was due, and an hour before his usual bedtime, he crept up on his mother (she was reading a magazine in the kitchen, Dad was watching football in the TV room), tapped her on the shoulder, and asked if there were any empty shoe boxes lying around in a voice that didn't have any air in it. That infamous land-forms project blew up into emergency meetings and academic testing, but had since become somewhat of a family joke between Luis and his mom. It had scarred his father for the remainder of Luis's academic life.

Tommy: "Oh, shit. I've heard him do that. Luis, that's totally your dad." Josh and Tommy giggled, high-fived each other, and whispered more stuff about his dad.

"Yeah, but not exactly." Luis always felt small, there was never a moment when he wasn't in some way aware of his lack of size and physical maturity, but in the range of degrees of small, right then, he felt downright subatomic; a life and a relationship defined by interrogation over stupid homework. Was there anything more childlike? And he felt marked or stained by his father. Was *he* that easy to read? And he was superpissed at Tommy and Josh for laughing, for acting like they knew anything. They didn't know a goddamn thing.

Josh: "What about me? Do me next."

Tommy: "Yikes, bro."

Arnold rubbed his hands together then held them out like he was surrendering. "I don't know if I see anything. Wait. Your mother is the hardo."

Josh: "Eh, yeah, true. But both of my parents are hardos."

Arnold: "I'm thinking she washes your clothes every day, right? She strips your bedsheets like twice a week, I'm thinking. Makes sure you always have clean underwear, right?"

Tommy: "Ew!"

Josh: "Pfft. Like you guys wash your own clothes."

Luis did, but he didn't fess up to it.

Arnold: "You'll go home and put that shirt right into the washing machine because it's what she makes you do now that you're older. To try to give you more privacy, yeah? She talks about you becoming a *man,* like every day?" Arnold shrugs and laughs.

Josh is laughing, too, but he turns red at that statement. "It's like he can see me naked!"

Tommy: "And jacking off into your sheets!"

Josh screamed with mock outrage and wrestled Tommy.

Luis said, "Jesus Christ, I guess those two are actually drinking their beers today."

Tommy shouting from beneath the assault: "What else you got on Josh? Need more dirt!"

Arnold: "I don't see much more from Josh. I can't turn it off and on like a faucet. I see what I see when I see it."

Josh shuffled over to Arnold, scuffing his sneakers on the granite, like his feet were too heavy to bother lifting, and shook his hand. "Cool trick or powers or whatever. I'm impressed. But, come on, everyone's parents are hardos, right?"

Arnold said, "Most. My mother was so not-hardo that I'd end up staying with the hardest of hardos. The Rev wasn't my dad but he acted like one, and he was the worst. Mom had or has this little meth problem." He paused and the boys didn't say anything and Arnold shrugged before continuing. "The Rev used to have a batshit-crazy problem, but now that he's older and not the Rev anymore, he has a fat-shit lazy problem. That I can deal with, you know?"

Arnold stopped again, and Luis thought he was going to say more and he figured that was what this was about. Arnold wanted to open up about his shitty upbringing. That was okay by him. Luis would listen and he'd commiserate, and tell Arnold yeah, everyone's parents are messed up, and Luis would say something he'd never told anyone before: admit that he'd already decided he'd never become a dad, that when he was old enough he was going to up and move to LA and help make scary movies. He didn't have to be the star or even an extra, as he'd be fine being the key grip or whatever, as long as he got to be a name on the credit scroll at the end.

Arnold said, "So not everyone's parents are hardos. Right, Tommy?"

Tommy was sitting down, on the outskirts of their circle, his back up against the gnarly tree, which was totally Tommy: smiling in the sun, happy to be a part of whatever was going on, content to comment here and there, but usually more than happy to be on the perpetual sideline.

Tommy snapped to and said, "Huh? I guess. Or—I don't know." Tommy bounced looks back and forth between Luis and Josh, clearly in a near panic over what Arnold was going to say or ask and what he would then have to say about having no dad.

Arnold should have been able to tell that something was up with Tommy by his rabbit-in-an-open-field reaction. Luis said, "Hey," but stopped, because what the hell was he going to say that would protect Tommy from that uncomfortable conversation? If he told Arnold not to guess about Tommy's parents, or if he came right out and said Tommy's dad ditched his family and ran away and then died in a drunk-driving accident, would Tommy still have to talk about his dad? Tommy would say it wasn't a big deal, but no, it was. How could it not be the biggest of deals?

Arnold ignored or didn't notice Luis's "Hey." He walked toward Tommy and sat a few feet away, at the ledge of the split, the same spot at which they were all sitting before he showed up. He said, "Someone important to you, that someone is gone? Right?"

Tommy didn't say anything. He stopped looking at Luis and Josh, and tried to hold Arnold's stare, but he kept looking down to the rock and to the split, to the emptiness to his left.

Arnold: "Your father?" He was still speaking in questions, questions that were their own answers.

Josh stood there with his mouth open. Then he sidled closer to Arnold and Tommy, and sat down on the boulder.

Arnold: "He's been gone for a while?"

Tommy looked away, past them all, and nodded. It wasn't so much that his head moved but his whole torso, like he was rocking in place. A full-body yes.

Luis was getting pissed, and it wasn't because Arnold was totally focused on Tommy and here Luis was with his trivial homework-dad diagnosed and tossed to the side. That wasn't it at all, and it wasn't that he was already into his second beer. He said, "Don't make him talk about that if he doesn't want to."

Arnold: "I'm sorry, Tommy. I didn't mean to make you feel bad. Sometimes when I start seeing, I can't stop. It sort of takes over, and—"

Tommy: "No. No worries." He drank the rest of his beer in one sip, and held the can upside down to prove it was empty. "Finished. You know what?"

Arnold: "What?"

"Beer kinda tastes like sucks."

Luis: "*The* sucks. Get it right."

Arnold: "It kinda does. You want another one?"

Tommy said, "Yeah." He took a second one, put it down next to him unopened, and then he started talking about his father and what he remembered about him. He'd never really done that before, at least not with Luis around. Josh knew Tommy way back when they were kindergarteners, and Luis didn't become friends with them until fourth grade, so Luis had always assumed that Josh had to have talked to Tommy about his dad at some point. But then again, he wasn't sure. Luis never asked Josh what he knew about Tommy's dad. It was this unspoken thing that Tommy's dad was gone and they would all deal with it. Dealing with it could mean different things: trying not to talk about his own dad around Tommy; trying (and often failing) to keep Luis's parents from fawning over Tommy like he was a homeless boy and made of glass; Luis and Josh making sure they did something with Tommy on Father's Day and on the anniversaries of his father's leaving the house and his death. On the increasingly rare occasion Luis made a father joke or some unthinking, throwaway reference to a father, any father, Luis would say, "Sorry." That was it. Sorry. And Tommy would say, "No worries," and that would be the extent of any discussion.

Tommy grabbed a twig and passed it between his fingers. His head was down and he wasn't looking at any of them as he talked. "I don't remember much about my dad. I remember his face was scratchy with beard stubble all the time. I remember jumping onto his back from the couch. And that's about it. I only really remember what he looked like from pictures and I don't really remember what he sounded like. I have his voice inside my head somewhere, I think. I don't know. It's weird.

"My parents got separated, divorced, whatever, when I was four and Kate was two. I don't remember much. I remember them fighting some-times, and Mom would bring Kate into my room and tell me to play nice. I'd be there with my big bin of plastic dinosaurs. It'd be night, close to bedtime. Mom would shut the door and they'd start yelling at each other. I don't remember what they were saying. They were so loud. And I remember being scared but telling Kate that it's fine. That was my little-kid catchphrase, yeah? *It's fine.* Kate sat there and she wouldn't move, wouldn't do anything. I'd pretend she was a mountain or a cliff or something and I'd, like, balance the dinos on her and pretend to scream when they fell off. So weird I remember that.

"Then, you know, one day at breakfast, Mom told me that Dad was going to live somewhere else but he was still my dad and he loved me very much and I'd see him but not every day, and that I could talk to him on the phone too, if I wanted. She promised I'd still see him, said it like a hundred times until I said, *It's fine.* I know it wasn't the next day, but it seemed like it, and it was breakfast again, and she was telling me that Dad wasn't calling because he went away and she didn't know how long he was going to be away, and that was all she said, I think. I don't know. I was only four, right? And then, one morning I got up and my grandmother was there in the kitchen with Mom, and Mom told me something happened to Dad, something really bad, and that he died, and he was gone. I remember dressing up for the funeral but I kept taking off my clip-on tie. We were in church forever, and then after we stood in line and all these people I didn't know sticking their huge-ass faces into mine, telling me I was a little man or some shit like that and rubbing my hair. I got so pissed at that. Didn't want the tie, but didn't want them messing up my hair, you know, I was supposed to be dressed up and looking nice. Mom didn't tell me how he died until I was in fourth grade. I used to bug her to tell me and she'd say, *When you're older, when you're older.* There was this one random day I asked again, in the car, on the way back from school, expecting her not to tell me anything. Mom flat-out told me, right there in the car, that Dad wasn't handling things too good, he was very unhappy, that he ran away and was gone for eight months and no one knew where he was and then he was out drinking, shouldn't have been driving, and she thinks he was driving home, maybe, because of where he crashed. Over in Canton, not too far way, crashing into that big, stone railroad bridge, and that was it. He died.

"He pops into my head at these totally random times. I'll go days, maybe even weeks, without thinking about him. Then there'll be days where I'm like totally obsessed with him. I get stuck there sometimes, wondering what he would look like, what he would think of me."

Tommy paused. Luis didn't think he was done yet. Tommy scraped the small twig against the rock, wearing it down to a nub. He looked up, smiled at us, and added, "Or would he be a cool dad or a total hardo, right?"

193

Josh said, "And, like the most important, what would his zombie contingency plan be?"

Luis couldn't believe he said that. It was probably the best worst thing he'd ever said, and they all laughed. Tommy the loudest.

Tommy: "Yeah, I've totally thought about that! Seriously! What, you a seer too now?"

Josh : "I'm gonna practice and get good at it."

Tommy: "And you know what's weird, since summer started, I have been thinking about my dad a lot. Like *a lot*."

Arnold said, "Nah, that's not weird. Not weird at all."

Tommy and Josh needed time to work off their buzzes before dinner. They were in no rush to get home, and they walked their bikes over the rocky, winding paths of Borderland. There would be no repeat of the painful mock-DUI demolition derby from a couple of days ago, especially not after everything Tommy had told them about his dad.

Instead of being maudlin or contemplative, Tommy laughed at everything Josh said, even if it wasn't supposed to be funny. Was it the two beers? For a kid that never said more than three words in a row (unless it was about zombie preparedness), he couldn't stop talking, going on and on about Arnold and his seer abilities.

Luis was miserable and tried to hide it by being

nonresponsive. He knew it was better to not say anything, even if he couldn't quite admit to himself that he was jealous of the attention Tommy had received today from Arnold. Two days ago it had been Luis and Arnold making the deeper connection and talking movies, and the other two had been relegated to the background, quietly listening in, nervously plotting how to dump out their beers without anyone seeing. Today, it was as though Arnold had dismissed Luis, determined him to be less interesting, less special. Proof? This second day at the rock had ended with Tommy and Arnold exchanging Snapchat usernames, and worse, Arnold had offered Luis and Josh his username as an oh-yeah-you-guys-can-send-me-messages-too-if-you-really-want-to afterthought. Luis didn't even bother storing it in his phone.

Tommy said, "The zombie stuff, sure, yeah, whatever, right? But there's no way he could've randomly guessed that shit about your dad. That was amazing. He's like a real psychic or something. Don't you think that was amazing?"

Luis said, "*Amazing*, bruh. I get it. Yeah. I guess."

Tommy: "You guess?"

If Luis continued to argue against the amazingness of Arnold, they'd call him hardo and mock his always being the contrarian (it was a matter of time before one of them said, *Classic Luis*). He actually agreed with Tommy, that what Arnold had said today was legit and strange and more than a little scary.

Luis said, "I don't know. Like, parents get all over kids about homework. It's what they do. He could've been talking about anyone's dad or—" and he quickly added, "—or mom," as though he could cross out the *dad* reference, still aware of the no-dad-talk-around-Tommy rules that had been in place for the entirety of their friendship, or in place pre-Arnold, anyway. "He could've said that same thing about Josh's parents."

Tommy: "Classic Luis."

That stung a little, even though he knew it was coming and he sort of deserved it. He hoped that Tommy would understand what he was trying to do with his point-counterpoint, even though Luis didn't quite fully understand it himself.

Josh: "Nah. He totally described your dad. That was all him. Mine doesn't go nuts over homework like yours does. Not even close."

Luis: "Whatever. I'm just sayin' he might not definitely be, you know, psychic. Maybe he's like doing a—a live version of catfishing, or something."

Josh drunk-laughed. It was fake and high-pitched and couldn't have been more mocking or dismissive. Luis wanted to cry and kick him in the balls at the same time.

Tommy shook his head yes with a big, fake, open-mouthed smile. Then said, "Nope. I don't get it."

Luis: "So Arnold says something about home-work and my father, right? Then he watches my reaction, and yours. You guys went totally stupid—"

Josh: "Chirps!"

Luis: "—whenever he said something that was true, or even close to being true, so he knew he guessed right and just kept going."

Josh: "Nah." He dropped his bike, its frame clattering off a football-sized stone at the edge of the path. "Piss break." He stomped off into the woods. Luis and Tommy walked a few yards ahead, and then they dropped their bikes, too.

Tommy looked at Luis with a hopeful, we're-done-talking-about-this-right? look.

Was Luis implying that Arnold was ultimately trying to manipulate them? Maybe. And Luis couldn't articulate that his jealousy was mani-festing as professed skepticism, which was rooted in his near-constant feelings of inadequacy. Luis was aware that he'd never seen Tommy so outwardly happy. He felt bad that in a very real sense he was trying to tear that down. But he still kept picking at it.

Luis: "Arnold said 'someone important' was missing, yeah? Say that to anyone and then they go *Whoa, my grandmother died two years ago, how did he know that?*"

Tommy: "He didn't say just someone. I mean, he did, but, you know, he was talking about your parents and Josh's and then you guys were talking about like all parents and then he looked at me. He looked right at me and—and I don't know, it felt so weird. Then he said—"

Luis: "He said *someone important* was missing. That's what he said. He didn't say your dad first, and kinda let you fill in the blank."

Tommy really seemed to consider this, and as he did so, he went through a subtle physical transformation: his head tilted down toward the ground, nervous eyes mostly hidden by his bangs, arms wrapped around his middle, shoulders gone slouchy, bending his back forward, contorting his body into a question mark. That Tommy wasn't more popular at school was at times a mystery, given that he was graceful, tall, handsome, and not totally blighted with acne. But it was this punched-in-the-gut posture Tommy carried throughout most of the day at school, as though some unseen sadness manifested in him physically and the desperate herds of classmates could sense this flaw, this otherness, within him. No one picked on Tommy or made fun of him like they did Luis and Josh; they stayed away from Tommy, and maybe that was worse.

Tommy said, "No. That's not what happened. At all. He knew about my dad. I can tell. He just knew."

Luis stopped himself from saying *If you say so* or *That totally proves it,* or similar go-to snark when he's in the endgame of the argument. He wasn't sure he wanted to win.

Josh stumbled out of the woods, shouting, "I'm gonna be covered in ticks."

Luis picked up his bike and started walking ahead. He shouted back at Josh: "There ain't no tick that can find yo' dick!"

Tommy was the last to pick up his bike. Picked it up like it was a delicate artifact, but then he caught up quickly to Luis. He said, "You're so wrong, you know. So wrong. But let's pretend for a second you're not, okay? So—why would Arnold do that? Guess and pretend he can see stuff?"

Luis: "I dunno—"

Tommy: "Exactly."

Luis couldn't tell if Tommy tripped over his own feet or if he lurched at Luis purposefully, but Tommy was suddenly looming in his space, looking down on him. The two boys didn't make contact, but their bikes knocked their front tires, hard enough Luis almost lost his grip on the handlebars. Was the nicest guy in Ames attempting to physically intimidate him?

Josh jumped on his bike and pedaled quickly ahead of them. He stopped at the edge of one of the brackish ponds. He tossed his bike, bent down, and splashed dirty water onto his T-shirt.

Tommy and Luis both yelled, "What are you doing?" at the same time.

Josh: "My stupid shirt still smells like beer!"

Luis said, "You're being stupid," when he knew

that Josh wasn't being stupid. That he would do the same thing.

Josh: "My mom'll smell it and then she'll kill me and then she'll ground me forever."

Tommy: "Don't forget to get behind your ears. Hardo Mom will check."

Luis: "You're right. She'll never ask why your nipples are wet with pond."

Josh: "My nipples *are* wet."

Tommy: "Sexy!" He ran over to the pond's muddy edge, right next to Josh, put a hand on Josh's back, and pretended to push him in. Josh cupped water in his hands and threw it at Tommy.

They left the pond. Luis hung back behind Tommy and Josh. They flung mud and dirt off their sneakers at each other and resumed their deep discussion about the hows of Arnold's seeing and recounting their reactions to it. Tommy was back to being adamant that Arnold had psychic ability, and that he couldn't have guessed everything he guessed.

Luis went quiet and listened closely to his friends. His jealousy and anger passed into a resigned sense of unease. He wasn't unsettled because of Arnold per se; whether or not Arnold was actually some sort of psychic or a con man wasn't the main issue. Luis was afraid that he and his two best friends—his only friends, really—were such hopeless, desperate losers that they were an open book, open for anyone to read.

Elizabeth Talks to Dave, Dinner for Two, Notifications at Night, a Fight, a Sketch

After Detective Murtagh left the house with copies of Tommy's diary pages tucked inside a folder, Elizabeth's mother and daughter abandoned her in the living room. Kate slouched to her bedroom, and Janice said she was going to clean one of the bathrooms and maybe the kitchen floor, too.

With the avalanche of stress, the lack of sleep, continued red-line-level caffeine intake, Elizabeth's heart races through a two-minute punk song of beats. She thinks about how easy it would be for her to lie down on the couch or curl up on Tommy's bed and die of a broken heart, and she briefly indulges in a daydream where Tommy returns home to attend her funeral, and everyone there is happy he's back, and they recognize the Faustian sacrifice Elizabeth made on behalf of her son. The faceless Arnold is at the funeral, too, hiding in the back of the crowd.

Elizabeth shakes herself out of the daydream. She is not prepared to think about Arnold and the possibilities associated with him. He's there now, though, looming like a threat that is a promise. She wants him to go away and to have nothing to do with her son, ever.

Elizabeth makes another cup of coffee, spastic heartbeats be damned, and dedicates the rest of her day to phone calls, e-mails, and social media outreach, trying to keep the suddenly weakening flame of media interest in Tommy burning. During the initial hours of Tommy's disappearance, all the Boston news crews reported live from Borderland and documented the police and their dogs and the search teams clad in orange vests as they scoured the park. With the search radius now extended beyond the park, it's as though the media no longer have a focal point beyond a missing boy. Without a singular setting for their saga of loss and hope, the reports and interview requests are waning. The Find Tommy Facebook page traffic is already down 50 percent from two days ago. There have been no new tweets (other than her own) with #FindTommy in the last ten hours.

Elizabeth reaches out to an online support group for parents of missing children and teens. She introduces herself with a terse any-advice-is-welcome post on the group's message board. Response is instantaneous, as though a group of parents are on standby, ready to swoop in the moment someone new reaches out. Elizabeth is grateful, but she can't help seeing herself a year from now, sitting hunched in front of the glowing computer screen, staring at this same message board thread waiting for the next post. Or maybe she'll become another voice in their chorus of the damned, haunting the message board for the chance to share her digitized cautionary tale with one more person on the off-off-off chance they might know something about what happened to her still-missing son.

Much of the advice the group shares with her is common sense, but still it's good to hear. None of the members speaks in platitudes or prayers. No one spews the things-happen-for-a-reason bullshit. Thank God. These parents care, commiserate, and offer a tougher brand of emotional support. They are hardened realists who categorically do not trust the system that failed them and continues to fail them and their missing children. They tell Elizabeth that given Tommy is a teenage male and not a young boy it will become increasingly difficult to keep the media's long-term interest, which is her only real chance of ever finding him or finding what happened to him.

Inspired and terrified by the group, Elizabeth makes one more phone call before dinner, and it is to Dave Islander, a townie who is an editor and a reporter for the local weekly newspaper. Dave promised her a weekly update/feature on Tommy until they found him. That is very kind of him, and she is sure he meant it when he said it.

She once played on a co-ed softball team with

Dave five or six summers ago at the urging of two coworkers at the DPW who were not-so-subtly trying to play matchmaker. It was a ridiculous idea, but the kids were a little older, and Elizabeth really hadn't done anything social for herself and by herself since William died. She agreed to play and was relieved to not be the worst player on the team. She hit well and could play first base and pitch adequately. Dave was the best player on their not-so-good team. He was in his early thirties, short, fast, and hilariously reckless with his body on the base paths and with his prodigious throwing arm from the outfield. The team went out for drinks after a handful of their games. The bars were always too loud or too crowded, and no one on the team knew Elizabeth well enough to know that a bar was the last place in the world she wanted to be. Elizabeth went anyway, mainly because she felt the pressure of the whole team willing her and Dave to make a connection. She didn't drink any alcohol and kept looking at her watch the whole time, wondering if Kate and Tommy were in bed or if they'd ganged up on the overmatched teenaged babysitter, and it all made her feel like such a mom and twenty years older than her teammates instead of her actual five to ten. Still, she looked forward to those stolen hours of games and occasional postgames. Dave was self-deprecating, charming in an Eeyore kind of way, pleasantly quirky, but not quirky enough for her to ask him on a date. She got the sense that the feeling was mutual, as he never asked her out, either. He ruptured a disc in his back the following summer and had since put on some weight that he carried with the oversized shame and regret of a scarlet letter.

She says, "Hi, Dave? It's Elizabeth."

"Hey there, Elizabeth."

Now that she has him on the phone, she isn't sure what she wants to say or should say. There isn't much Tommy news that she can share, really, so she says, "How's your back doing?"

Dave says, "Fucking horrible. I want to take it out to the parking lot and curb-stomp it." He chuckles softly at himself and Elizabeth smiles at his inability to dial down the Eeyore act. "Anyway, I'm glad you called. I'm actually working on a column about Tommy as we speak. Haven't been able to get much from the police department. What do you got?"

"What do I got? A whole lot of crazy." She has the urge to unzip herself and let everything spill out as though he's an intimate confidant: tell Dave that she saw Tommy in her house or some form of Tommy, and was initially so sure what she saw was him, had to be him, but with each hour that passes she doesn't know what to think. What if she tells Dave diary pages are being left in the house by the spirit or ghost or double of Tommy? Saying that out loud would sound totally ludicrous, even though she believes it, or is still willing to believe it. Is there a difference? What if it is Kate leaving the pages? Why would Kate do that? If it was someone else, who? And how did they get the pages there? She wants to tell Dave no one in the house is really talking to the others when they've never needed one another more. They're all exhausted, broken, and struggling, or not struggling, but drowning, failing, crumbling, whatever goddamn *–ing* you wanted to use. Maybe Elizabeth should insist she and Kate see a counselor. There is no maybe about it. Elizabeth has rewatched for the four-hundredth time the surveillance clip her app recorded. That shadow isn't there anymore and would Dave want to take a look and see if he can find Tommy in there, anywhere?

"I'm sorry, Elizabeth. I really don't know what to say. Can't imagine. Um, you still there?"

"Yeah, sorry, still here," she says and then tells him about the police search expanding to other towns, malls, and the like. Dave asks if there is anything else. She tells him about going to some of those local towns herself and passing out fliers and how most people were friendly and helpful.

He asks, "Is there anything else?" It's the second time he said that.

She asks if he saw that the sign at Split Rock had been vandalized to read *Devils Rock*. He hasn't been out to the park yet because of his back, of course, but he heard the police were having a hard time keeping older kids from hanging out there and that they made a kind of shrine to Tommy.

She says she heard a folk story about Eastman facing and then tricking the devil out at Split Rock.

"Huh. Where'd you hear the story?"

"From, um, Tommy?" She pauses and when Dave starts to fill in the gap for her, she talks over him. "Yeah, he, uh, he wrote a little about it in a diary of his."

"Lived here all my life but never heard anything about a Devil's Rock. I'll look into it. E-mail what he wrote about that story, okay? Anything else?"

She can't tell if his *Anything else?* is what a reporter is conditioned to ask and continue to ask until there's nothing else to say. She's worried that the expanded search and Devil's Rock story isn't enough for him. With the support group instructions still ringing in her ears, Elizabeth decides to tell Dave about Arnold.

She says, "We just today found out that Tommy and his friends were hanging out at Borderland with an older boy earlier this summer."

"Older boy?"

"Yeah. Or a guy, a man. A young man, in his early- to midtwenties, maybe. The boys don't know his age for sure. They, uh, ran into him at the 7-Eleven in Five Corners and they—" she's not sure how to describe what happened on that afternoon "—they hit it off, I guess." She winces at the awkward-sounding phrase. "And then went to Borderland." She stops there and isn't going to tell him about the boys drinking beers with him. There is no way she will chance having Tommy painted as some early-teen alky and give the media and public a chance to conclude *Oh, he's just another troubled teen who should've known better, should've been taught better* and turn up their rocks-in-glass-houses noses and give themselves permission to forget about Tommy forever. "We, um, don't know who this guy is yet and we don't know, obviously, if he has anything to do with, you know, the disappearance, but still, we—" she pauses again, aware that she's making it sound like she's Robin to the police's Batman "—the police are looking into him. They're looking into everything possible, you know."

"Okay. This is good."

Is it good? Seems like an oddly terrible thing to say. She hears him scribbling notes down. She can't help but feel like she's making a mistake or betraying a trust. Why shouldn't that information get out there? It can only help. When his column hits, maybe other news outlets will come calling again with this new character added to the story.

Dave says, "What else do you know about this guy? Can I have a name?"

"I only know his first name and that's it."

"Can I have it?"

"No. I don't think so. Not yet."

"You sure?"

"I'm not sure about anything. I gotta go, Dave. Thank you for everything. Really."

"Hey, yeah, okay. Please. Least I can do. You call whenever, okay? I'm here and I don't sleep."

"Me neither. Bye."

After she hangs up her phone rings almost instantaneously. It's Allison. She says that according to Luis and Josh, Tommy may have communicated with Arnold via the Snapchat app. The detective admits she's never contacted Snapchat before and isn't sure how much they'll be able to recover, given the app is famous for images and messages that disappear within ten seconds, but they are going to request any and all information they can get from Tommy's account.

Janice leaves late that afternoon, soon after Elizabeth gets off the phone with Allison. She says she has to go home, take care of a few errands, check in on her cats. Janice uses the phrase *has to go* as though there is no other choice. Yes, her neighbor Charles is watching the house, but her cat, Bear, will get mad and stop using the litter box if Janice is gone for too long and the other one, Moose, will refuse to eat or show her black-and-white face for days after Janice's return. Mom is under no obligation to relocate to Ames for the duration of Tommy's disappearance, and Elizabeth assures her that she has already been a huge, life-saving help. Janice promises to be back within a day or two, if not sooner, especially if there is news. Still, her leaving feels like an admission of defeat. Their little three-person vigil is as ineffectual as everything else that has been done in the ongoing search for Tommy.

Elizabeth considers going out to a restaurant for dinner with Kate, but the idea of cleaning herself up and rousing Kate into doing the same, and then leaving the house and facing the public as their incomplete two instead of three is a Sisyphean task. Rousing Kate especially. Her earbuds are always in now, including when she sleeps. Short of video camera tech help, Kate doesn't speak unless spoken to. Elizabeth has even resorted to communicating by text. Kate won't eat, drink, or change her clothes without being harassed into doing so.

Elizabeth defrosts a vegetarian lasagna that one of her coworkers made. With the meal prepared and the ceramic dish set in the middle of the table, Elizabeth regrets not going out. She could've driven down to Providence, which is only thirty minutes away. They could've had a nice meal on Federal Hill or maybe surround themselves with Brown University students and hipsters on Thayer Street. No one would've known who they are down there. Could she have really crossed state lines and be that far, both physically and meta-phorically from wherever Tommy might be? Probably not, but it would've done both her and Kate some good. Their house is closing in on them.

Elizabeth's square of lasagna is cold in the middle. She stands up, taps Kate's hand, and pantomimes taking out imaginary earbuds.

Kate pulls out the earbuds and leaves her phone in a tangle of white wires next to her plate.

Elizabeth: "Want your piece heated up a little more? Mine's kinda cold."

Kate nods.

She microwaves both pieces for too long. The cheese melts into scorching lava pools. A flash of irrational anger fills her, and she visualizes throwing the plates against the wall and seeing if the lasagna would stick.

Elizabeth sighs, tells herself to get a grip, and grabs a damp dish towel from the top of the oven to use as a makeshift oven mitt. She slides Kate's now-steaming plate back to her and says, "Um, if it's still too cold, you let me know. Could still be frozen. Hard to tell." Elizabeth smiles and tilts her head to peek under the curtain of Kate's purple-streaked hair.

Kate bites the inside of her cheeks like she did when she was really little and playing the you-can't-make-me-laugh game. She sticks a fork in the bubbly cheese and says, "Looks frosty."

Elizabeth: "So. How are you doing? Dumb question, I know."

"Terrible."

"Me too."

"I know."

"You keeping in touch with Sam or any other friends?"

"Yeah. Mostly Sam."

"Good."

"Can I ride my bike to her house tomorrow?"

"Yeah, sure. I think that's a great idea. Make sure you ask if it's okay first, and not just show up."

"I will."

Elizabeth imagines a never-ending tomorrow with everyone gone and her wandering through the house like a ghost who doesn't know she's a ghost. She'll need a plan. Stay busy. Make phone calls. Set up more Google alerts. Keep chatter going on the Facebook page and her support message board. She will not go into Tommy's room. Maybe she'll set aside an hour, run a bath, and let herself cry loudly.

Elizabeth: "Been talking with anyone else?"

Kate shrugs. "People." She plucks a hair elastic from around her wrist and puts her hair into a ponytail. "Can I put, like, an ice cube on my lasagna?"

"If you want. Sounds kind of gross."

Kate cuts a still-steaming wedge from her piece and takes a bite with her lips curled as far away from her teeth as they can go. "Ow!"

"I know, I'm sorry. Here, cut it up and wait a minute or two." Elizabeth slides Kate's plate over and follows her own instructions, which have instead become a narration.

"Mom."

"Almost done."

"I could've done that."

"I know."

"My tongue hurts." Kate drops her head and sticks her tongue into her drink.

"Classy."

"Is Nana coming back tomorrow?" She talks with her tongue still stuck out and dripping.

"Ew, put that away, you're making a mess."

Kate giggles.

Elizabeth says, "I don't know. Probably in a few days."

"Tell her she can bring Bear and Moose here. They can sleep in my room."

"I did. She's afraid Bear would spray all over the place."

"Nah, he'd be fine."

"Nana said he sprayed like a hose the last time he was at someone else's house."

"Bear likes me. He wouldn't do that to our house."

"Yes he would."

"Nah."

"I know you love him, but he's kind of an asshole."

"Mom!" Kate fakes shock and covers her ears. She leans to the side of her plate and plants her elbow on the table, holds up her suddenly moon-sized face with her fist and says with a smirk and without blinking, "All cats are assholes. It's what makes them so cool."

"True. Watch your language, Miss Kate."

"You said it first."

"It doesn't matter."

"You like it when I swear."

"What? No I don't." She's right, though. Elizabeth loves this smart-ass version of her daughter so much it breaks her heart, because it's impossible that she can love equally all the versions of Kate to come.

"You do. I can tell. Ass bum piss!" Kate giggles, covers her mouth with both hands, and her eyes go wide, daring Elizabeth to be mad at her.

"What the *bleep* fuck is ass *bleep* piss?"

That Elizabeth high-pitched bleeps out non-swears and leaves the actual swears uncensored sends them roaring into laughing fits. The two of them whistle and wheeze, faces go red, mouths open, hands on their stomachs, eyes squeezing out tears. Elizabeth is on the verge of losing total control, and the laughter is dangerous. It feels like anything can happen, that she is capable of doing anything, including flipping the kitchen table and their chairs and then screaming and never stopping.

They both settle down eventually. There are aftershocks of giggles, deep sighs, and quick rehashes of the exchange and impersonations of each other's reactions and expressions. And then they eat. Kate finishes her lasagna first, though she surgically removes the bits of broccoli.

Elizabeth: "Wow. Someone was hungry."

"Yeah. Now I might puke. So full."

"Well, you needed it." Two weeks ago this kind of exchange about food would've launched Elizabeth into flights of worry about Kate's eating habits and her body image and extrapolate it to how Kate or any girl could possibly make it through puberty and middle school and high school unscathed, unscarred. That worry is still there, but Elizabeth has filed it away into the deal-with-it-later folder.

Elizabeth: "Drink some water. Or I can make some tea. I have the Black Raspberry that you like. Yesterday Cheryl brought over some honey from her bees, too. It's so good."

Kate takes a small sip of water. "Nah, I'm good." Then she looks down at her smartphone and the tangle of wires with something like regret and resignation. She will put the earbuds back in and go back to hiding inside herself, because that is the new normal.

"Should we watch a movie or something? I can make some popcorn."

Kate shrugs big, shoulders going almost past the top of her head. "Dunno. Not feeling a movie. I'm kind of tired." She reaches for her phone.

Elizabeth says, "Kate, can I ask you something?"

Kate unties her hair and it falls over her face as she looks down. She transforms into the girl behind the curtain again. "Sure, I guess."

"What do you think is happening with the diary pages? How are they getting there?"

Kate shrugs. "I don't know. I guess I believe like you do. That Tommy's somehow leaving them for us. Sharing them with us."

"You're not leaving them out, right?" Elizabeth has to ask it, to try it on.

Kate rolls her eyes and says, "Nope."

"This guy Arnold. Tommy never talked to you about him?"

"Like I already said. Never heard of him until this morning. Anything else?"

"No. Yes. I don't know. Tell me something. Talk to me. Anything. Please."

Kate says, "Do you still believe Tommy's ghost or whatever is leaving the pages out, Mom?"

"I—" She pauses. It sounds so crazy when it is said out loud like that, but she does believe it, even if she can't come right out and say it. "I— I'm still not sure."

"Still not sure." Kate wraps the earbud wires around the fingers of her left hand, tight enough that her flesh bulges out red in between. "I wasn't gonna say anything about it because I'm not sure if it, like, was anything real, okay? Just like you. And I was like half asleep or all asleep when it happened."

"When what happened?"

"I think maybe I saw someone outside. Last night. Looking in my window."

"Wait. What? Who did you see?"

"I dunno. I woke up, middle of the night. I didn't have to pee or anything, I just woke up. Nana didn't wake up, I don't think, she was lying on her side, facing away from me, and I sat up, looked over my shoulder and out my window. I thought there was someone standing there and, I don't know, standing there and looking in."

Is she telling the truth? Elizabeth can't tell. She is speaking carefully, fumbling around for the right words. That isn't Kate, normally. When she talks, she does so without breathing and impulsively, without thought of consequence. Is Kate making this up or detailing a dream in an attempt to distract and obfuscate? Is it possible that there was someone standing outside her window? Was it the someone who's been leaving the diary pages in their house? A deranged news junkie? A drunk high school kid on a dare? Or, as Tommy described it in his diary, a devil creeping

217

the woods? Did Kate see what other people in Ames have been claiming to see at night? Did she see what Elizabeth had seen? Did she see Tommy?

Elizabeth: "Jesus, did you see a face?"

Kate: "Not really. I remember seeing something there in the window when I wasn't looking at it but kinda looking at it? I mean, I sat up, turned to my left, like I was gonna get out of bed, and I wasn't like head-on facing the window but I could see something, like, sort of over my shoulder, over there." Kate pretends to be looking across the kitchen and motioned toward the wall on her periphery with her left hand. Kate then sags, blowing air out through her lips, "I don't know, it's like—"

"I get what you're saying. You saw something out of the corner of your eye."

"Yeah, that's it! But I can't remember exactly what I saw. It was like a shadow there, but not exactly. It was less about seeing, okay, and like, I felt someone there looking in. I could feel it. Like a sense something was taking up the space outside my window. I jumped up out of bed and looked and looked and there was nothing there. Then I stood on the bed and put my face against the window and couldn't see anything." After her initial hesitancy, Kate gets more excited and animated as she speaks, almost manic, as though excited to have this story to tell. "I remember looking at my clock and it was like four something and—"

"Four something?"

"Like maybe 4:30. Ish. I think?"

"That was when I got the second notification from the camera. Last night. The notification that came with the little video clip."

Kate: "Right. Huh. Okay. I was gonna wake up Nana but she was sleeping hard. I wasn't really afraid. Definitely weird, yeah. I was so sure someone was there. Eventually I went to sleep and when I woke up, things got crazy in the morning with us and all that window stuff felt more like a dream, didn't seem as important, you know."

"You should've told me this morning. We could've told Detective Allison."

"I guess. Sorry."

"Did you hear anything?" Elizabeth stopped herself from asking if she smelled anything.

"No, like what?"

"Someone walking around outside or inside. Knocking on windows. People talking." There's a waver in her voice she can't control. Elizabeth is in her head watching the surveillance video clip from last night, and the shadow she saw next to the front door. "Or, I don't know, trying to get in our front door. Anything. Did you hear anything?"

"No, nothing like that. I was awake for a little while, I think. Didn't hear anything. Maybe I was dreaming. It didn't feel like I was."

"You were probably dreaming."

Kate furrows her brow and scrunches up her face like she can't believe what Elizabeth said. "Seemed really real to me. You don't think I saw what you saw in your bedroom?"

Elizabeth doesn't answer her. Kate's seeing-a-shadow story feels different from what she experienced. It feels like a threat. Elizabeth stands up and grabs their lasagna plates and carries them over to the sink. She says, "Will you help me reboot the camera in the living room? Maybe we can mess with some of the settings and stuff. I want to be 100 percent sure it's working right. And then we'll double check that the doors are locked."

Before going to bed, Elizabeth and Kate slightly adjust the angle of the camera so that more of the house is included in the shot. Instead of pointing it directly at the front door, they position the camera so that the door is tucked in the bottom left of the screen, and the result is a fuller shot of the living room and most of the kitchen. They delete and reinstall the surveillance camera app on Elizabeth's phone and then run a bunch of tests and practice runs. They manage to get the motion-detecting sensor reacting the way it's supposed to react. If the front door opens or if either of them walks anywhere within the shot, the camera turns on and records the event as a video clip. The smartphone notifications work as well, and Elizabeth chooses an obnoxious honking sound to accompany the message. There is no way she'd sleep through that.

They both fall asleep on the couch with a *Mythbusters* marathon running, the volume muted. Kate wakes Elizabeth up a little after 11 p.m. to tell her that she's going to her room.

Elizabeth stands and considers making herself a cup of coffee and staying up all night. Instead she backs away from the couch and shuts off all the lights. Darkness fills the warm, sleepy space she and her daughter just occupied. She turns on the surveillance camera with her phone, the small red light glows in the newly barren, unexplored living room.

Elizabeth skips washing her face and brushing her teeth, and crawls directly into bed. She plugs her phone into the charger and scrolls though her texts.

Janice sent a message a few hours ago while she and Kate were asleep on the couch: *Back home. Safe. Will call tomorrow. Get rest. I love you.*

Elizabeth texts back: *Thnx. I'll call when I wake up. I love you, too.* She stares at her words contained in the blue dialogue bubble.

Janice responds quickly with, *Night, my dear.*

Elizabeth types, *I'm so tired*, but then erases it. She types, *I miss Tommy so much.* Erases it. *What the fuck are we going to do?* Erases it. She starts crying. She types, *Night, Mom,* and finally hits Send.

Janice sends one more text. *I sent you an e-mail link to an article about something called felt presences. You should read it when you get a chance.*

Elizabeth doesn't respond and she doesn't check her e-mail. She lies on her side, and tears slide across the bridge of her nose, down her cheek, and onto the pillow. She closes her eyes and plucks at the individual spider threads of all that's happened, and she follows them into the dizzying web of what can and could happen until she's hopelessly lost and vulnerable to the gentle fang of sleep.

Just after 1 a.m. the car horn alert blares. Elizabeth bolts upright in a full body spasm and inadvertently flings her phone over the foot of the bed and to the floor, where it lands with a chunky thud and pinwheels toward the end table. Elizabeth is at the bedroom door before her phone finishes asteroiding across the room. She yanks the door open, dives headfirst into the hallway. There is a huddled, blocky, dark shape coming out of the kitchen and down the hall, and Elizabeth can't stop and almost plows into it.

An involuntary yelp leaks out of Elizabeth.

Kate says, "Oh my God! Mom! Are you okay? It's me! What's going on?"

Elizabeth: "Jesus H.!" She slaps at the wall and finds the light switch.

"Dude. Bright light." Kate is standing there squinting, lost inside a black, oversized T-shirt (is it one of Tommy's?) with a cup of water in her hands, an almost fully grown Cindy Lou Who prepping to snarkily ask why everything is gone.

Elizabeth: "Honey, you scared the crap out of me."

"You scared the crap out of me! Why are you running out here?"

"You know, the— " Elizabeth points into her bedroom and shakes her hand up and down, priming the pump until the rest of the words come out "—the goddamn camera motion-sensing alarm thingy went off."

"Oh, right. Oops. Sorry. Hey. Can I, uh, see the video?"

"Seriously, Kate? No. No. Go back to bed."

"How am I supposed—"

"Just go, Kate. You're not watching it now."

Elizabeth walks away from her grumbling daughter and into the living room, and the car horn alarm sounds from her phone back in the bedroom. Now *she's* set off the goddamn motion detector.

"For crying out loud . . ."

Kate: "I got this!" and she skitters into Elizabeth's bedroom.

"You don't need to—ugh."

She stands in the middle of the living room. There aren't any notes left on the rug.

Kate's voice comes through the camera's mic. "I can see you, Mom. What are you doing? It looks weird."

"Nothing. Put my phone down and go to bed. Please."

"Okay, fine. I'm watching my video first."

"This isn't a game," Elizabeth says and curls her toes in the rug. There's no response. She doesn't know if Kate is still watching/listening or if the camera is recording her on its own or if those words are lost forever, like all words are lost eventually.

Elizabeth doesn't move from the spot until she hears Kate shuffle across the hallway and her bedroom door closes shut. Once back in her room and under the covers, Elizabeth watches the ten-second clip of Kate in the kitchen and getting water. Kate waves at the camera and the car horn alarm goes off (it's far away and muffled, but Elizabeth can hear it) and then the clip ends. Elizabeth chuckles softly and says, "That little shit."

Before trying to go back to sleep, Elizabeth opens the surveillance camera app on her phone and rechecks the notification settings. It's been set to silent mode. The tab for the audio alarm is dull gray (off) instead of green (on). Vibration notifications are shut off, too. The alarm was clearly on and working as of a handful of minutes ago. Elizabeth quickly rebuilds the timeline: alarm sounded, she ran into the kitchen, stumbled into Kate, the alarm went off a second time when Elizabeth tripped the motion sensor, and Kate went into Elizabeth's bedroom to shut off the alarm. Kate did not have to open the program and change the settings to quiet the alarm; all she had to do was let the alarm expire after ten seconds or hit the red Okay button that appears on the phone's screen along with the camera-is-recording notification message. Why would Kate open the app, navigate to the settings screen, and then shut off all future notification alarms? It wasn't something you could do with one mistaken keystroke or finger swipe.

Elizabeth climbs out of bed, goes across the hall, and opens Kate's bedroom door without knocking. The room is dark with the shades draped over her windows. Kate is in bed with her glowing phone a few inches from her startled face. Elizabeth's own voice comes through Kate's phone's speakers, shouting, "For crying out loud," then after a brief silence, "You don't need to—ugh."

Kate sits up, eyes as wide as sinkholes, and she dives her phone under the bedcovers. "Mom? What, what is it?"

Elizabeth turns on the overhead light and stands next to Kate's bed. "What are you watching?

Kate? Was that me? Was that me on your phone?"

"Mom—"

"That was me on your phone, wasn't it? Give it to me."

"You can't take my phone. I—"

"Kate Sanderson, give me your phone right now."

Kate stops arguing and hands the phone over. She says, "I was watching the new videos. From just now."

"What videos? The ones from the surveillance camera? What do you mean? How can you do that?" On Kate's screen, the video is paused at the spot when Elizabeth tripped the motion sensor walking from the kitchen into the living room.

Kate: "I put the camera app on my phone, too."

"What? Why?"

She shrugs. "The app was glitchy on your phone. My phone is newer, right, so I thought the app would work better on mine. And I've been watching the live feed at night, sometimes. Helps me fall asleep."

"How come you didn't tell me?"

"I forgot."

"You forgot."

"Yeah."

Elizabeth: "So you've been able to control the camera this whole time without saying anything to me. You've been able to turn it on or *off* whenever you want. Is that what you're telling me?"

"I haven't messed with it like that, I swear. I just watch the feed sometimes."

"And you shut off the alarm notifications on my phone, too. You went into my room and you turned it off, Kate. Why would you do that?"

"Mom, you asked me to go into your room and shut off the alarm."

"You didn't have to shut off all notifications. You know that!"

"Please stop yelling at me, Mom."

"Why did you shut off the notifications, Kate?"

"I don't—I didn't even realize I did that. I mean, yeah I opened the app, and everything, to watch the video of me, and I shut the notifications off from the app, I guess. I thought that's what you wanted. I'm sorry—"

"Kate. Stop. Just stop. I can't deal right now." Elizabeth wipes her eyes and face and sighs deeply. In her head, Elizabeth sees Kate shutting off the notifications on her phone so the alarm wouldn't go off when Kate came back out later, and Elizabeth sees Kate turning off the camera last night with her own phone, dropping the diary pages on the floor, returning to her room, and then turning the camera back on after. It wasn't Tommy leaving the pages. It was Kate. It had to be. And she feels like a fool for believing otherwise.

Elizabeth says, "Christ, Nana was right."

"What do you mean?"

Part of Elizabeth hates herself for interrogating

her daughter, and if hiding Tommy's diary is how Kate is coping with this impossible situation, then Kate should be excused and forgiven her odd behavior. Another part of Elizabeth wants to wring everything out of Kate like she is a wet towel.

Elizabeth: "Okay. Where's the rest of Tommy's diary, Kate? It's late and I'm tired and I want the rest of the pages. We can talk about why you've been leaving the pages out later, but—"

"Mom, I'm sorry I shut off the stupid app. Okay? It was so loud and we didn't need to hear it going off when it was you out in the living room."

"You shut if off because you were planning to go back out to the living room after I went back to sleep and then drop Tommy's pages on the floor and—"

"Why are you saying all this now? I thought you believed me. I thought you believed it was Tommy."

"—*and* you didn't want me waking up and seeing you doing it."

"I was just shutting off the noise. That's it. Goodnight, Mom." Kate sinks into her bed, pulls the blankets over her head.

"Nope. Not tonight." Elizabeth shoots across the room and tears the blanket and sheets off of Kate and off the bed and onto the floor.

"Hey! What are you—come on! Stop it." She looks so little and vulnerable, twitching like a bug when the rock gets overturned. Kate tries covering herself with her arms and then hides her head between the pillows.

"Out of bed, now. Come on. Let's go. I want you to give me the rest of the diary. Look, you don't even have to tell me why you've been doing it if you don't want to. I know . . . everything is all, all messed up, and—"

"I don't know what you're talking about."

"—and it doesn't matter, really. I mean, it does matter; what you're going through matters. I just—I just want the rest of the diary. Okay. That's all I want. Please. And I want it right now."

"Mom, I thought you believed me!"

"Tell me. Right fucking now, Kate. Where is it?"

"I thought you believed it was Tommy." Kate retracts her knees into her chest, sits up against the headboard of her stripped bed, and doesn't say anything more.

"Fine!" Elizabeth walks over to the old elementary school desk, a refugee from the DPW take-it-or-leave-it. Years ago, she and Kate painted the desk and its little wooden chair candy apple red and added black-and-white dots so that it looked like a ladybug. It was one of a handful of DIY projects in the house that looked like it was supposed to. The desk is way too small for Kate now, but she still uses it. The paint is peeling and chipping away, and most of the surface is tattooed with scrawled band names and song lyrics. Seeing some of Elizabeth's own favorite nineties bands writ looping and large on the side of the desk almost stops her from doing what she's going to do.

With one sweeping backhand motion of her left arm, Elizabeth roughly knocks Kate's dusty minitrophies, trinkets, and knickknacks off the desk. She lifts the top and roots around inside the desk, tossing out pens, pencils, loose paper, Post-it note cubes, phone chargers, Tommy's old GameBoy.

Kate flinches but she still doesn't say anything.

"Is it over here?"

Next is Kate's purple floor-to-ceiling bookshelf that is both a library and stuffed-animal menagerie. Elizabeth yanks out fistfuls of books, and they fall and crash like thick hailstones.

"Is it in here?"

From the bookcase Elizabeth storms through the bedroom like a hurricane, kicking and knocking things over on her path to Kate's closet. Elizabeth wrenches the door open, denting the plaster with the knob.

"Is it in here?"

The closet isn't very big or deep, its contents barely contained. At the bottom is a green plastic shelving unit. She pulls the drawers out of the frame and dumps out their contents onto the floor behind her: photos and drawn pictures and chewed-up magazines and birthday cards and corrected homework assignments and yellow report cards and packs of Lego kit instructions and clothes for the antique dolls Kate only ever played with when she was alone in her room.

Elizabeth yells, "Is it in here? How about here? Or here? Or here . . ." and when the unit is empty, she picks it up, grunting like a bloodthirsty giant, and throws it behind her. It rolls, slides, and crashes into the foot of Kate's bed.

Kate is blank-faced and staring quietly at the destruction of her room.

Elizabeth is crying now, and screaming through her teeth, and she doesn't stop tearing through Kate's things. She yanks all the clothes off their hangers and throws them fluttering out of the closet. Elizabeth knows that what she is doing, what she is perpetrating, is a disaster, a calamity, and it will change their lives and her relationship with Kate forever. In the aftermath of the evening she will sit with Kate on the bed, hold her, and repeatedly tell her that she is sorry. But in the great and terrible now, there are still the stacks of sweaters and sweatshirts piled on the built-in shelf above the hangers. Her hands reach out to them—

From somewhere behind her, in the yawning canyon of the bedroom, Kate says, "Mom, I have it. I'm sorry."

Elizabeth stops, backs out of the closet, and turns around, momentarily unsteady on her feet.

The room before her is a disaster, the rubble of her daughter's young life, there at her feet.

Kate stands in the middle of it all, and she has a book cradled against her chest. The cover is black and has no decorations that Elizabeth can see. Kate starts in with the apologies and self-recriminations and tears and she falls into Elizabeth's arms, stuffing Tommy's diary into her hands. Kate doesn't say the words *It's Tommy's*. Elizabeth knows it's his.

Kate's head is still down and pressed against Elizabeth. She says, "For like two days after Tommy didn't come home you were like in a coma, shut down, when you were home you barely moved or said anything and I'd never seen you like that and I was so afraid, and then the morning after you saw his ghost in your room it was like you were back to normal, back to you, and it was like it was almost okay again, or it could be okay again, so I wanted to help you keep believing, you know, believing that he was still here, that he would come back again, and so I left the pages out so you could still hear his voice and keep believing that Tommy was here in the house with us and sending messages. I was just trying to help, I swear. And I'm sorry, I'm so sorry."

They cry, they hug, and they apologize to each other. Elizabeth could stand there holding and hugging her daughter forever as long as it meant nothing terrible would ever happen again.

When Kate calms down she admits to finding the diary in the bottom drawer of his dresser, buried beneath old pairs of jeans, and then she kept it where she used to hide her own diary from Tommy; under her bedframe, wedged beneath the box spring and one of the support beams. And now that she has admitted to having the diary Kate doesn't stop talking and she says that having and reading his diary gave her a reason to get up and get out of bed each day, and how Tommy continually talked to her in the diary, it was like the diary was shared, it was theirs, and they were having a secret conversation, and she wanted it to last as long as possible. She also admits to manipulating the camera with the app on her phone, and shutting off the camera when she dropped the pages last night and then turning it back on after.

Kate points at the diary and says, "One of the last entries is scary and I was going to show this, the whole book to you before, I swear, but I don't know, I wanted you to still believe in Tommy and I'm sorry, I'm sorry, and then it kept getting harder and harder to admit it and, I don't know, it's like I wanted to believe too, and—"

"Okay, Kate. It's okay. Thank you for telling me now, and please, you can tell me anything. You have to be able to tell me anything, especially now, right?"

"Yes, I will. I promise. So Mom, the camera went off twice last night, right? Once was me.

But I have no idea why the camera went off that second time, when the pages were already on the floor and that video you thought you saw the shadow in and it happened like at the same time when I saw the shadow in my window. That wasn't me. I swear. I swear to God that wasn't me."

Elizabeth: "Okay. We'll look at that again later. Come on. Let's get a drink of water."

They walk into the kitchen, Kate following Elizabeth, and Elizabeth with the diary in the crook of her arm, a bird protecting an egg under her wing.

Elizabeth opens the unadorned cover. Protruding from the book's spine are the jagged remnants of torn pages, like rows of worn-down teeth. There are three pages with writing intact within the diary, and then after the three pages, more jagged remnants from torn pages.

The first intact page is a block of text. The second page, at first glance, features what looks like a large sketch of a zombie in the upper left corner, literally looming over the text below it. Tommy has shown her so many of his zombie sketches throughout the previous year and they all kind of blurred together in terms of tone and feel. This zombie is less cartoonish than the ones she has seen. Maybe *cartoonish* isn't the right word, but there was an undercurrent of his sense of humor, of his playful silliness, inherent in his zombie drawings: the odd and impossible bend of an arm or a leg, a goober tooth, rolling googly eyes. That the frail and ridiculous human body was condemned to an eternal pratfall was the ultimate zombie gag, and while Tommy wouldn't have been able to articulate it that way, he understood zombies were a gallows kind of funny in his artwork.

The zombie on this diary page doesn't have a trace of funny in it. Primordial in its grotesquerie, the drawing is wrong, just wrong, as it communicates an unspoken, deep, and terrible truth while being more abstract than his usual sketches. The normally sharp lines of his comic book style gave way to subtle shading, and a vague, unnerving topography; the exaggerated tallness and thinness of the torso and limbs, the body as an impossible, elongated smear, as though he furiously tried to rub the body out. The zombie's head is oversized and misshapen, as craggy as a mountain topped with a forest of hair. The eyes are two small black circles, like button eyes, spotted in the middle of swollen and puffy flesh, bruises on the page. Cheekbones avalanche and pool above a swollen and ruined mouth.

Elizabeth touches the drawing, sticking her finger to one of the eyes as though testing the temperature, and expects her finger to come away ink-stained black. Rot and decay is the violent promise, and this zombie is Tommy. A zombie

Tommy. There is no question it's him, regardless of whatever the accompanying text might to say.

Elizabeth touches the picture again, testing for wet ink. She stares at her finger and then at the drawing and there's a nagging thought that she's missing something. Something obvious.

Kate, "I can't look at that for like more than a second. It's too—"

Elizabeth says, "Oh my God," and then pushes away from the kitchen table. That night in her bedroom with Tommy, with the shadow crouched and hiding, and then right before it disappeared, she saw a flash of a face, and it was this face. It had those same dots for eyes. She saw this face.

Kate: "What, Mom, what?"

Elizabeth in that instant decides she's not going to tell Kate and she's going to keep this to herself, forever if she has to. She says, "Sorry. Like you said, that picture. It's terrible and I don't want to look at it anymore."

Arnold's such an amazing guy. The coin he gave me yesterday is sick. I put it in a plastic bag to keep it safe. I didn't tell Luis or Josh yet but I pinged Arnold on snapchat late last night. Couldn't sleep again so instead of playing Minecraft by myself I tried Arnold, and he was awake too. I showed him some of my drawings.

He said they were amazing and that he would try to set me up with some friends of his he knew working in indie comics. How cool is that? He sent me pictures of more coins he had and he made. He said he was sorry about my dad and then asked me to draw a picture of him, of what I remembered him looking like. I thought it was a bad idea but I did it and I drew it quick and dirty, and even though it's a terrible picture It's on the next page it ~~felt good doing it~~ ~~and~~ he probably knew that I would feel better about it, about everything. It's so easy talking to him so I sent him our Minecraft server address and told him to meet me on there. He did. I was worried Josh or Luis would be on and they'd be mad I invited Arnold to play in our world but they weren't online. I mean Josh sounded totally mad yesterday when he thought Arnold was already playing in our world. Kid needs to chill. I showed Arnold around our map and he promised he wouldn't change anything, wouldn't get in our way, mess any of our stuff up. He said he understood why Josh or Luis

would get upset because it was ours.
Such a cool guy. I told him I was
sorry about his mom like he told me
he was sorry about my dad. He said
she was still in jail, he thinks. He
actually wasn't sure and I asked him
about his uncle, The Rev. He told me
that when he was like ten he used to
go to carnivals and these things
called tent revivals and watch the
Rev work the crowd and do his
SEEING thing and as mean and
scary as he was to Arnold then, he
still started showing Arnold how to
do the seeing thing, what questions
to ask what to look for how to put
it all together, plus talent that
you're born with. Arnold said I had
that talent too, he was sure of it,
and he'd teach me how to get better
with it. We messed around on
Minecraft for like an hour and before
we both signed off I asked him if he
was still living with his uncle and he
said yeah, he wished he didn't have
to. He used to hate the Rev like
poisoned poison but now he kind of
felt bad for him. Arnold said he was
planning on moving on soon. I asked
him if he was going to stick around

the area because he said moving on and not moving out. He said he wasn't going anywhere far. Phew, right?

 Kate, I don't know what to do. This is not me. It started off as the dad-drawing but I changed it and I know it looks like me, yeah, holy shit it does, but it wasn't supposed to, and in a weird way it feels realer that it does look like me. I don't want to talk about it but something awful happened and now this looks like what I saw. I saw this and I'm afraid I'm going to see it again, afraid that he's going to be there all the time, in the dark corners of every room I'm in and in the woods and behind every tree and at night he'll be there next to my bed, or in the closet, under the bed, in the hallway, in the bathroom, standing outside my window. Watching. He'll be in my head when I close my eyes always. I thought I could write about this but I can't.

I'm sorry. I think I saw Dad. Or I thought I saw him and saw exactly what he looked like when he died, after his car accident, like right after it happened, the mostly dead HIM and I was so sure I saw him, like SO sure but now I don't know, I think I'm wrong or maybe not totally wrong and I did see him but didn't see him and I want to take that fucking stupid seer coin and bury it or put it over one of my eyes like a patch, blind myself so I'll stop seeing him. I'm sorry

The third and final page with writing has only two sentences, writ achingly small.

Don't leave.

I'm still here.

Elizabeth snaps photos of each page with her cell phone, never once taking her eyes off the drawing. She e-mails the pictures to Allison with a subject heading of *a few more pages from Tommy* and *call me in the morning* in the body of the message. The morning before, when Allison was at the house, Elizabeth thanked her for her hard work, support, and compassion. A day and night of madness later, she is angry at the detective who she now decides is emotionally detached to the point of being indifferent, is not forthcoming with information and leads, and is not leading the investigation with any kind of urgency or efficiency. That all of this is still happening and nothing has been solved is proof of the town's cruel ineptitude. Nice people she's known most of her adult professional life but clearly not up to the task before them.

The sent e-mail *woosh* sounds from her phone, and it's as though she has banished the photos to a vast nothingness.

Elizabeth then e-mails her photo of the page with the sketch to Dave Islander, the local weekly editor, along with a brief explanation about how it came from Tommy's diary. She wonders if he'll publish it, and she hopes that having as many people view the sketch as possible will somehow dilute its awfulness.

Allison at the House, Kate Visits Josh, Hobo Nickels

The article won't appear in print for a few more days, but a little after 9 a.m. Dave Islander uploads his latest piece on Tommy Sanderson to the *Ames Patch*, the catchall local online news site. The article opens with a brief description of Split Rock and how it's become a makeshift shrine for Tommy. Along with the stash of gifts, flowers, and messages left at the site, the venerable brown trail-marking signpost for Split Rock has been crudely vandalized to read *Devils Rock*.

Islander then breaks the news that Tommy was befriended by a man in his early twenties, identity and whereabouts unknown. During the summer the man hung out with Tommy and his friends at the 7-Eleven in Five Corners and also met the boys inside Borderland State Park. Ames and state police have no official comment as to whether or not this yet-to-be-named man is a person of interest in their investigation. Islander then details a seeming epidemic of reports/complaints of late-night trespassing from numerous residents with homes abutting the state park. High school-aged kids sneaking into the park after hours has never been an uncommon occurrence, and the police have been extravigilant in that regard. However, since the night of Tommy's disappearance, a group of residents have consistently reported a person walking or cutting through their property and into the park, with five residents even claiming that someone stood outside their windows, peering into their homes and bedrooms.

Islander segues from there into an obscure local folktale about the devil stalking the woods of Borderland and ultimately being tricked into disappearing by Oakes Eastman at Split Rock. How obscure? Islander could find only a few print references to the tale, with the most recent being a book called *Forgotten New England Ghost Stories*, published in 1993 by the now-defunct Willow Press.

Islander writes that Tommy and his friends were "obsessed" with the devil/Eastman story, so much so the boys renamed Split Rock to Devil's Rock, a name that seems to be catching on with local kids given their makeover of the SPLIT ROCK sign. Islander ends the article with Elizabeth's photo of Tommy's drawing, and it is presented as evidence of a young teen's obsession with the devil-versus-Eastman folktale, which is ostensibly a story about a clandestine rendezvous in the woods with a mysterious, charming, and dangerous stranger. The implications and connections Islander makes to the unnamed male who befriended Tommy are obvious and ominous.

Once posted, the Islander article quickly explodes in social media. On the Patch's Facebook page there are hundreds of comments, with more people claiming the shadowy figure has been walking through their properties at night. There are renewed calls to close down the state park to the public and for a curfew for Ames teens. #FindTommy trends on Twitter with thousands of article shares and retweets. The disturbing image drawn by Tommy is dubbed "shadowman" on twitter and it's what dresses up the clickbait headlines in online news feeds. The article is even picked up by the national online news-gathering site Gawker. By late morning the traffic overwhelms the Patch and the bandwidth dries up. By lunch all the Boston media outlets are reporting on the unnamed male, and they have redescended upon Borderland. Two news vans are parked outside the Sanderson home as well.

Two camerapersons and reporters with microphones follow Detective Allison Murtagh up the walkway to the Sanderson house, asking questions that she doesn't answer. Elizabeth opens the door before Allison has a chance to use the bell and she walks inside without pausing.

"Thank you, Elizabeth."

Elizabeth wears cargo shorts and a blue T-shirt.

Her hair is still wet from a shower. "It's been a madhouse all day. Come on in. Can I get you a coffee?"

Allison says, "Actually, I'd love a coffee." She only had two hours' sleep and was up late with her father at the nursing home again; he is still in considerable pain after a fall in the bathroom. That's she even thinking of her father at all in the presence of Elizabeth makes her feel guilty.

"Sorry about all that out there." The way Elizabeth says it, it's clear to Allison that she isn't sorry, and wants to talk about why she isn't.

"Why are you sorry?"

"Well." She pauses in front of the cabinet with two coffee mugs. "All that out there is because of me, right? Not because of me, that's not what I mean. Because I told Dave, the local weekly guy, about Arnold and sent him one of the diary pages. Dave promised to help me out with support from his paper, and all the advice I get from this support group I belong to is to do everything I can to keep Tommy in the public eye. I'm not trying to make things harder for you guys, and nothing personal, but I think the press is Tommy's best chance to be found."

"Elizabeth, you don't ever have to apologize to me. You keep doing what you think you need to do."

Elizabeth's rigid defense posture visibly softens. She pours two cups of coffee and adds milk and sugar to both without asking. She says, "So, you guys aren't mad?" as she passes Allison her cup.

"No way. I'm not mad."

"Yeah, well, I know a bunch of other guys in your department are probably mad. Drummond probably. Stanton definitely."

"Eh, Stanton's always grumpy, if we're being nice. Especially if it means he has to answer a few more phone calls. Don't worry about him or anyone else."

"Phone's been ringing like crazy all morning and I can't keep up with all the tweets and posts to the Find Tommy page. Everyone asking about the mysterious older guy. I didn't tell Dave the man's name was Arnold. I don't know why. I just didn't."

"I did notice that."

The kitchen table is covered in a dissected newspaper and what looks like pages from an instruction manual. Elizabeth says, "Sorry. The kitchen's kind of a mess. We can sit out in the living room. Have a seat on the couch. I'll move the little side table over."

"Don't make a fuss for me, I'm fine." Allison follows her out and sits next to the table.

Elizabeth: "So what did Luis and Josh have to say about Arnold? Did you have any luck with Snapchat?"

Allison gives Elizabeth an update of what's been going on for the last thirty-six hours.

Josh and Luis do not know Arnold's last name.

They claim to have met up with Arnold a total of five times during the summer with the last time being more than a week before Tommy disappeared. None of the boys have Arnold's cell phone number, and all of their cell phone records bear that out. Collecting Snapchat data isn't quite the same. If they had Tommy's phone in hand there is forensic software that can recover any sent or received Snapchat images from the phone's data.

As far as Snapchat the company goes, they have been cooperating thus far and haven't yet asked for a warrant or court order given the emergency situation. The police can only retrieve images from the company that haven't been viewed by the user within thirty days of being sent. After thirty days, the unviewed images are deleted from the company's servers. There are not any unviewed images that have been sent to Tommy's account within the current thirty-day window, unfortunately. They have been able to attain a log of the last two hundred snaps that Tommy sent and received. The log doesn't include images, but is more like a map of who he was in contact with. There is one username in the log of "arnoldfrnd." Tommy sent and exchanged snaps with that user, twenty-one in total, with seventeen sent in one night about two weeks ago, and the four most recent snaps sent two days before his disappearance. Allison and her colleagues have an e-mail address and phone number for that user. Attempts at contact have come up empty so far, and the phone number belongs to a pay-as-you-go or burner phone, or he's using a number created with a burner app.

Elizabeth: "Oh, God. Using a burner is not good, right?"

"It makes it harder to find him, certainly. I want to be clear that in and of itself use of a burner doesn't necessarily imply criminal intent or behavior. Pay-as-you-goes are a convenient and cheap alternative to standard phone contracts."

Allison continues with the update, telling Elizabeth that the police have been reviewing surveillance video from the 7-Eleven at Five Corners. They've pored over hours and hours of film thus far with a focus on late June, when the boys were newly out of school and they first met Arnold. They've isolated three different dates and times with Tommy, Josh, and Luis in the store and hanging out front. The surveillance angle is from behind the register, with the sliding glass front doors in the upper middle of the video frame. Within the third of the three videos, there is an approximately seven-minute clip with the boys outside on their bikes, gathered to the left of the front door. They take turns popping or landing the front tires on the concrete parking stop as they are talking to another male. It's not the best, most clear shot with where they are sequestered in the upper-left corner of the frame. Plus the sizable magazine rack and an energy drink display blocks out much of the view out of the bay window, and outside there's a large trash can in the way. They haven't been able to pull or isolate a clear, identifying shot of the male's face.

"Nothing? Can't zoom in on him?"

"No, we can't." The video is maddening. Allison spent most of her morning watching and rewatching the clip, and whenever Arnold (she does presume the man in the video to be Arnold) was about to turn and directly face the camera, he didn't, or he veered off in another direction, or one of the boys stepped in front of him, almost as though their movements were choreographed. "The store's surveillance camera is not very sophisticated, severely limiting what we can enhance. As good as folks in the forensics department are, they can't magically make what wasn't filmed in high definition high definition."

Elizabeth raises her hands and lets them fall against her lap. She looks away from Allison and at the small camera on the TV stand across from the couch. "Cameras, cameras everywhere, but—" and then she looks at back to Allison and then away again, as though caught looking at something she shouldn't have been looking at. "But not a drop to drink. Or something like that."

When Allison came over yesterday morning for

249

the diary pages that mentioned Arnold, she noticed the camera perched on the TV stand. "I totally understand your frustration and we're doing—"

"I don't think you do understand my frustration. And it's more than frustration, Allison. It's a hell of a lot more than that." Elizabeth isn't quite yelling but it's close. She looks away and wipes her eyes.

"Of course. I'm sorry, Elizabeth. Truly, I am. I want you to know we're all working—"

"Yeah. Okay. I know. Sorry to interrupt. So you're saying we don't know anything for sure yet about this Arnold guy, but does this mean you can issue an Amber Alert now?"

Allison explains that while they already have issued a nationwide BOLO (be on the lookout) for Tommy, they cannot issue an Amber Alert unless there is clear evidence of abduction. "We haven't eliminated any possibilities. Given how thoroughly the park has been searched, it's unlikely that Tommy is injured or lost within the park, but, still, we don't know if he's been abducted or if he's an endangered runaway."

"I know. I get it. But he wouldn't run away. He wouldn't do that to me and he wouldn't do that to his sister."

Allison doesn't say anything.

"Is that what you believe, that he ran away, and now, maybe with this Arnold guy?"

Allison can't tell her that she's seen it before; young teen blinded by the allure of danger and the charms of an older person, particularly when alcohol and drugs were involved. She can't tell her that people always do things that their friends and loved ones never imagined they would do. Not only is everyone more than capable of making the worst decisions possible, those kinds of decisions are frighteningly commonplace and easy to make.

She says, "I haven't made up my mind, and it's my job to remain open to all possibilities until the evidence leads us to the truth."

Elizabeth says, "I can't stop thinking about that picture Tommy drew. I know he says it's really someone else, someone he saw, had been seeing, I guess, thinking it was maybe even his dad, but my God it looks so much like Tommy. Like some horrible self-portrait. I mean, when I picked up the page, that's what I saw before reading any of the rest of it, and it knocked me over. It was Tommy, and when I saw it I thought—I thought right there on the page is the terrible thing that happened to him."

Despite the bloated facial features, Allison agrees that the drawing does look like Elizabeth's son. She says, "Does it look like his father too?"

Elizabeth stares at Allison for a beat. "Maybe. A little. I can't tell. I can't unsee what I already saw, you know."

Allison won't tell her that her coworkers—people that Elizabeth knows as well as she does—are mimicking what's happening in social media, referring to the figure as shadowman. Allison puts her coffee cup down on the end table and pulls out her pocket notebook and pen. "Tell me again: How long ago did your ex-husband disappear and then the car accident?"

"Just over nine years ago. He died April nineteenth. He disappeared eight months before that."

"I know we talked about a lot of this already, but I feel like we're potentially overlooking something. Did Tommy talk to you about his father, more than usual, this summer, or in the spring, maybe around the anniversary of his death?"

"No. Tommy hardly ever talked about him. I can tell you exactly the last time we talked about William. It was the day before Christmas. Breakfast. I went and got donuts and bagels and we were going to head up to New Hampshire and my mom's place. Tommy was teasing Kate, pretending that she still believed in Santa, and it was totally getting under her skin, so I made a joke about their dad believing in Santa until he was eighteen years old. Kate and I talked more about William, how we met, what he got me for our first Christmas together, that kind of stuff. Tommy didn't say anything. He's a stereotypical teen boy in that way, you know? Won't talk about anything that's difficult or emotional. But he stayed there and listened to us. He took it all in."

Allison: "That Arnold somehow made that . . . um, connection to his father's death really seemed to make an impression on Tommy. And it seems clear, at least from the diary, that Tommy has been thinking about his father a lot this summer. He even writes about disappearing, too."

"Yes. I know. Reading all that has been, well, devastating, frankly. I'm always asking him to talk to me, to tell me anything, and I'm not trying to pry or lead him into anything he doesn't want to talk about. He's not rude or a bad kid, or anything like that, and we'll talk about his favorite TV shows and movies and stuff. Tommy's the sweetest, kindest boy you could ever meet. He doesn't like to talk about the heavy stuff. Or not with me, anyway."

A door opens and closes, and Kate shuffles out into the kitchen.

Elizabeth calls out over her shoulder. "Kate? I'm in the living room with Detective Murtagh."

Kate says, "Okay." She rubs her eyes and walks a tight little circle in the kitchen before opening the refrigerator door and pulling out a bottle of orange juice.

Elizabeth: "Can you hang out in your room for a few more minutes? I'll come get you when we're done."

"Okay. But I want to go to over Sam's house soon."

"You can. Just give us a few more minutes."

Allison says, "It's up to you, but I don't mind if she's here."

"I rather have her not here for now." Elizabeth stands up, and Kate leaves the kitchen with her glass of juice. "Thank you, Kate."

Allison asks, "Can you give me a list of William's friends on the off chance Arnold is someone who knew William or is connected to him somehow?"

"Oh, jeeze, his old friends and coworkers. I can give you names, but I haven't spoken to most of them since his funeral."

Allison says, "That's fine. We can work with that. Now, this might sound like a weird question—"

"It's all been weird."

"That third page you found this morning, the one that says 'Don't leave. I'm still here.' " She pauses to clear her throat, unhappy with how her voice is sounding. "Any idea what that means? Do you think Tommy is quoting someone, maybe William?"

"What? No. I don't have any idea what that means. Why do you think it's something William said?"

"It struck me that Tommy wrote about wondering what his father's last words were in his diary. Remember? I'm trying to piece together how obsessed Tommy had become with his father's accident, any possible connection to Arnold, and how it might've played a role in his disappearance."

Elizabeth puts down her cup of coffee on the floor, folds her legs up onto the couch, closing up and off. Allison just lost her. She doesn't blame her. Her questions about her dead ex-husband sound like she's grasping at the shortest of straws. She might as well move on to the next question, the one she's been waiting to ask all day.

"Where did you find the most recent diary pages?" She doesn't add the observation that it's more than odd she keeps finding them, parsed out, once a day and like a wake-up alarm.

Elizabeth exhales deeply. "I found yesterday's in the middle of the living room floor."

"The living room floor?"

"Yeah, there." Elizabeth points at the floor and then folds her arms across her chest, cupping her left elbow in her right hand. "And I, um, I have to tell you. I haven't been finding Tommy's diary pages bookmarking random other books. Not this morning, but the previous three mornings they were left there on the rug."

Allison looks at the floor and it's as empty as an unused theater stage. "I'm not sure I follow. How did they get there?"

"Kate. And I'm sorry I—or—she wasn't more forthcoming about the diary and stuff. It's been a mess, you know? But she admitted to finding his diary last night and that she was tearing out the pages and then getting up at night and leaving them out on the floor for me to find in the morning, because, well, Jesus, it's a long story, Allison."

Allison doesn't know quite what to say and stumbles through something that's supposed to be commiserative. "Okay. Yeah, I can't imagine how difficult this is for Kate, and what she might have to do to, um, cope."

Elizabeth looks over her shoulder and down the hallway. "Yeah. Kate had been so adamant about it not being her, you know, leaving the pages out, that at first I thought it wasn't her." Elizabeth pauses and looks into her lap, like she's given the most embarrassing confession. She says, "And then I kind of let it go on, you know, because . . . because this all has been so hard to deal with. Impossible. Just fucking impossible, and if doing this—" she points at the rug, and the speed and momentum with which she speaks increases, and to Allison this ramble sounds like a rational-ization, and not as honest as what she said when she looked into her lap a few moments ago "—was how Kate needed to deal with it, or cope like you said, then okay. But Kate and I had a big fight, late last night, or early this morning. And, I didn't handle it well, I'm afraid." Elizabeth laughs softly at herself. "Understatement of the year. I yelled, kind of went crazy, tore apart her room, looking for the diary, and made a mess of everything. Everything." Elizabeth abruptly stops, cuts out.

Did Allison say that people were always capable of the worst decisions out loud earlier, or did she think it? She's been so knocked off her axis by this unexpected revelation and turn in the conversation, she isn't sure. "I think you and Kate are holding up amazingly well, and I'm sure Kate will forgive you for yelling at her. Did she eventually admit to leaving out the diary pages?"

"Yeah, and she gave me the rest of the diary." Elizabeth hands her the book.

The front and back covers are black and the spine thin. The book feels as fragile as an ancient artifact. There couldn't be more than fifty pages in the book even before some of the pages were torn out. Allison opens it. The page with Tommy talking about his late-night chat with Arnold is the opening page, buffeted at the spine by the jagged edges of previous pages torn out. Allison carefully peels back each edge to count the missing pages. She counts twice and there are six, which accounts for the previously found entries. She then care-fully flips past the intact entries. Between the "I'm still here" page and the rest of the unused note-book more pages have been torn away. She says, "There're pages missing after these last pages you e-mailed me." She holds the diary open at the spine to show

Elizabeth the perforated edges. "There are—" she counts "—five pages missing. Did you ask Kate if there were more entries and if she had them?"

"Yeah, we saw that. And Kate swears the book was that way when she found it. After everything we went through last night, I don't think she'd be lying about having more missing pages."

Allison closes the diary and says, "Okay. Should we talk about that small camera you have mounted on the TV stand?"

"Yeah." Elizabeth nods her head. "I thought, especially when the pages first started showing up, that there might be a chance, you know, that it was someone else, not Kate, leaving them out."

"Who?"

"I—I don't know, maybe Luis or Josh, or some other kid from school was sneaking into the house, leaving the pages. I'd left our doors unlocked in case Tommy came back, so I don't know, I thought maybe it could be Tommy doing this, too." Elizabeth stops, looks away, and rubs her eyes. She's clearly uncomfortable answering the why of the camera.

Allison needs to restate the last part. "You thought Tommy was coming home and leaving out the pages for you to find?"

"No. Yes, but not exactly, I mean. I'm not explaining this very well. But I bought the camera thinking one of two things would happen: we'd catch on video who was leaving

258

the pages, or Kate would have to admit to doing it."

"What did you get on video?"

"Not much. The camera's been kind of glitchy. Or I thought it was. Kate was actually secretly controlling it so I wouldn't see her leaving the pages out for me—and she admitted all this to me. I let her set the whole system up. She synced it to my phone and to her phone, too, without telling me. She's very tech savvy and I'm not, and last night, she muted the alarm we'd set up with the camera notifications. There's a clip from yesterday morning though that Kate says wasn't her."

Elizabeth takes out her phone and moves closer to Allison on the couch. Elizabeth shows her a still of the room from 2:11 a.m., and then a video from 4:34 a.m. Other than the diary pages on the living room floor, there wasn't anything else out of the ordinary that Allison could see. Elizabeth played the video three times and appeared to grow more frustrated with each viewing.

Elizabeth says, "At first I thought—"

Kate says, "Hi?"

Kate is behind the couch, telephone-pole straight with her hands held behind her back. She wears a loose white T-shirt from a summer lacrosse camp, and there are thin backpack straps over her shoulders. She wears jeans with holes and frays on the tops of the thighs, a giant hole like a denim mouth over her left knee. Her hair is

259

up in a tightly tied ponytail. The purple streaks blend in and fade into her dark hair. Her chin is up, and she looks so much like her mother, but there's another's face underneath. Allison wonders if Elizabeth sees her that way, too.

Kate waits until both adults are turned around and facing her before continuing. "Um, Detective, did Mom tell you that I woke up the other night and saw someone standing outside my window?"

Allison looks at Elizabeth quickly, then back at Kate and says, "No."

Elizabeth: "I was about to tell her, and show her the video you said wasn't you."

Kate doesn't take her eyes off Allison and says, "The one that was just a snapshot of the room, that was me. I had the camera take a shot of the room, then I like shut it off—"

Allison: "How?"

"With the app on my phone. And then I dropped the pages out there, then turned the camera back on. But that second video—I have no idea why the camera went off. It wasn't me. And I think it went off at like the same time I saw what I saw outside the window. It could've been a dream, I guess, but it seemed totally real, and it was scary."

Allison: "I bet. Could you tell if it was a man or woman? Did you see a face?"

"I couldn't see much. Hard to tell how big it was or anything like that. It was dark in my room and dark outside, but it was like an even darker shadow standing there, you know, in the shape of someone, outside my window, and then it, I mean, whoever it was, was gone pretty quick. When I got out of bed and looked out the window, that shadow wasn't there anymore." Kate pauses and says, "There seems to be a lot of that going around in Ames."

Allison: "A lot of what?"

Kate: "I dunno, dark shadows of someone looking in on people's houses. It's kinda scary. People all over Twitter and Facebook are talking about it, calling him shadowman, and talking about that big article this morning, yeah?"

Allison: "We have received a number of complaints very similar to your description."

Kate: "Mom, did you tell her about seeing a dark shadow in your room, that first night after Tommy disappeared?"

Elizabeth tilts her head and stares hard at Kate, and then she coughs and breathes deeply again. "No, Kate."

Kate: "Why not?"

Elizabeth looks at Allison as she talks. "It's not the same as what she said she saw, or what other people are reporting. I was in my room and I'd just woken up, went to the bathroom, still groggy—"

Kate: "Mom."

Elizabeth holds up a stop hand at her daughter. "—let me finish. It was one of those half-asleep,

261

late-night things, eyes seeing shapes that aren't there. Anyway, I thought I saw something near the chair in my room. But I got up and went over to the spot and it was nothing. Really."

Kate: "Mom, you've been saying you saw the shadow of someone hiding next to the chair, like a person was crouched down or something, and you said you thought it was Tommy."

Elizabeth: "Kate—"

Kate: "It's true."

Elizabeth: "Listen, I—"

Kate: "Why are you being like this?"

Elizabeth is yelling now. "Kate! That's enough!"

The two Sanderson women abruptly end the exchange before Allison resolves to intervene. The silence is as long as it is uncomfortable. Elizabeth is looking down into her lap, and her arms are crossed again. Kate is still standing behind the couch. Her rigid posture has relaxed, or sagged. She adjusts one of the straps on her backpack.

Allison is not quite sure how to proceed. She wants to hug them and shake them both violently while demanding to know what the hell is going on in this house. She says, "Kate, can I ask you something?"

"Yeah."

"There are more pages missing from Tommy's diary. Five of them by my count." She holds up the diary opened to the second section of the spine where there are missing pages. "Did you tear them out?"

"No way. I swear. When I found the diary, it was like that. Those pages were already torn out." Kate is calm and her expression doesn't change, her eyes are hard and unwavering. Unreadable. If she's lying, it's a righteous lie in which she fully believes.

"Do you know where those missing pages are? I know you found the diary in his room, did you find anything else with Tommy's writing like this?"

"No. Just his drawings and stuff. I haven't found anything else like the diary and I haven't found any missing pages anywhere. I'm going to my friend's house soon, and you can feel free to check my room while I'm gone if you want."

Allison: "If it's okay with your mom, I think I'll take you up on that offer, and I think we should go through Tommy's room as well."

Elizabeth nods. Kate remains motionless, a picture of a teen's assured defiance.

Allison continues. "I'm sure you realize this already, Kate, but based on the pages we've received so far, especially ones that mention Arnold, assuming there are more pages, it's possible they contain critical information." Allison hopes she doesn't sound condescending. She wants Kate's trust. Allison also doesn't want to sound too desperate or too impersonal.

"Information that could help us locate Tommy."

Kate says, "I know and that's why I'm totally telling the truth now. And I do have something else for you, Detective." She brings a hand out from behind her back and she holds something small, and what appears to be the top of a plastic sandwich bag sticks out from her closed fist. "I found these two coins on top of Tommy's bureau." She opens her hand, holds up the bag, and shakes it. The two coins inside jingle. Kate readjusts her backpack straps, then reaches over the couch and hands the bag to Allison.

Allison opens it and looks inside but does not shake the coins out onto her palm.

Elizabeth says, "I'd forgotten about these."

Allison: "You've seen these coins before?"

Elizabeth: "Kate showed them to me a few days ago. Tommy used to collect coins like crazy when he was younger. Fourth and fifth grade, mostly."

Kate: "One coin looks like a nickel, but it has this weird empty face and then a big eye hanging above it. I think maybe it's the seer coin that Tommy talks about in his diary. When he said Arnold showed him pictures of the coins he worked on, and then on the page with the picture, Tommy said something about wanting to put the seer coin over his eyes, yeah."

Elizabeth: "Oh, Jesus Christ . . ."

Kate keeps talking, "And, you know, Tommy says Arnold called himself a seer, right?, so who knows, I started thinking that maybe Arnold gave Tommy the coins or something."

Allison carefully manipulates the coins in the bag.

Kate, looking over Allison's shoulder, says, "That one is just a penny. But the Lincoln head has like a big crack in it."

Allison: "Have you taken out the coins? Touched them with your hands?"

Kate: "Yeah."

Allison: "That's fine. We'll still try to get some prints off these if we can." Allison inspects the coin with the tails side of a nickel and the heads side with a silhouetted face in profile and a large, roughly etched eye hovering above. Allison opens her notebook. "Can you show me where you found these?"

Kate: "Uh-huh. Like, now?"

"Yes, please."

The three of them go to Tommy's room. Kate walks in without hesitating, her thumbs hooked in the backpack straps. Elizabeth hangs back and allows Allison to go next.

It's brighter in this room than it is in the hall-way with natural light pouring through the windows and reflecting off the light blue walls. Tommy's bed is made. His room is clean, tidy, staged. Tommy's books and comics are stacked neatly in the bookcase along the wall and the bedframe bookcase. His desk is huge, a peninsula jutting out into the middle of the room, and made of thick, serious wood. Its top is well organized, with pens and notebooks in their spots and a dormant laptop, graffitied with stickers and a Sharpie. Next to the desk is a milk crate filled with more notebooks.

Kate says, "I found the bag up here, and it was inside the metal tin, near at the top."

Tommy's bureau isn't as neat as his desk and is cluttered with hats, superhero action figures, and loose change. The metal tin sits in the back middle, a raincatch for pocket-sized trinkets.

Allison asks, "Do you know where the bulk of his coin collection is?"

Kate shrugs. "No idea."

Elizabeth: "It's gotta be in here somewhere."

Allison pulls out a pair of latex gloves from a jacket pocket and puts them on. She feels the Sanderson women watching her. "I may come across something that we might want to pull prints from."

Allison brings the tin to the front of the bureau and sifts through it.

Kate: "Mom, do you guys need me anymore? Can I ride my bike to Sam's house now?"

Elizabeth: "Bike? I thought I was going to drop you off."

Kate: "I want to bike over."

Elizabeth groans and runs both hands through her hair. "I really wanted to give you a ride over. I don't like you out by yourself right now."

"It's fine, Mom. I've been doing it all summer. It's not even that far and I haven't done anything in days and I feel like a slug."

Elizabeth looks at Allison for some sign of approval, or maybe disapproval. Allison doesn't give either. Elizabeth says, "I guess so, as long as your leaving now is okay with Detective Murtagh."

Allison: "Yes, of course. But is there anything else you need to tell me before you leave?"

Kate's "Nope" is instantaneous to the end of the query. She rises on her toes and falls back to the floor, itching to be gone.

Elizabeth: "You can stay for a few hours. Be back before dinner. And make sure you have your phone on. Is it charged?"

Kate is already walking out of the room. Her blue pack bounces with each step. "Full charge, Sarg."

"Be careful."

Allison calls out. "Kate?"

Kate is in the hallway, but turns around and stands in the doorway. "Yeah?"

"You said we could check your room, and thank for you that. Do you mind if we see what's in your pack?"

Kate shrugs, walks into the room, shimmies out of her pack, and holds it out to Elizabeth. "Sure. Take a look. Just my phone, headphones, our picture flip book we've been working on all summer, granola bar, and . . . two lemonade juice boxes."

Allison stands next to Elizabeth and watches as she goes through it. The contents that Kate catalogued are all there, along with a few stray pens and pencils, and a brown book.

Elizabeth: "What's this?"

"I, um, started a new diary."

Elizabeth takes it out. The book is small, secret-sized, definitely not big enough to be the book from which Tommy's pages have been coming. She turns and flips it in her hand, as though confirming its small dimensions. She inspects the front and back covers, both decorated in a neat but loopy scrawl, different from Tommy's handwriting.

Kate: "You're not gonna read it, now, with me standing here, are you? It's just, you know, my diary. I don't want you reading it. Not now. It's my stuff. Maybe later." She reaches for the book hesitantly, and Elizabeth turns away.

Allison would very much like to read it but won't press her on it if she balks. She's confident that she'll be able to find the missing pages (if they're in the house) in either of the Sanderson kids' bedrooms.

Elizabeth flips through the pages slowly.

"Mom! I said don't. There's nothing there for you."

Elizabeth hands the diary to Allison. "Can she

flip through and not really read it, to make sure that it's all your handwriting and no one else's?'"

Allison verifies the pages have Kate's and only Kate's handwriting, and color of the ink is purple and blue and sometimes green. It's about a quarter full. She hands it back to Kate.

Kate stuffs it back in her pack.

Elizabeth says with a voice that's supposed to be soothing, but has an obvious edge to it, "I know, I'm sorry. Just making sure, right? We'll talk about this when you get back."

Kate gives her mom a hard stare and zips up her pack, loudly. Allison can't help but think of what she would've said to her own parents at that age: *No we're not.*

Kate: "I'm going now. Bye."

Elizabeth talks to the back of Kate as she walks out of the room. "I'm going to call you in half an hour to make sure you got there and that your phone is on."

Elizabeth and Allison listen to Kate go out the back door. Elizabeth says, "She hasn't been out of the house, really, since Tommy went missing. She needs to get out, see her best friend."

Allison: "It'll be good for her."

Elizabeth nods but her stare is aimed outside the room, and the house, and following her daughter.

Allison says, "You're welcome to stay and watch me, but you don't have to be here in the room, either. I'll call you in if I have any questions."

"I'd prefer to watch, if that's okay."

Allison starts with the built-in bookcase and then the bookcase along the wall, methodically removing each book, occasionally asking Elizabeth if she recognizes the titles. She checks behind and under the bed. Next she goes through his desk and then the milk crate of notebooks. She sits at Tommy's desk and reads every page of every book, looking for more entries, mentions of Arnold, and signs of pages having been removed. Elizabeth reads over her shoulder, and Allison hears her reacting emotionally to what she reads. She laughs at some of the cartoons and clicks her tongue or swallows heavily at the more teen angsty pictures and proclamations, and she sighs at the "school is like drowning" title page.

Elizabeth says, "Oh jeeze," and mumbles apologies as Allison flips through pages of lurid nudes and sex scenes.

Allison says, "He's a teen boy. I don't think there's one who hasn't drawn a penis."

After the milk crate, Allison moves on to the bureau. She goes through his drawers first. Elizabeth is no longer hanging over Allison's shoulder. She sits at Tommy's desk, and she goes through some of his notebooks and sketch pads again. Allison doesn't blame her for not wanting to see what's inside her son's bureau drawers. There isn't anything there, no signs of a diary nor any drug/alcohol paraphernalia. From the bureau she moves on to the closet, which smells like a locker room. There's a half-full laundry hamper on the floor. Elizabeth mumbles something about getting around to washing his clothes. Allison goes through the pockets in the dirty shorts and jeans. Nothing.

From Tommy's closet they move on to Kate's room, which is a disaster and smells of dust, wet sneakers, and unlit, too-sweet scented candles. Allison tries not to step on anything but there're clothes, hangers, books, and assorted preteen debris all over the floor.

Allison has to say something. Against her better judgment, she tries to be lighthearted in the face of what was the result of a traumatic experience in this room. "Whoa. I thought my room was a mess when I was a kid."

Elizabeth says, "This isn't Kate's fault. I went a little nuts last night looking for the diary. I threw everything out of her closet. I didn't find it. Kate gave it to me."

Allison won't find the missing pages, either.

Kate's bike is fire engine red, with tires thick enough to belong on a monster truck. It was Tommy's first gear bike, which he outgrew over the course of two summers. Mom was crazed, given how much she'd spent on it, and tried to sell the bike, but never got a serious offer. Last summer Kate wanted a new bike and not Tommy's old one, but Mom shrewdly struck a deal with her; Kate could paint it any color she wanted (it was originally silver). Kate getting to paint the bike sealed the deal and she got to put new tires on the bike, too. It wasn't that she was so into off-roading or trail riding; Kate reasoned the wider the tire, the less likely it became for her to ever wobble and fall. Kate ended up loving the souped-up bike. Tommy was totally jealous of the tires and often rode her bike without asking, which was both a source of fury and pride. That Tommy thought her bike was cool meant she'd never relinquish it.

She plows through the backyard, the overgrown grass grabbing at her tires. She eventually picks up enough speed to weave between two thick fir trees (a neat trick, one she hasn't always been able to pull off without crashing or scraping an arm or leg against coarse bark) onto a small path that Tommy wore out through the brush that leads to the edge of their neighbor's property. The path is also a shortcut to their street. Kate navigates the snakey path and rides smoothly over a little lip and onto the blacktop. She doesn't look back at the news vans parked behind her, confident that they won't follow as long as she doesn't turn to look at them. At the end of her street Kate takes a left. She's not going to Sam's house.

It's a cooler-than-normal late August day.

There's no humidity and an underlying crispness in the air that makes autumn easier to imagine. Her fat tires chew up the blacktop and spit out small bits of sand and rock. The sun is bright, and Kate regrets leaving the house without sunglasses. She thinks about taking her bulky helmet off (it's a charcoal gray/black and it makes her head look like a mushroom cap) and letting the wind blast through her hair, but she won't stop the bike. Now that she's out on the road and by herself, she doesn't want to stop pedaling ever. The urge to be the one who disappears suddenly becomes a compulsion. Maybe the people who go away are the ones who are not afraid, not sad, and not alone. Maybe there's a place where they gather and say things like *What is to be done with all the silly people we left behind?*

Kate turns off Massapoag Avenue and its shallow, dirt-covered shoulders and onto a sleepy residential side street. She rides down the road's exact middle without yellow lines to guide her. Shortly after the street curls to the left she hops a tall curb, which is no match for her greedy tires, and then powers her bike through the dried-out front lawn of Josh's house. Almost all the way across she says, "Oops," out loud, remembering that Josh's parents freak out over their grass. She makes it to the driveway and gently lays down her bike, a fallen apple in front of the closed garage doors. She takes off her mushroom helmet and leaves it on the handlebars. As she walks to the front door, she hopes that she sees the rut her tires chewed through the lawn only because she knows it's there.

Kate rings the bell.

Josh's mom is a pair of eyes peeking through a small rectangular window. Kate waves. Mrs. Griffin opens the door. She wears jeans and a black fleece zipped all the way up to her chin. She says, "Kate?" like her name is a puzzle.

"Hi, Mrs. Griffin."

"Hi, yes, wow, I wasn't expecting—it's great to see you." Josh's mom leans her head over and past Kate. "Is your mom here, too? Are you here by yourself?"

"It's just me." Kate shrugs. "I rode my bike over. Wanted, you know, to get out of the house, be in the sun."

"I can imagine. Are you doing okay?" Mrs. Griffin groans at herself and says, "Of course I know things aren't okay, but are *you* doing okay?"

"Yes and no. A lot of sitting around and waiting." Kate stops talking and gives a half smile, a derp face, as Tommy would call it. It's obvious that Mrs. Griffin doesn't know what to do with her. And that's fine. Other people should be made to feel uncomfortable, too.

"Your mom let you come over by yourself?"

Now that she's admitted to leaving out the

diary pages to Mom, Kate decides to be direct with everyone, and to say whatever comes to mind. Without painfully deliberating and weighing every word of each response, talking will be easier. "Kinda. She thinks I went to my friend Sam's house. Which I will do. I didn't lie to her. I'm going there, but only after."

"After what?"

"Can Josh come outside? Maybe shoot some hoops with me for a little while? Sam won't play basketball with me, and she'll sit in her room and talk about Tommy, and I want to be outside for a little bit first. It'll probably do Josh some good, too, don't you think?"

"Um, yeah, okay, I think so. He's home. In his room. I'll ask him. But—" She pauses and looks out over Kate's head again.

"But what?"

"If a news van or anything like that comes by while you guys are outside, I'm going to have to call you in. Is that okay?"

"Sure. No problem."

"Thank you. It's just—we've been getting a lot of calls and, um, messages today, from different places, and it's been, I don't know." She stops and shakes her head.

Kate says, "Yeah. Us too. Mom handles all that."

"I'm sure she does. She's a strong person, your mom. Anyway, this was very nice of you to

275

come over, Kate. Do you want to come in? Need a drink or anything?"

"Nah. I'm good. And I'll wait over in the driveway for Josh."

"Josh. Right. Are you sure?"

"Yeah."

Kate walks down the stairs and thinks about not waiting for Josh and going into the backyard and then into the woods from which Tommy disappeared. Maybe in her own diary she could create a short comic in which she calls out Tommy's name into those crowded trees and her voice is enough to bring him back. Instead, Kate sits down cross-legged on the driveway next to her bike. She stares out at the empty street and the houses that look like they've always been part of the landscape. She imagines the houses as the backs of giant sleeping monsters, and she wishes to see what it all will look like when the houses finally get up and crawl away. The garage door whirs to life behind her and Josh walks out, bending under the still-rising door when it's halfway open. He has a basketball cuffed against his left side. It's Boston Celtics green and white, an outdoor ball, the kind that is all rubber, smells like a tire, and bounces as wildly as an excited electron.

Josh says, "Hey." His hair is just-got-a-haircut short. It's thick, bristly, like wire. His Washington Nationals T-shirt is so dark blue it's almost black. His baggy light blue shorts go past his knees and down to midankle. His basketball sneakers are big and red, untied, and on so loosely there's no way his feet won't fall out when he takes a step.

Kate says, "Hey. Is that the best ball you have?"

"My good ball is in my dad's car."

"Gimme."

Josh lets the ball fall toward her. Kate snags it, takes two hard dribbles to the net and throws up a shot with two hands. She knows she'll never be a basketball player for any team yet is self-conscious that she still shoots with two hands instead of one. Her T-shirt comes up over her stomach, and she pulls it back down in midshot. The ball bounces hard off the backboard even though she didn't intend it to. The ball's first two bounces are over her head, and she has to sprint to chase down the rebound before the ball lands on the lawn.

Josh says, "Is there anything going on, or, um, new with Tommy?"

"No."

"I'm sorry."

"I know. Everyone is sorry. I'm sorry you were the last one to see him." If it sounds like an accusation, then good.

Josh hides his hands in his pockets and edges out toward the basketball hoop. He looks behind him, toward the bay window, as though looking for someone else who heard what Kate said to him.

She says, "I gave Mom the rest of Tommy's diary." Her having finally given up the diary to Mom is an act of acceptance, although whoever said *Acceptance is the price of freedom* has a funny definition of freedom. Kate doesn't feel free; in fact she feels like a quitter, and feels sadder than ever, believing like Mom does, that their Tommy is truly gone, and gone forever. In a few weeks Kate will give her new therapist honest attempts at further articulating why and how she thought she was helping Mom by initially keeping the diary and tearing out the pages and leaving them in the living room, although she'll never be able to adequately explain her actions. And with the passage of time, those actions will belong to another person, someone she'll miss but who will be no longer an influence on her life.

Josh: "The detective was asking me stuff about the diary yesterday. And I saw the picture of the shadow-man-thing he drew today, too."

"Right. So that's about it. But looks like there are pages missing, though."

Josh doesn't say anything.

Kate says, "Is your mom watching us?"

"Yeah. Probably."

"Let's shoot." Kate shoots, pulls down her shirt. This shot goes in. Josh taps the ball back out to her in that annoying, nonchalant way of boys, making it look like giving any sort of physical effort beyond breathing is the uncoolest thing in the world. That's what they call a hardo, right? She hates it, and wonders why would Josh, of all kids, act like that in front of her, and now. Josh isn't Luis, the one she has an obvious crush on. If he's not equivalent to a big brother, Josh is like a first cousin, one you see at all the family gatherings and with which you swap your most embarrassing stories about your freaky, related parents.

Kate rotates the basketball in her hand and says, "I thought you hated the Celtics."

"I don't *hate* hate them. I won the ball at Canobie Lake Park."

"You won it?"

Josh shrugs. "Yeah."

Kate thinks he's lying. She thinks she can tell when he's lying. She throws the ball to him hard. He's slow to put up his hands and the ball hits him in the gut. He struggles to swallow a reaction and not touch where the ball hit him.

She says, "Your turn."

Josh shoots. His form has an odd hitch and wiggle to it, with the ball down by his hip, he turns, or swivels, and desperately heaves it up there, as though his arms aren't strong enough. It takes a long time to get the shot off, but he makes it.

Kate says, "Fancy."

Josh smiles and says, "Catchphrase, right?"

His saying Tommy's saying to her, it might be the nicest thing anyone has said to her in a week. She says, "Maybe."

Josh goes through his ritual contortions again and makes a second shot in a row.

Kate says, "Did Arnold give you any coins like he gave Tommy? I found them. On Tommy's bureau."

Josh doesn't say anything and dribbles the ball between both hands slowly, awkwardly. Even Kate notices how slow and uncoordinated he's gotten, compared to how fast and athletic he was when they were all in elementary school together. How does that happen?

Kate: "There's one coin that looks like a nickel but has a weird eye on it."

Josh shoots the ball and front-rims it. It bounces back to him. He says, "Yeah. I saw that coin. Arnold gave each of us a coin."

"He did? So you got one, too?"

"Yeah."

"Can you show it to me?"

Kate's cell phone goes off. The ring tone is the opening riff of the Clash's "London Calling." It's her mom's favorite song. Kate thinks it and the Clash are just okay. Joe Strummer's voice sounds like an old, drunk person saying *Fuck you,* and it makes her feel sad for him. She likes the other singer better.

Kate holds a finger against her lips and says to

Josh, "Don't say anything and stop dribbling." She answers the phone. "Hi. I made it here, Mom."

Elizabeth: "Great. Can I talk with Nancy for a second?"

Nancy is Sam's mother. No she cannot talk to Nancy. Kate says, "She's in the bathroom. I'll call before I leave. Bye," and she hangs up.

Josh: "Who's in the bathroom?"

"Don't worry about it. Go inside and get the coin that Arnold gave you. I want to see it."

"I don't have it. I gave it to Tommy."

"Really?"

"Yeah."

"The cracked Lincoln head penny?"

"Yeah."

"I found that one, too."

"I figured."

"He'd put them both in a plastic sandwich bag."

Josh looks back toward the bay window like he's waiting for his mother to tell him that he has to go inside.

Kate says, "Yo. Shoot the ball."

Josh dribbles a little. He doesn't shoot.

Kate: "I gave the coins to Allison."

"Allison?"

"Um, Detective Murtagh."

"Oh, yeah. Right."

"You didn't know her first name?"

"Not really."

"Haven't you guys talked?"

"Yeah, of course, for like hours."

"She's searching my room now. Did you let her search yours?"

"No. I mean, she hasn't searched my room but she hasn't asked to." Josh talks slow, like he's stuck in time. "She can if she wants, you know."

"Why did you give it to Tommy?"

"What?"

"The crack-head penny?" Kate laughs despite herself.

Josh smiles. "I don't know nothing about a crack-head penny."

"Seriously. Why?"

"I dunno. Tommy's the coin guy."

"Was?"

"I didn't say 'was.' "

"You sure? Gimme the ball if you're not gonna shoot. It's my turn anyway."

"I said, 'Tommy *is* the coin guy.' Not 'was.' "

"Okay. I believe you." Kate is convinced she can tell whenever anyone is lying; sometimes it's so easy to tell. And Josh, he's the easiest. Always has been. It had to be part of why Tommy and Josh have been lifelong friends. Josh is safe like that.

Kate shoots and the ball goes in off the backboard. She wasn't trying to use the backboard. "Why did Arnold give you guys the coins?"

• • •

It was their fifth time with Arnold at Devil's Rock. First week of August, and the hottest day ever, the kind that slumped his shoulders and jellied his legs and threw his internal thermostat out of whack. Josh's forehead, right along the hairline, was melting. It was around noon and there wasn't much shade to be had on the rock.

Luis suggested that they go sit by some trees instead, or even chill inside the actual split. Josh protested that they'd too easily get caught drinking. He was in near a panic about being caught, more so than usual, because he had brought the beer. His father had an old fridge in the garage he kept stocked with water and beer. Mostly beer. There was a random collection of odd-duck bottles, each from a different brewer on the door shelves. The rest of the fridge was full with water and white cans of light beer. The light beer was marginally more drinkable than the darker stuff in bottles. And you couldn't hide how much you were or weren't drinking with a bottle, so he made sure to bring only the light beer cans. Luis made mock complaints like he was a beer snob already.

The boys sat in what little and fleeting patches of shade they could find on the rock. Arnold was restless. He paced and hopped over the split a bunch of times. He made Josh nervous.

Tommy burped loudly, then said, "I played

283

Minecraft last night for like the first time since school got out."

Luis: "Should've texted me."

Tommy: "It was way late. Like 2 a.m."

Luis: "Hardo."

Tommy: "I wasn't up to 2 a.m. I woke up and couldn't go back to sleep."

Luis: "Your first wet dream?"

Josh: "About Luis's mom!"

Tommy said, "Chirps!" like it was the next line in their script. The banter ended there as Tommy went away, somewhere inside himself. It was so Tommy. He had this switch he could flip and he'd disappear into his own head right in front of you. He was there but he wasn't there. You could almost feel that electric charge of Tommy's fully engaged personality shut off. It wasn't an affect, a woe-is-me posture, or a pose, or something he did for attention. This was a part of who he was, and Tommy had been doing it for as long as Josh had known him. Josh had spent more time than he'd ever care to admit wondering where it was Tommy went and what exactly he was thinking. Today, he figured Tommy was back in his room and thinking about why he couldn't go back to sleep. Maybe Tommy had dreamed about the devil standing outside of his window.

Forget the beer and the rock and Arnold and even Luis, Josh wanted to go home now and get online with Tommy, spend the whole day playing Minecraft like they had just over a month ago, back when they were so different than they were now.

Tommy: "I was on our server. And I don't know what happened but things looked way different." Unsaid was the question of whether or not Josh or Luis had been playing and adding buildings and/or destroying what they'd built.

Josh: "What, like errors? Glitches?"

Arnold said, "You have any corrupted chunks?" Pools of sweat ink blotted his red T-shirt around his armpits and on his chest up by the collar. He still kept jumping across the split, alternating the foot upon which he landed.

Luis: "Corrupted Chunks. Band name."

Arnold: "There are region fixers you can download to correct the errors, recover the parts of the world."

Luis said, "That's so cool."

Josh rolled his eyes. After Luis's initial reluctance and stand-offishness toward Arnold, he had since morphed into Arnold's chorus, a parrot. How could a kid who was normally such a relentlessly contrarian wiseass go so totally in the other direction and not see it? Who had replaced Luis with this lame imitation?

Tommy: "I don't think there're errors or anything like that. Just, like some of the rooms in our home base were different and some of the small bases were in different parts of the map than I remembered."

Luis: "Don't look at me. I haven't played in months. Probably Josh changing and hiding shit on us again."

Josh: "Easy, hardo. I did it one time, over a year ago. *One time,* and he still gives me shit."

Tommy: "He's a giver."

Josh: "I haven't been playing at all."

Luis: "Yeah, right. You probably rebuilt—"

Josh interrupted with "Shhh. It'll be okay, Luis. You'll get over it someday."

Luis threw an empty can at him, and the metallic clank of can off rock echoed through the surrounding forest.

Arnold ignored the skirmish, and he started talking about some of his own Minecraft discoveries and strategies. The boys listened and drank. Or at least Josh pretended to drink. He'd brought the beer hoping that the offering would help take off the pressure of having to drink the stuff himself. The last time they were here, Luis had been relentless with jokes and comments about Josh being a lightweight. Arnold had told Luis to chill, but it was halfhearted, and Tommy and Arnold had ended up talking to each other about the fungus that turned South American ants into zombies, which made things worse for Josh. Whenever Tommy had Arnold's full attention, Luis would turn on Josh, and then later, when it was just the three of them or just him and Luis, it was like none of the verbal sticks and stones had happened. Josh didn't get why Luis was acting like this now. At school Luis never made fun of Josh, and unlike Tommy, who retreated into his own world, Luis would run madly into the daily middle school skirmishes to defend Josh against any and all tormenters.

Arnold kept on talking Minecraft and the first time he made it to the End. He didn't really describe it, but he didn't have to because all the boys had been there.

Tommy chimed in. "Took us forever to beat the Ender Dragon for the first time, and it was kind of disappointing, right? We got that end poem message thingy at the portal, but I expected more of a big deal, yeah? But it was dark, like dark-dark, and nothing but endermen milling around, and I don't know, it felt lonely."

Josh and Luis looked at each other and laughed at Tommy. Tommy shrugged his patented yeah-I-know-what-I-said-is-weird shrug and took a small sip of his beer, and let his bangs fall over his eyes.

Luis said, "You need a hug, bro?" He said *bro* in Tommy's way of saying it: *bruh*.

Arnold said, "You know what's weird?"

Luis: "Josh's right nut is three times smaller than his left nut." He couldn't get it all out without breaking up at his own joke.

Josh laughed. It was funny. So much funnier than the constant drink-up harassments.

Arnold: "That is weird. But not what I was gonna say. I played Minecraft last night too, right around the same time Tommy was playing. And it's the first time I've played since—since before I met you guys, I think."

Josh said, "Of course the seer knew you were playing, Thomas." He said Tommy's name like "Tom-ass."

When he first met Arnold, Josh had thought the whole seer shtick was exactly that, and Josh had pretended otherwise because it was fun and it was what their summer had become. Tommy had his big mystery to contemplate, and Luis had someone he looked up to and wanted to impress, and Josh was content to simply play along because, well, for good or bad, that was what his role had become. The others seemed so happy and they were willing to include him. It was enough. Now he wasn't so sure that there wasn't something off or unsettling about Arnold. The repetition and sameness of their meeting place and discussions and beer drinking felt purposeful, like they were being worked on or worn down.

Luis said, "So it was you who messed up the place!" He pointed a mock-accusatory finger at Arnold.

Josh was horrified. Had Tommy invited Arnold to the server? *Their* world? His already hot and sweating face flushed, the color red pushed and pulsed beneath his skin.

Arnold spoke in a formal voice, "I assure you that I caused no trouble in your region and played with a sound mind and pure heart."

Josh: "You were playing on our server?"

Tommy: "What's the big deal?"

Arnold: "No. No worries. I was on some public one. Not yours."

Josh: "How'd you know Tommy was playing then?" His voice was whiney and he hated himself when he sounded like that, but he couldn't help it.

Arnold: "Huh? Nah, I didn't know."

Josh: "You just said you did."

Arnold: "I didn't say I *knew* he was playing. Me and him playing at the same time was random."

Josh: "Random?"

Arnold: "Yeah."

Josh: "So, a coincidence?"

Arnold laughed a little. "Random. co-inky-dink. Yup."

Josh: "The devil's in the coincidence, right? You said that."

Luis: "Dude. What are you getting at? Why do you always have to be such a hardo?"

Josh didn't know what he was getting at, but even in his rising anxiety, he enjoyed that Luis was bothered by his questions. Josh said, "*Dude.* Relax, I'm just joking around. That's what he told us, remember? Coincidence. In the story about the devil and the rock and everything else."

Arnold wasn't annoyed, at least, not that Josh could tell. He still slowly and nonchalantly hopped over the split and back. "Are you saying I'm the devil?"

Josh's insides pooled into his toes, the same feeling he got in school if the vice principal threatened him with detention. "I'm not saying, I'm just saying. If the horns fit." He giggled, not because it was funny, more like a pressure valve releasing steam. He giggled because he couldn't believe he had said it out loud.

Arnold pawed around his head with one hand, fake-looking for horns. "Nah. Nothing there. I had them removed. Grinded down with a power sander."

Tommy: "That sounds ouchy."

Josh laughed and felt tears filling his lids, and he didn't know why he was getting so upset or what he was going do if he started crying in front of them all.

Arnold said, "I know that my devil story is like the greatest." He held out his hands and rolled his eyes at himself, allowing both Luis and Tommy to grumble playful insults at him. "And I know you all know it's just a folktale, but let me tell you all something. For reals. Everything that happens is a coincidence, and at the same time there's no such thing as coincidence."

Luis pointed at Arnold and said, "He speak funny."

"Watch." Arnold kept on leaping over the split. "If I slipped and fell into the split right now—" he jumped across and back "—would that be a coincidence or karma or whatever you want to call it? No, because I'm taking a chance that I might fall with each jump, yeah? I mean, if I fell in, would you be surprised?"

Tommy: "Yeah, actually I would."

Arnold: "Right! Yes! *You* would, but at the same time, when the park ranger guy shows up after I fell in and bashed my head open, and you'd have to tell him that I had a few beers and I was jumping over the split a bunch of times and then missed once, the ranger'd be all like, oh, okay, Darwin award winner takes a rock dive and bites it. Right? It would be an accident but not an accident at the same time. Get it? It's hard to explain, but everything that happens is connected to something that happened before it."

Tommy said: "So you mean everything that happens to us, is like, all mapped out already?"

Arnold: "No, no, it's not all mapped out. Shit can happen and change, there's still chance, and infinite possibilities, and everything, but there's this—what—a connection. More of a connection than people think. When one thing happens, it turns into the next thing, and then the next thing. Yeah?"

Luis: "Go home, Arnold. You're drunk."

Arnold: "Wiseass."

Luis beamed at him. "You sound like the math guy from *Jurassic Park*."

Arnold laughed and kicked a twig at Luis. He walked away from the split and sat down on the rock, closer to Josh than the other two. "I'm not saying this right—okay, it's like this. You ever think about something and then it happens?"

Josh: "I don't know. Maybe. I guess." Maybe it was like when before he went to bed and he thought about Arnold and the devil story then he had nightmares about a man standing outside his window. Josh had constructed detailed images of the scene on the rock with Oakes Eastman, and how the devil was trapped in the split, scurrying and scrabbling back and forth, so quickly, like a blur, and that blurring would loop in his head if he let it. So his thinking about the story would lead to him having a man-standing-outside-his-window dream, and the dream would make him think more about the story and then he'd dream again.

Luis: "Nah, I call bullshit."

Arnold: "Like, haven't you ever been thinking about someone randomly and then boom, they call you or text you?"

Josh wasn't sure if he had, but he nodded. So did Tommy.

Arnold: "Or you get a song in your head, you're

singing it and you don't know why, and then you hear it on the radio or someone talks about the song without you bringing it up? Or how's this: You're hanging out at a 7-Eleven talking Minecraft, and this total boss comes up to you and starts dropping mad knowledge?"

The boys all laugh at the same time and in rhythm.

Luis: "Or if you're thirsty, someone gives you a beer."

Josh tosses him a can.

Luis: "That's so weird!"

Arnold downed the rest of his beer. "Nice on keeping these cold, by the way, Josh."

And with that Josh climbed down from the peak of his Arnold mistrust. He relaxed. That thanks-for-the-cold-beer comment from Arnold was really all Josh wanted out of the day, to feel like he wasn't a fourth wheel.

Josh tossed Arnold another beer. This would be his third. There were only two left in Josh's back-pack.

Arnold: "People talk about right-place-right-time as a way to explain coincidence, and letting themselves admit that maybe there's a connection there, to something. Something bigger."

Tommy: "What is it?"

Arnold: "I don't know. It's like sometimes I can sense it and almost put it into words, but can't. What I'm really describing is seeing. *My* seeing, yeah? That's what it is. Sometimes, it's like I know what I'm looking for, and I can see the connections happening before they happen. From a mile away. Not all the time."

Tommy: "But sometimes."

Arnold smiled. "Right."

Tommy: "So coincidence is like connecting the dots?"

Arnold shouted, "Yes! Exactly!" He nodded his head and shook a finger at Tommy. "Tommy gets it. I had a feeling you would."

Tommy laughed a goofy little laugh and wiped the back of his hand across his mouth, as though he was drooling. Luis had gone quiet and plucked at the pull tab of his beer.

"Hey, I have something for you guys." Arnold leaned back on the rock so he could get his hand inside his front jeans pocket. Josh was instantly terrified he was going to pull out a pipe or a joint or something worse, something he'd never consent to trying.

Arnold pulled out a small handful of change. He opened his hand and carefully plucked out a coin and tossed it to Luis.

Luis caught it with two hands. He held the coin close to his face, pinched between two fingers, and examined the front and back. After a thousand and one facial expressions, never settling on one, he asked, "What the hell is this?"

Arnold: "It's a hobo nickel."

Luis: "A what? Whoa, it's all messed up. Shit—that looks like a zombie face." He laughed. "It's a zombie face, isn't it?"

Arnold: "Yeah. Not my best work. But at least you can tell what it is."

Tommy: "Hey, I know what a hobo nickel is."

Arnold: "I thought you might. You're a coin collector, yeah?"

Tommy scratched his head. "Yeah. Wow. Or I used to be."

Josh: "Wait. What? Since when?" He looked at Tommy and Tommy didn't really look back. Then to Arnold he said, "And holy shit, how'd you know that?"

Luis mock-whispered across the back of his hand, "He's the seer . . . or Tommy said he knew what the fuck a bobo nickel was, so it was a good guess."

Arnold laughed. "Hobo nickel, dick."

Luis: "I prefer Ricardo."

Arnold threw his empty can at him.

Luis: "Not the face!"

Arnold: "Ricardo is partly right, but I guessed Tommy was a collector before today."

Josh had both hands on top of his head. "But how'd you know? I didn't know?"

Arnold: "Hold on. We'll get to that in a minute—"

Luis: "Awesome. Great. Neat. So someone tell me why hobos are putting zombie heads on nickels?"

Arnold: "You tell 'em."

Tommy shrugged and said, "People have been, like, etching images on nickels since what, the early 1900s." He looked at Arnold like he was the teacher and wanted some sign of approval before continuing. "The metal in a nickel is wicked soft and easy to work with and, um, reshape?"

Luis: "Hobos. Is there anything they can't do?"

Tommy: "Yeah. I guess. They'd make them and sell them for food and stuff."

Arnold: "Yeah, sort of. You know the word *hobo* doesn't mean 'homeless,' exactly. Or it didn't used to. Ever see a picture or cartoon of a dude carrying a stick slung over his shoulder with like a bag at the end? That's a hobo, and hobos traveled long-distance from job to job. One of the guys, like a roadie, for my uncle, when he like went on tour with his revival tent, told me about the nickels, showed me how to do it, too."

Josh: "So why do that to the coins?"

Arnold: "Pass the time, mostly. During the train rides between gigs they'd hack away at nickels. And, I don't know, because they could."

Luis: "You made this?" He held out the zombie-headed nickel.

Arnold: "Yeah."

Luis: "Where's your stick bag?"

Arnold: "Left it at home."

Luis: "I'm just kidding. It's really cool. This is for me? Seriously?"

Arnold: "Yeah. Have at it. You're the zombie movie guy, right?"

Luis: "Nice. Thanks. Man, this zombie head looks like something you'd draw, T." He threw Tommy the nickel.

Arnold: "You like to draw?"

Tommy shrugged. He always shrugged. He passed the coin over to Josh, who had his hand out. He said, "Yeah. A little."

Josh looked at the nickel quickly, and it did look like one of Tommy's goofy zombies. He said, "Dude, shut up. Tommy draws all the time and he's awesome at it. Like seriously good."

Luis: "He's fucking great. And he's gonna make famous comics or cartoons someday."

Tommy hid his head inside his shirt and muffled his voice. "Thanks, but I'm not that good."

Josh stood up and pointed at Arnold. "Hey, hold on! You didn't know this. You didn't *see* Tommy could draw. What happened?"

What could have been a look of annoyance flashed across Arnold's face. Josh wasn't sure. Arnold said, "Like I told you. I can't and don't see everything." He picked another coin out of his hand and flicked it over to Josh.

Josh dropped it and the boys hooted and hollered at him as the dark, copper coin rolled around between his legs. It was a penny. And it looked like a normal penny, from the 1950s. "I got it, relax. Bad throw . . ."

Arnold said, "I started your nickel but didn't finish it yet, so you can have this penny. It's pretty sick. See anything weird about it?"

Josh: "No . . . oh, there's a like a big crack across Lincoln's head."

Arnold: "Right through his forehead, and out the back." Arnold pointed a finger into the back of his head. "Or maybe it starts in the back and goes out through his head. Kind of a famous penny. An assassination penny. Get it?"

Josh: "Oh yeah. Shot in the head." He passed the penny to Tommy right away. Tommy ran a fingertip back and forth across the penny, worrying at the crack in the head.

Josh tapped Tommy's shoulder, just in case he was getting ready to go inside his own head again.

Tommy said, "That's kinda creepy. Somebody carve it, make it look like this?"

Arnold: "No. Probably a crack in the die cast. Happens a lot."

Tommy: "So weird how it's perfectly through his head like that."

Arnold smiled. "Totally. Random. Coincidence." He laughed.

Josh reached out and tapped Tommy's shoulder again. "Hey, since when are you a coin collector?"

Tommy: "I got started in fourth grade. My dad used to collect coins, and my mom decided to give me and Kate what he'd had, and I started adding to it. I didn't get too nuts into it or anything." He gave the penny back to Josh.

Did Luis know this about Tommy's coin collecting? Probably not, given that Luis had yet to brag that he knew about it. Josh rubbed his finger along the crack in Lincoln's head like Tommy had. He couldn't feel it.

Arnold said, "Yo. Tommy. Don't drop it." He tossed a coin.

Tommy caught it one-handed. He smiled and said, "Thanks," in a little, lost voice, that made Josh feel awkward on his behalf.

Josh didn't wait for the coin to be passed over to him. He scooted over next to Tommy and looked over his shoulder. The heads side of the coin had a blank profile of a face and above the face was an oblong eye, very much like the eye on the back of a dollar bill. Even though it wasn't as detailed as the zombie nickel, the simple etching on this coin was more smooth and accomplished.

Arnold: "It was actually tougher to make that one than the zombie one. That one I got to use most of Jefferson's face. Here I had to wipe him out, totally, start over. And that eye was a bitch. Totally worth it though. Looks good, right?"

Tommy said, "It's great. Amazing."

Arnold: "Do you know what it means?" He talked like there was no one else on the rock, no one else in the park.

Tommy: "No."

Arnold: "Yeah you do. Think about it. Connect those dots."

Tommy sat and thought. Tommy was one of those kids you could see think. He said, "So, the person on the coin, is, um, a seer?"

Arnold: "Yeah. You got it. And I'm giving you this coin because I think you're gonna be a seer. A real good one."

Luis started cracking up. It was loud and fake and he slapped his legs, and Josh loved him for it. Josh and Tommy laughed a little, too.

Josh: "Kid is such a dick."

Arnold laughed, too, and he sprang up onto his feet and scrambled over to Luis, started dead-arming his shoulder and jamming fingers into his ribs. Luis was still laughing, so was Arnold. Before now, Arnold hadn't made any kind of physical contact with the boys, and it was like a barrier or border had been crossed. Despite the laughter, there was an edge to the play fight, and it carried an all-too-familiar message of dominance, of pecking order.

Arnold shouted, "That's it! Off my rock, Ricardo!"

Luis laughed hard, screamed no, kicked out his legs trying to get his feet under him, and wriggled like a dog that didn't like to be picked up. Arnold had him all bottled up.

Tommy ran over, bear-hugged Arnold from behind, and tried to pull him away. Josh was the last to join the fracas, and he hesitantly grabbed one of Arnold's forearms, which was surprisingly thick with muscle. The wrestling pile broke up, and the three boys scattered to different ends of the rock, Arnold in the middle. Everyone laughing and talking trash, and Arnold went after Josh first. He knew Arnold would go after him first. It didn't take a seer to anticipate that. Josh got low, and leaned a shoulder into Arnold's chest. Arnold overpowered him and slid him back to the edge of the rock like he was nothing more than a garbage barrel being brought to the curb. Josh twisted around so that he faced away from Arnold, and to Josh's horror, his feet were on the edge of the rock and his torso was hanging out over it, leaning way past the tipping point. Arnold said something, a growl, and Josh couldn't make out what he said, and he screamed, "No!" at the moment when he was sure he would fall into the rocks that were twenty feet below him, his frenzied brain going into emergency planning, mapping out where to put his hands and feet when he landed to minimize damage. But he didn't fall off the rock, he stumbled backward away from the edge. He wasn't sure if Arnold had pulled him back or had simply left him to go battle Luis and Tommy again.

Josh sat down next to his backpack. He had a bloody raspberry on his knee. He didn't remember scraping it on the rock. For the second time that afternoon he fought back tears. He opened the second-to-last beer and took a sip. He still hated it so much.

Multiple voices shouted, "Okay," and "All right," and someone announced that it was, "Too fuckin' hot for this shit," and then the wrestling match was over. The other boys returned to their corners, laughing and saying *ow,* and proudly describing their future badges of honor, where they had scrapes and would have bruises.

Tommy walked past Josh and gave him that sad, sheepish smile that said, *We'll be all right.* He sat down next to Josh, pulled out the seer coin from his pocket, and said, "This is really cool, thanks, man."

Arnold was still breathing heavy from the wrestling match. He brushed off his arms and T-shirt. He said, "Add it to the collection."

Tommy: "I will. But—"

Arnold: "But what?"

Tommy: "I'm not a seer. I don't even think I'd want to be one."

Arnold: "I can't help you with the last part. But you are. Hey, let's try it out, yeah?"

Tommy: "Try what out?"

Arnold: "You seeing."

Tommy: "How?"

Arnold: "You're going to tell me how I knew you were a coin collector."

Luis: "I know! I know! You were dropped on your head as a baby and it gave you super-powers."

Arnold gave him the finger and said, "Seriously, Tommy. Think about it. And tell me. You can totally do it."

Luis: "Yeah, bruh, let's hear it!"

They all watched Tommy, and nothing in the world could've possibly made him more uncomfortable. Josh wanted to tell Arnold to leave him alone and for Luis to stop staring, but Josh couldn't help but stare, too. Tommy fidgeted, rocked in place, looked around like he wanted to make a break for it, but then he slumped, a prisoner resigned to no hope of escape.

They waited for him to say something. They waited for a while. Tommy finally picked up his head and looked at Arnold straight on. He never looked at you straight on, not with a serious look, anyway. Everything was a glance, a shy smirk, or a look from the side, or slightly tilted. He said, "That second time we met you at the 7-Eleven. You gave me five bucks and I got a Twix for me and an energy drink. After I paid, I walked back out and was looking through the change. I did it quick, but I remember checking a few dates, like maybe there was an old coin or something in there. You joked if I was keeping the change. That's it. Right? Only a coin collector looks hard at his change like I did."

Josh had never heard Tommy talk like that before. He sounded how most adults sounded to him; measured, guarded, but oddly confident, as though they believed in what they were saying more than they believed in themselves, and it sounded sad, too, because the truth always had negative implications, and underneath, a sense of there being more than what was actually said.

Arnold said, "Goddamn, you nailed it, T-money." He laughed. No one else did.

Tommy exhaled, like he was exhausted.

Josh looked at his bloody knee, which had started to sting and throb, and said, "Come on. That's not seeing. That's, what, remembering, and, I don't know. It's—"

Luis jumped in with "—deduction."

Josh: "Right. Yeah. What he said."

Arnold waved his hands at us like they couldn't possibly be more wrong. "That's how seeing starts, boys. You gotta make those first connections. It takes a little work to find how those early coincidences aren't so coincidental, and then—then you're able to do it enough and it all opens up for you."

No one had an answer for that. Josh thought he made sense and wasn't making sense at the same time. He tried to do as Arnold said. He tried to connect the dots as to where Arnold came from and why Arnold would hang out with them, three unpopular eighth-graders-to-be. Josh got up and sat with his back against the gnarly tree and quickly poured out some of his beer behind him.

Tommy passed the coin between his fingers, and said, "Let's talk about something else," and he went back to talking Minecraft. He wanted to make a Borderland server, and the main trails and area over by the estate was the overworld, plenty of space for creepers and zombies and endermen to roam. No one objected to the reset in conversation topic. Luis suggested that Devil's Rock would be in Nether, and the rock and the tree would be made out of obsidian (blocks you couldn't break), and wither skeletons would spawn from the split. Tommy disagreed and wanted the rock in the overworld to use as his zombie fighting base, of course.

They left when the beer was gone. Luis and Josh climbed down the rock first. Josh's backpack was a maraca filled with empties. He asked where he was going to get rid of them. Luis suggested the pond, but he wasn't serious. Neither noticed that Tommy and Arnold weren't with them. They had stayed behind on top of the rock, standing with the tree between them. Tommy had the seer coin in the palm of his hand, and Arnold pointed at it and they talked. Josh couldn't hear what they were saying. Luis said something under his breath, then shouted up at them.

"Let's go, suckbags!"

Josh wasn't a seer. He wasn't good at making connections and feared that would always be the case. But this was what he knew for certain: He knew that while Luis idolized Arnold, it was fleeting, like rooting for an underdog team that wasn't your team, or a first crush. What Luis felt about Arnold ran too hot and too cold. He'd turn on and abandon Arnold eventually, and likely over a perceived slight. It was different with Tommy, though. Watching the two of them climb down the rock, Josh knew that Tommy would follow Arnold to the ends of the over-world.

Elizabeth and Felt Presences, the Last Entries, Kate and Josh Twice

It's 7 p.m. There's a pizza box on the stove. Five slices of sausage and mushroom left. Kate walks in the back door, goes straight to the kitchen, and takes a soda can out of the fridge. She says, "I'm not hungry. I ate at Sam's."

"I know that." Elizabeth leans against the sink and has her arms crossed, hoping that she can communicate how furious she is without going temporarily insane. Elizabeth doesn't want to start a fight again less than twenty-four hours after the atomic meltdown in Kate's room. "I talked to both Nancy and Josh's mother. If I'm going to let you leave the house by yourself, you can't lie about where you're going."

"I didn't lie. I went to Sam's house. I just didn't go there first." Kate says it without conviction and turns away from Elizabeth, an admittance that she knows she's wrong.

"Kate. You can't go off on your own without telling me. Especially not now."

"I know. I'm sorry, Mom."

"Thank you. What did Josh have to say?"

"Not a lot."

"You sure?"

"Yeah."

"Why'd you go?"

"I wanted to shoot hoops."

"And what else?"

"And I wanted to talk to him." Kate turns back around and brushes the bangs that have fallen out of her ponytail away from her eyes. "Oh, yeah, Josh did tell me that Arnold made that weird nickel and gave him and Tommy those coins."

"Did Josh tell the police that?"

"I don't know."

"I'm guessing he didn't. Allison didn't seem to know anything about the coins this morning. Why wouldn't he tell her about something like that?"

"Dunno. Maybe he didn't think it was a big deal."

Elizabeth fires off a quick e-mail to Allison on her phone. She asks, "Any more 'oh, yeahs' for me?"

"What?"

"Is there anything else Josh said I need to know?"

"No. I don't think so."

"Okay. Do you want to know what Allison and I found when you left?"

"Yeah. What'd you find?" Kate stands with her back against the fridge, ramrod straight.

"We didn't find anything."

"Nothing? No more diary pages?"

"No."

"Maybe he chucked them. He talked about burning up his first diary, right?"

"Yeah. He did." Sounds more than reasonable, but she can't tell if Kate is truly surprised that they didn't find anything more, or relieved, or if she knew all along they'd never find it because she hid them. After giving up the diary and confessing to leaving out the pages, Elizabeth thought for sure Kate wouldn't keep anything else from her. But now Elizabeth has doubts about Kate and the missing diary pages. Maybe Kate has managed to concoct another not-quite-a-lie scenario, like today and her going to Josh's house before going to Sam's house. Either way, she's finding out the truth tonight as she's going to pull an all-nighter.

Kate: "Hey, what did Allison say about that surveillance video after I left? You showed it to her, right?"

"Yeah, but she didn't say much. Didn't really see anything other than the pages on the floor." Elizabeth has continued to watch the video in private moments, hoping and not hoping to again see the shadow that she saw there on the first viewing. Hoping and not hoping to see the face that's in Tommy's diary somewhere else.

Kate takes a sip from her soda can. She reaches over and lifts the cover of the pizza box and makes a face at the pizza.

Elizabeth says, "I thought you said you weren't hungry."

"I'm not. Just looking."

"I can make you something if you want. French toast?"

"I'm good."

"That was nice of Nancy to give you a ride home. I should've gone out and said hi."

"There are four news vans out front now. Reporters with cameras and everything came running over when we pulled in the driveway. Nancy was like a superhero and cleared a path for me."

"That article this morning. It's totally blowing everything up. Have you read it yet?"

"I got the gist from tweets and texts when I was at Sam's. We read them together."

"Like what? What have people been sending you?"

"It's no big deal."

"No, no, no. You don't get to do that."

"Mom. It's not that bad, they're just—"

"What, trolling you?"

Kate smiles at her mother's using of the word *trolling*. "Twitter, yeah, some trolling that I block, whatever. And some kids from school, texting, asking if the rumors about Tommy are true."

"What rumors?"

"That he was doing bad stuff."

"Drinking?"

"Yeah. And drugs, and some people were asking if he, like, worshipped the devil, or something, when they went out there in the woods."

"Jesus, where are people getting this shit? Here I was debating whether or not I was going to say anything to you about other online stuff because my saying something will make you go read it."

"Read what?"

"I was going to tell you to stay away from the Facebook page. There're some real assholes posting ugly, nasty stuff, and it makes me so angry I can't even think."

"Tell me."

"I don't even want to say it out loud. Some of it is kind of like what you saw already with the devil worship stuff, I guess, but worse. They go to awful, hateful places, and . . . Never mind. Just don't go. Please. I shouldn't have mentioned it. I don't want you reading it. I'll deal with that page."

"Mom. We're in this together."

Kate's general default setting of loyalty and earnestness has always been a shock to her. Elizabeth had been neither when she was Kate's age. She was angry and rebellious and actively searched for reasons to be so. She stopped wishing long ago that her daughter would be just like her and think just like her. Instead, Elizabeth now hopes that Kate will never lose that earnestness even as she must harden that outer shell that bruises and cracks so easily.

"We are. But I don't think you should see—"

"Let's go to the page together and then I can show you how to screencap the trolls' comments, tweet them out, you know, and totally shame them publicly."

"We should probably leave them alone. Ignore them. They'll go away. They don't sound like the most well-adjusted people."

"Mom, they don't go away. That's why they're trolls." Kate sounds like she talks from experience, and Elizabeth is overwhelmed by a giant wave of sadness with a riptide strong enough to suck all the unmoored out to sea.

"I'm not feeling up to that right now."

They go quiet and have a standoff in the kitchen. Each afraid to be the first to move. Kate's phone rings.

"It's Sam. I'm gonna take this."

"Okay, go ahead." By the time Elizabeth softly adds, "I'll be in the living room if you want to come out later," Kate has answered the phone and walks into her bedroom.

Elizabeth paces around the couch twice, then retreats to the dining room and the computer desk instead of the couch. As she waits for the computer to wake out of sleep mode, she flips through one of Tommy's sketchbooks that she brought out with her. It was probably his first one, or the oldest one that he saved, and the drawings (mostly robots and dinosaurs) have a hint of blocky-ness and lack proper proportion, but the talent to come is apparent. You can see it. On the inside cover she stuck the little square piece of duct tape that he'd stuck on his laptop cover over the logo, the one with the hungry cloud monster doodle. She let Allison take the laptop back to the station. Elizabeth kept the duct tape doodle.

Elizabeth doesn't go to the Find Tommy Facebook page and instead checks her e-mail. Twenty e-mails from the top is an e-mail her mother sent her yesterday. She opens it.

Liz. Found this article about 'felt presences.' I really think you should read it. Maybe it'll help explain a few things. Love. Mom.

She takes her hand off the mouse and presses down a corner of the duct tape square, which is curling up off the cardboard.

Her phone vibrates in her pocket. It's a text from her mother. She says to herself, "Perfect timing as always."

Janice's text: *They're talking about Tommy on Fox News. It's horrible. Please don't watch.*

For the two millionth time since the ordeal started, everything inside Elizabeth turns into a liquid electricity that rises up into her head before bottoming out, leaving her momentarily hollow, and then all the fear, anxiety, and despair rushes back, and refills her.

She reads the text again and smirks at herself. She'd pulled the same thing with Kate when she'd told her not to go to the Facebook page knowing full well that she would go directly to that page. Janice is telling her not to go watch because she actually wants her to go watch, and then, afterward, she'll have the righteous authority to say *You should've listened. I told you not to watch.*

Elizabeth walks to the couch, on her tiptoes, trying not to be heard moving around again. A practice run for later tonight when Kate is asleep. She turns on the TV and searches the guide for Fox News. It's a standard cable news talk show setup: a middle-aged white guy host with three supposed experts in something, each on their own live feed from somewhere not in the studio. The experts are two middle-aged white guys and one not-middle-aged blonde woman.

Elizabeth watches them for almost ten minutes. She alternates between writhing in her seat and being statue still, frozen by the horror of the media Medusas as they talk about Tommy's disappearance. They talk about how Tommy comes from a broken home and lament the inexorable disintegration of the traditional family. They quote an anonymous source within the Ames police department saying that Tommy was into "not-so-good stuff" and making terrible decisions. They talk about underage drinking and speculate on drug use and further illegal activities. They talk about the latest report, broken this afternoon by Fox News of course, that cites anonymous classmates of Tommy's who describe him as a loner and obsessed with the zombies and anything related to the occult. They talk about the occult in the context of the rise of atheism. They talk about folklore and Satanism and its potential role in Tommy's disappearance. They talk about the locals seeing a mysterious person or persons walking through their yards and standing in front of their windows at night. They wonder if what's going on in Ames is evidence of a larger satanic cult or conspiracy and they talk about how "shadowman" is trending on twitter. They talk about the mysterious man referenced in the *Ames Patch* article. They talk about what kind of relationship Tommy might've had with this person of interest. They call him a person of interest while law enforcement has yet to do so. They talk about pedophilia and other perversions associated with occult activities. They are loud and are almost yelling, sounding like they're arguing with one another, but there is no argument; they're all in agreement. These talking heads do not shy away from further speculation and extrapolation from the facts and nonfacts. It's as though Tommy's disappearance has become a national Rorschach test; they blurt out whatever it is they think they see in the chaotic inkblot. They do not once refer to Tommy as someone who needs help, and the only descriptors they use are "misguided" and "perhaps deeply troubled."

Elizabeth shuts off the television. Instead of burrowing under the couch cushions or sprinting out the front door and going house to house smashing TV screens, she writes a text to her mother.

I shouldn't have watched. I'm going to put my fist through the TV screen.

Janice: *I know. It's awful. I'm coming back down tomorrow. Leaving here at noon. Need me to pick anything up?*

Elizabeth sends her a list of groceries. As she types *milk 1%* and *diet soda* and *1 lb turkey* and *cheese* and *bread* she wonders how it was she got here, to this particular moment; calmly texting an ordinary grocery list seconds after shutting off a national cable news show discussing the evils of her missing son.

She goes back to the computer. Her e-mail box has twenty new e-mails since she last checked ten minutes ago, most of which are notifications of posts and messages on the Find Tommy Facebook page. She returns to the e-mail her mom sent last night and clicks on the article link.

The article is hosted on a new long-form essay

site, the kind that people link to on social media even though they probably have read only the headline and the first paragraph. She wonders if her mother has read the whole thing.

The article is about Third Man Factor or Syndrome; a widely reported phenomenon of a ghost, spirit, or what the author calls a "felt presence" that appears during a traumatic, terrifying, or stressful experience. These presences are often described as formless shadows. The article includes a brief summary of perhaps the most famous Third Man account: that of Antarctic explorer Ernest Shackleton. With their boat frozen in the ice, Shackleton and two other men trekked for thirty-six hours across a mountain and glacier-filled South Georgia to a whaling station. The three men barely survived the harrowing trip, spending weeks convalescing in a hospital after-ward. Shackleton and his crewmates reported that a mysterious fourth man had joined them and had walked silently alongside during the latter stages of the trek. The mysterious man never spoke, but his presence was a comfort and helped to keep them moving forward. When Shackleton and his companions finally arrived at the whaling station the mysterious man was gone. Shackleton's experience inspired lines in T. S. Eliot's *The Wasteland* that refer to a "third man" always and mysteriously accompanying two others as they walk down a road. It's the lines in that poem for which Third Man Syndrome is named.

The article goes on to discuss other mountain climbers, sailors, and disaster survivors who reported similar Third Man experiences. Scientists argue such extreme conditions and stresses provoke these hallucinations of another person being present, perhaps as a physiological coping mechanism. The Third Man or felt presence phenomenon is not unique to survivors of trauma. People who suffer from Parkinson's disease and other neurological disorders have symptoms that include the felt presence sensations. The article's author draws a clear line of connection from the trauma of the near-death experience to the intense emotions of extreme grief the bereaved experience after a loss. Felt presence accounts from heartbroken people who claim to have seen or sensed the presence of a recently deceased loved one are as commonplace as the traditional ghost story. The author then goes into more scientific detail, discussing current studies that cite the possible roles of dopamine and other neurochemicals as being the source of the hallucinatory phenomena.

Elizabeth loses the thread and rereads the final paragraphs multiple times before giving up. She says, "Goddamn it, Mom."

Doubt gnaws at her. Is it possible what she saw was a grief-induced hallucination and her now-soupy brain is simply associating the picture

Tommy drew with what she saw, or thinks she saw? In her head, Elizabeth is back in her bedroom on that night one week ago: she throws her sneakers at the chair again and they bounce and tumble away and Tommy is still there, in shadow, yes, but he's there, crouched next to the chair, his legs pulled against his chest, his head tilted, his hair over his eyes, and then the face, the terrible face, and then his smell.

Elizabeth does not haunt her support group message board or the Facebook page, and ignores the swelling swamp of post and comment e mail notifications. She instead searches the stories referenced in the felt presence article, and from there she searches for and reads other first-person accounts. There are all manner of websites devoted to such paranormal phenomena, from the slickly produced (their margins filled with ads for books and DVDs) to the achingly sad blogs that haven't been updated for years, blogs with virtual tumbleweeds and feature walls of text, detailing the raw, stream-of-consciousness ramblings from the confused, broken, and damned. Her Internet search splinters outward, like cracks in the ice of a frozen pond, and she reads about bilocation: a living person projecting (willingly or not) their spirit/double to another place. There's a legend about a French schoolteacher at a European boarding school in the mid-1800s who repeatedly projected her double in full view of her students. Her double would appear at the black-board, mirroring the teacher's movements before disappearing. Once, while the teacher was working in the garden, her double appeared to sit in a chair in front of the entire student body at assembly.

Kate opens her bedroom door and announces that she's going to bed. Elizabeth jumps up from the computer and shrinks the window as though caught looking at stuff that she shouldn't be looking at. Elizabeth ducks into the hall and quickly says that she's going to bed soon as well. She's always been a terrible liar. They do not wish each other a goodnight. After Kate closes her door, Elizabeth takes a lap around the living area, shutting off the lights. She considers turning on the security camera but decides not to. She doesn't want it going off every time she flinches or reaches for the computer mouse.

The glowing computer screen is the only light on in the living area. She sits down and reads more about bilocation and doppelgängers. Reports of bilocation often occur under the similarly stressful circumstances described in the felt presences / Third Man article. But in folklore, doppelgängers represent everything from mischievous spirits and demons, portents of imminent disaster, a vision of the near future, or a temporal shift, to a shudder in dimensional time and space. There is no shortage of pseudo-historical apocrypha regarding doppelgängers. The famous poet Goethe claimed to have passed his doppelgänger on a quiet road to a German town, only years later to realize that his double was a vision of his future self traveling the same road but in the other direction. More chilling are the tales of the doppelgänger being the harbinger or omen of death: Percy Bysshe Shelley (husband of Mary Shelley) had visions of his doppelgänger confronting him and pointing out to the Mediterranean Sea in the weeks before his own drowning; Queen Elizabeth I of England died shortly after seeing her double lying prostrate in her own bed; English poet John Donne ran into his wife's doppelgänger walking the streets of Paris with a baby cradled in her arms, while back home their child was born dead.

When Elizabeth next looks up, disengaging from the computer, she realizes that two-plus hours have eroded away. Her eyes are tired and stinging from all the on-screen reading in the dark. Janice had obviously sent Elizabeth the link to the felt presence article to provide a rational, scientific explanation for the Tommy sighting in her bedroom. But now Elizabeth's head is full of tales of doppelgängers and shadowy presences and the harbingers of doom.

Elizabeth turns on the small desk lamp, opens the desk drawer, takes out Tommy's diary, and stares at that terrible picture, the shadowman that has since gone viral on the Internet and news. She can't look at it for too long for fear it will burn a hole through her retinas, and then the image will be seared inside her head and she'll never be able to think of anything else without seeing it. She is dreadfully certain this awful, shadowy image that looks like Tommy—even if he wrote that it wasn't him—is the *something* that happened to her son.

Elizabeth powers the computer down and puts the diary back in the desk drawer. She limps into the kitchen on stiff legs, quietly fills a glass with water, and then goes into the living room to wait . . . for what? Tommy to come back? A shadowman at the door, in the windows, or in the room with her? For Kate to sneak out of her bedroom and drop the missing diary pages?

Maybe she should sit on the couch with a bottle of wine and see how deeply into it she can get. She doesn't really like wine, but there isn't any beer in the house. She imagines adding "get beer" to her mom's text grocery list. Then she wonders if Tommy ever stole any beer from her. Not that she ever kept a lot in the house, usually a mishmash of types and brands, usually more than a couple of bottles or cans but never more than twelve, not that she kept inventory. Was it solely because of Arnold that Tommy started drinking beer? Thirteen years old is early for that, isn't it? Were there kids drinking when she was in middle school? Probably, but she can't remember any names or faces. There were vague groups of kids they called the burnouts; the mysterious and dangerous ones who met up in the woods after school, the ones no one seemed to notice or talk to when inside school. Years from now, to so many of his classmates, Tommy will be a cautionary tale, a legend, an odd bit of folklore, a shadowman.

Standing in the dark next to the couch, Elizabeth whispers, "I'm sorry," out loud to no one and everyone. She asks, "How did I not know, how come I couldn't smell it on him when he came home?" And the only answer she has: *I was supposed to know*. If she had known, would confronting him about it have changed anything? Would he have admitted to it and admitted to hanging out with this older guy, Arnold? Would she have grounded him, not allowed him to go out or even go to Josh's house to sleep over? Would her removing some of the dominos in the secret chain that tumbled them all to this hellish now have kept Tommy from disappearing?

She sits heavily on the couch, and the green light on the base of the security camera blinks into life. Did she sit on her phone and accidentally turn it on? Elizabeth spills her water as she reaches for her phone, which isn't in her pocket. She left the phone next to the computer, didn't she?

She struggles to stand up without further

soaking herself and shouts "Goddamn it!" at the tipped water glass and the Valdez-sized spill on the couch, and a muffled, metallic doppelgänger of her voice echoes back from somewhere down the end of the hallway. The camera's green record light is still on. Elizabeth turns toward the kitchen and says, "What the hell is going on?" Her voice echoes again, on slight delay.

Kate screams, "Mom!" from her room repeatedly.

"Kate? What is it? Kate?" Elizabeth runs through the kitchen and into the hallway.

Kate's bedroom door flies open, and Kate runs out like she's being chased, like she needs to desperately escape something. She runs straight into Elizabeth, almost knocking her over. She's crying hysterically.

"Honey, what's going on?"

"I don't know! I woke up and I was so scared and it felt like there was someone in the room with me, watching, and I was so scared and I couldn't say anything and I couldn't move and then your voice started coming out of my phone on the floor but I still couldn't move and I tried calling out to you and Mom, I don't know. I don't know what's going on, I don't—"

"Shh, it's okay. You had a bad dream. You're okay—"

"No, Mom, I was awake. I was—"

"You're—you're all right." Elizabeth holds Kate tightly and looks all around the dark hallway.

She is totally spooked by this. Kate has never been one to have nightmares or night terrors, not like Tommy had when he was a preschooler. His nighttime freak-outs were weekly occurrences. "I'm here, slow down." She holds Kate until she stops rambling and crying.

Elizabeth: "Are you okay?"

Kate: "No. Yes, but no."

"Come on." Elizabeth starts to lead Kate back toward her room.

"Where are you going?"

"To your room—"

"No, I don't want to go. Can I sleep in your room, please, Mom? Please."

"Yeah, okay, sure, but look, I'm just going to turn on the light and shut off the camera on your phone."

"What do you mean?"

"Kate?"

"What?"

"The camera came on just now, when I was sitting out there."

"I didn't turn that on, I swear, Mom. My phone wasn't even with me in bed. It was on the floor, charging."

Kate hides behind Elizabeth as she opens the door and turns on the light.

Much of the mess from Elizabeth's tear-down of the room is still there, to her great shame. Elizabeth walks in gingerly, trying not to step on too much. Now that she's in the room, something feels off. Not right. She can't explain the off-ness. There is something wrong. Even with the light on and the two of them in there, Elizabeth doesn't blame her daughter for not wanting to sleep in there tonight.

Elizabeth edges deeper into the room, and the wrong feeling intensifies. She says, "Ugh, I'll pick up this place tomorrow, I promise. Where's your phone, Kate? On the floor, right? You didn't turn on the camera, Kate? Really? You're telling me—"

Kate: "Mom, I didn't. I swear. Cross my heart. I didn't."

"My voice came through your phone? The app doesn't turn on by itself." Elizabeth makes it to the side of the bed. Kate's phone is on the floor and charging. Elizabeth bends to pick it up and she's suddenly afraid of the dark under the bed, and Kate's windows with their closed curtains are inches away from the back of her head, and she can feel that small distance, like the bottoms of the curtains are fingers that want to stretch out and lightly brush the back of her neck, or blow open and expose someone standing there at the window, watching them.

As Elizabeth finally grabs the phone there's a loud, heavy thud from somewhere behind her, from somewhere else inside the house.

Elizabeth bolts upright and twists, trying to

turn around, and she almost falls onto the bed. "Jesus. What was that? Kate?"

Kate quickly shuffles out of the doorway and into her room, looking out toward the hallway behind her. She shakes her head. "That wasn't me! That wasn't me! It came from Tommy's room. Oh my God . . ."

"What do you mean?" she asks. But it did sound like the noise came from the room next door, from Tommy's room.

"Something fell. On the floor. Something big. I felt it like vibrating in my toes."

"Okay. Relax. Come on. We'll check it out," more to herself than to Kate. They walk into Tommy's room, Kate hiding behind her, and there's a large, comic art book on the floor in front of the bookshelf, splayed out like a dead body. It lies opened up, facedown, the broken spine pointed at the ceiling.

Kate says, "So . . ."

"No big deal. It just fell out of the bookshelf?"

Kate: "Yeah, because books do that all the time."

Elizabeth almost laughs at that purely genuine Kate reaction, and more than anything it makes her believe her daughter has been telling the truth tonight. She says, "Yeah, I don't know. Well, Allison and I looked through here today, remember? Must've not have put it back all the way or something. Left it hanging out?" Elizabeth gives a quick look up at the bookshelf and doesn't see any other, what, loose books. Books that are about to jump? She remembers flipping through the art book as they searched Tommy's room. It is well worn, the pages a little loose in the spine. Tommy clearly read and reread this book often. In the margins he'd practiced some of the outlined how-to techniques.

Elizabeth picks it up, carefully closes the book, and realigns the bent dust jacket.

"Mom, what are those?"

There are five loose pages on the floor. They are not pages from the art book. The pages are not white and do not feature garishly colored superheroes. The pages are yellowish, full of handwriting, and all crinkled up like someone balled them up to throw them away but then changed their mind and tried to flattened them back out. They are more of Tommy's diary pages.

Elizabeth flips the art book onto the floor behind her and drops to all fours, hovering herself above the pages.

"Mom? Are they—"

"Kate. Listen to me. You have to tell me the truth. Did you hide these pages in that book?"

"No, Mom. No . . ." Kate keeps talking and Elizabeth isn't really listening. Elizabeth paws behind her for the book and flips through it again. Earlier this afternoon she lingered over the pages of how-to-draw-torsos that feature heroic poses of Spider-Man and the Silver Surfer, and the comically large-chested self-portrait Tommy drew in the margin. There is no doubt she searched this book today and the diary pages were not there.

"Mom?"

If Kate hid the pages here, when would she have had the time or ability to do so? She would've had to hide the pages in the art book *after* she and Allison searched the room. Kate didn't come home until after the big search, and she and Kate spent the rest of the afternoon and evening together, she was never by herself until Kate went to bed. And even then her door was closed and it stayed closed. There's no way Kate could've snuck out of her room and into Tommy's to hide those pages with Elizabeth just around the corner, awake, and on the computer. Never mind somehow setting up the book to fall out of the bookcase later.

Elizabeth looks up at Kate. She says, "Me and Allison must've missed these somehow. Must not have seen them hidden in this book." She says it but doesn't believe it.

Kate doesn't say anything.

Elizabeth picks up the pages. The once-harsh folds and creases add shadows to the sprawl of text and crossouts. The pages bend and crinkle in her hand, as though the paper itself is attempting to speak to her directly.

The first page is full of Tommy's handwriting. The text at the very top of the page has a big, loose, wavy X crossed through it. She doesn't read anything yet. The next three pages after are walls of text, in handwriting that is small, clustered, desperate. The fifth page is a repeat of a couple of lonely sentences.

~~Dad used to play the penny game~~
~~with me. Let's play penny. Take a~~
~~hand full of penny's and tell me~~
~~guess the date. He said higher or~~
~~lower until I got it. Shiny pennies~~
~~are easy. The dirty ones are the~~
~~hard ones.~~
~~Kate I'm sorry don't read it just~~
~~don't~~ Arnold picked us up took us
for a ride and I thought we'd end up
at micky d's. We drove around and
drank beers with the windows down,
Arnold driving fast and chirping
tires. He drove us into Brockton,
wanted to take us back to his place
and show us how he made hobo
nickels and he took a bunch of turns
into like a sketchy area and Luis and
Josh were making jokes from the
back and flicking my ears, mad
drunk. Arnold parked on a street
that was crowded with tripledeckers.
Arnold parked in front of a gray one
that looked like it was gonna fall

down by itself. They all stopped laughing and telling jokes when we were out of the car, no one was around and we were the last people left on the earth and it was the best, I wanted it to be like that, Kate I did. Had no idea it was all wrong. Maybe I did. We walked up the driveway to the backyard, he said Come on. I was gonna ask why we didn't park in the driveway but I was afraid, I hate myself for always being afraid to say or do anything. I fucking hate it so much. In the back there was a little kid riding a bigwheel in a circle on the cracked cement. He waved at us, Arnold tossed the kid a coin, don't know if there was something cool like a monster on it then he told the kid to go home. Come on. That's all he said again. come on come on, and he went up the wooden back stairs that zigzagged up to the third floor. The three of us were buzzin hard I know I was and Josh and Luis looked at me like did we have to come here to see him make those nickels and they looked at me like I had the answers or maybe they were looking at me to

put a stop to everything ~~they always~~
~~looked at me like that I'm sorry~~
Arnold waited for us at the top and
we walked in the back door into
the kitchen and dishes and trash
everywhere and it smelled like
garbage and something else. Arnold
stood in the middle of it all and said
what a messssss, had like a hundred
ssss on it, then he turned and
walked into the next room, and I
want to write down what we were
all thinking but I have no idea what
we were thinkin and it all just
happened like it happened already
and we were watching it happen
again. Arnold said he had the nickel
stuff in his room then he shouted in
the other room, hey, come meet my
friends, and no one said anything
and we looked around the kitchen
not doing anything not knowin that
we could do anything and not
knowing that we could ever do what
we were going to do I swear and
then Arnold yelled for us to come in,
we did, a TV room with stained rug
and food wrappers and beer bottles
so many on a coffee table and on
the floor and an old TV on a small

stand, and there was an oldman on the couch, asleep sitting up wearing a gross wife beater, yellow in places and almost see through, tight dress pants that were unbuckled and fly down, tighty whiteys ballooning out under his gut. Luis said whoa and backed up. Arnold said it was okay he was passed out and couldn't hear us. We stood there and stared at the oldman for a long time, Arnold smiling and then Arnold laughing into the back of his hand and he looked at all of us like he couldn't believe we didn't think this was funny. He said what? it's just his uncle, barely even a real uncle, and I wish none of it was real, and he said let's wake him, he walked to the couch and slapped his uncle pretty hard on the side of his head and shouted, hey, wake up meet my friends, they want to meet Uncle Fat Fuck. Arnold laughed and Josh and Luis laughed a little too, maybe I did. The oldman moved a little, mumbled something, and Arnold laughed like crazy so we did too it felt like we had to. Then Arnold grabbed Josh, still laughing, said come here, your turn, go ahead, hit him, he won't even know won't even hurt, Josh leaned back and tried to pull away, knocked over bottles everywhere and Arnold let him go, we laughed at Josh falling down and I'm sorry about that too, next he told Luis to do it, just hit him, he said get mad and hit him, he said you get to do what I've always wanted to do, and then he told him to pretend he was those jerks at school who make fun of how little he is and he went on saying the worst stuff to Luis and about Luis until Luis slapped his uncle right across the face, so hard, the smack sounded like a shot and we all flinched, and Arnold started laughing again, so hard he couldn't breathe, and then Josh came up right behind Luis without anyone saying anything and hit his uncle in the same spot, his cheek turned red and then it was my turn it was supposed to be my turn and Arnold looked at me and then I did it. I hit him. I closed my eyes and my hand into a fist and punched him in the side of his head, it hurt, like punching a wall and his eyes rolled around and closed again and we laughed because I don't know we couldn't believe anything then we were all on him, and Arnold was shouting and asking how HE liked it, and we kept hitting and laughing and hitting and when we slowed down Arnold told us to help get him into the shower, to wake him up, and we pulled him onto his feet, he groaned and whined a little and we yelled at him to shut up without Arnold telling us to and we got him moving to the bathroom, too fast, we couldn't control him and he fell into the tub and Arnold squeezed by us and flipped his uncle around so he was on the floor leaning against the tub. He said wake him up, and we slapped his face and punched his chest but not as hard as we did in the living room and we weren't laughing anymore and then Arnold hit him as hard as he could grunting with each punch and he kept punching and the three of us stood there, we stood there and watched and the hitting sounds made me want to puke and Arnold wouldn't stop, then he found an empty bottle

on the bathroom floor and smashed
it on the oldman's head, his skin
cracked open his face covered in
blood, and he coughed and moaned,
didn't move his arms and sat there,
Arnold smashed three bottles on the
sink one at a time so the necks
ended in sharp spikes and he gave us
each broken bottlenecks and told us
to stick him, go ahead stick him he
said, it won't even hurt him, we
stood there waiting for the joke to
be over and he was whispering and
then he was screaming in our faces
and we still didn't do anything and
he grabbed me first, grabbed my
arm at the elbow and wrist and we
still didn't do anything and then he
was calm and because he was calm it
was like it was okay and he said
don't drop it and that was it don't
drop it, I thought that was easy I
could do that and I could pretend it
wasn't me and it didn't seem like
me and I didn't stop him and he
pulled me forced me and the chunk
of glass it went through the oldman's
shirt and I felt it sort of pop the
skin on his chest, slide in, and blood
filled up his shirt and I pulled my

hand away but the glass stuck there
stayed there and then he did the
same with Luis and Josh and he was
like gentle and patient and they
stabbed their broken glass into the
oldman's gut and Josh's went
deepest, the glass tip disappeared all
the way inside, then Arnold kicked
his uncle in the face and stomped
away and into the kitchen and
started yelling like crazy and he said
COME ON help ME and he shouted
other stuff and Luis and Josh ran
after him like they were afraid he'd
leave them there. I was by myself
and I crouched down got closer to
the oldman, the cut in his forehead
looked like a big crack and his eyes
were swollen shut and his nose
smooshed and I said I was sorry and
I was crying when I looked again his
uncle wasn't his uncle anymore he
was my dad and I KNEW it was him
because I was a seer, right? it was
him right after the car accident and
he had the car window glass pushed
into him and I had done that too
and I gently tried to pry out the
glass and tell him that I'd get help,
and I stood up to leave and he

MOVED he hugged legs against his chest and looking at him made me shiver so hard my teeth clicked together, Arnold came back and said come on and his uncle said something to me in a voice that I don't think was his, I should've said something back to him I don't know why I didn't and I wish I did. Arnold went into the bathroom kicked him three times I heard it shake the whole house then shut the door and led me out of the house and down the stairs, outside, to the street, past the bigwheel kid playing next to the sewer throwing in rocks and coins. So now I've been lieing awake at night wondering if his uncle is okay trying to convince myself that he'll be okay when I know he isn't and telling myself it wasn't our fault that we were forced into doing it then hating us for being so weak and awful I never thought we were so awful and I'm sorry Kate that we're such cowards we are and we deserve whatever terrible things that will happen to us and NOW that I'm writing it all down I know that I didn't see Dad when I looked at his uncle. I'm so stupid, I saw something I KNOW I did and I keep seeing it now all the time. Look at the picture that I drew a few days ago a few pages ago. it's not Dad ~~but it's someone because I think Arnold is right about one thing. there are no coincidences.~~ I know that now and no matter what happens to me I have to try to do something to fix everything. i'm sorry Kate I love you and mom so much and I hope you'll forgive me someday

~~I said~~

Don't leave

I'm still here

Kate stands behind Elizabeth in the nowhere space separating the kitchen and the living room. Kate's arms hang limply by her side and she leans into her mother, forehead resting between Mom's shoulder blades. Elizabeth awkwardly reaches behind her and rubs Kate's back. In her other hand is her cell phone. Her head tilts and her shoulder lifts to help cradle the phone against her ear as she talks to Allison. The diary pages are pinned tightly between her arm and her ribs.

Elizabeth hangs up and turns around. Kate stays rooted to her spot. She's stopped crying, at least. Elizabeth lifts Kate's chin and says, "Okay. Allison will be here in like five minutes."

Kate asks a lightning round of questions to which there are currently no answers. "Why did they go with Arnold? How could they do what—what they did? To that poor old guy? Did they—why would they let Arnold make them do those things? Why didn't Tommy help? What was Tommy talking about at the end? I don't get it. Any of it. Why—" she stops before asking *Why didn't he try to tell anyone what was happening?* Kate looks at the crinkly pages under Mom's arm and knows that he did try.

Elizabeth: "I don't know, honey. There's a lot of things that I don't know."

Kate: "Did Tommy tear out—"

Elizabeth stops her. "Look. I can't. Not right now. I, um, need to call Nana, too. Before Allison gets here. You okay for now?"

Kate says, "Yeah," only because she is supposed to.

Elizabeth rests a hand on Kate's head. "Go wash your face and have a drink. Warm milk, maybe? I'll be right with you. And we'll talk to Detective Allison together when she gets here."

Kate walks down the hall. She hears Elizabeth say, "Mom. It's me," into the phone in a papier-mâché voice.

Kate wanders into her bedroom instead of the bathroom and closes the door gently. Whatever was in the room and freaked her out earlier was gone. She isn't afraid anymore. She goes over to her bed and picks up her phone off the floor. She flips through her multiple pages of apps, tempted to turn on the surveillance camera again to watch and listen to Mom as she talks to Nana.

Kate navigates to her contacts list instead and calls Josh. He gave her his phone number earlier when she was over at his house. Their shooting hoops together didn't last long. Mrs. Griffin called Josh in to wash up for dinner after only like ten minutes out in the driveway, even though she'd never mentioned to Kate that they were close to eating dinner. Kate hopped on her bike, and before the garage door closed and Josh was swallowed up by the house, she asked for his phone number. More like she demanded it.

Josh doesn't pick up, and the call goes to voice mail. She calls again. He picks up on the third ring. He says, "Hello?" in a voice that doesn't sound very you-just-woke-me-up.

"It's me. Kate."

"Oh, hey. What's going on? Did something happen?"

She says, "We found the rest of Tommy's diary pages."

"You found it?"

"Yeah. In his room. Like he left them for us to

find, you know." She stops and waits for Josh to have to say something.

"Um, okay. Wow. What does he say?"

Kate gets right to the point. She doesn't think Mom will be on the phone long with Nana, so she'll have to hang up soon. "Tommy wrote about what happened with Arnold, about when you guys went to some old house or something and then all helped beat up and like, what, *stab* some old guy with pieces of glass. I mean, holy shit." Kate couldn't believe that Tommy not only watched but took part in the violence and then never went to the police himself or told anyone about what happened. That he would ever be part of such a horror show of events, and then make it worse by doing nothing, will forever mar how she feels about her big brother. She'll always wonder if there were other terrible secrets that he kept.

Josh whimpered, a sound a mouse might give after finally being stomped on by the petrified elephant. "Oh my God . . ."

"It was his uncle or something, right?"

"Yeah, I guess—"

"Josh, did you guys kill him?"

"No. My God, no. He was hurt bad but he was alive when we left, I swear."

"Oh, so he was like totally okay then."

"I don't know. I don't know. We don't know anything about him."

"Why didn't you tell anyone about this? Why are you guys hiding—"

"We didn't know what to do! And we didn't know how it happened, we never meant to hurt anyone. We were drunk and we didn't know how any of it could've happened. We were pushed into it and didn't—"

"You should've stopped, said something! Done something, anything! Why didn't you do anything, Josh?"

"We were so scared. I swear, we weren't trying to protect him or nothing."

"So, what, you guys were scared of getting in trouble? Didn't care about the guy at all?"

"No. It's not like that. I mean, yeah, we were scared about everything, and Arnold, when he drove us back, he threatened to hurt us, to kill us, I swear, and he said he'd hurt you guys too if we ever said anything to anyone."

It's not as easy to tell if Josh is lying when he's on the phone. "How about now, then? Or a week ago? Tommy is missing, you know? Gone. And you don't tell anyone about this guy? I don't understand why you didn't even say anything about Arnold that first night Tommy was gone."

Josh is crying. "I know, I know, but you don't understand. Arnold, in the car right after, he was freaking out, going crazy driving like a hundred miles an hour, drove right at a tree saying he was gonna do it, he was gonna do it! and swerved away at the last second, saying he was gonna do it. And he was yelling that he'd tell the cops it was all us, our idea, we broke into his house, we'd all get it for what we did to his uncle. Juvie. He kept saying juvie, and we wouldn't last five minutes in juvie. And then he said he'd find us before that anyway and do the same thing we did to his uncle to us and our families, only he'd make it count. He said that a bunch of times, making it count, and like from now on he'd be watching, watching us all the time. He kept saying—"

"Josh—"

"Wait, listen. That same night he was outside my window, standing there, looking in at me, watching and I was so scared because he wasn't lying, and he's been there like every night after and oh, shit, Kate, you gotta understand, we didn't know—"

Kate: "I can't believe you wouldn't help us find Tommy. That you'd protect Arnold because you're scared."

"No, it's not like that. We're not protecting him. We were trying to protect you guys, and protect Tommy, too. I swear. Not him—"

Kate is about to demand that Josh tell her why they snuck out to Borderland that night, but Mom knocks on the bedroom door lightly and then opens it.

She says, "Kate? Are you on the phone? Who are you talking to?"

344

Kate says, "It's Sam." The lie surprises her with how quick it is, and how easy it still is to lie. She hates the easiness. She says into the phone, "I have to go. The detective is on her way here, and I have to talk to her." Kate sounds robotic and knows it. "I'll talk to you later. Bye."

Kate wakes up to her vibrating phone at 2:15 a.m. She set the alarm after putting Mom to bed. Kate hasn't been asleep for long, and that makes her groggier. The night of her room is fuzzy around the edges, the continued slippage of reality feeling probable, inevitable. She gets up slowly, willing the creak of the bed frame and rustle of the sheets to not travel beyond her bedroom walls. She probably doesn't need to be so careful tonight, because Mom is passed out.

Detective Allison left a little before midnight with the last pages, totally confused (and clearly mistrustful) as to how the pages turned up in Tommy's room. Detective Allison pushed hard at Kate. Kate realizes that Allison now thinks it possible (probable?) that she kept the entire diary to herself because she had been trying to protect Tommy, hadn't wanted him to get in trouble based on what he'd written about doing to the old man. Allison was terse and stern, not the keeper of the peace from yesterday afternoon who had politely asked Kate to empty her backpack. In the face of her questioning Kate was calm and patient, and that part of it was easy, because she was telling the truth. She'd never seen those last crumpled up and flattened out diary pages before she and Mom found them on the floor.

Post–detective visit, Mom succumbed to a bottle of wine, drinking half of it in less than thirty minutes. Kate tried to ask Mom about earlier and how the camera turned on by itself and then the book randomly crashing out of the bookcase in Tommy's room, but Mom didn't want to talk about any of it. She was broken again, like the first day plus after Tommy disappeared. Mom simply told Kate how much she loved her and how they had to help each other through the next few days, and the rest of the days after that. Throughout Mom's drunken, spiritless pep talk, Kate imagined Tommy's shaking hand pushing broken glass into the old man's skin even though it filled her head with static. Mom refused when Kate offered to help her into bed, opting to use the walls to hold herself upright as she swayed down the hallway into her room. There was no more talk of them or of how as a team they were going to make it, any of it. Kate dutifully followed Mom into her room to ensure she made it to bed, anyway.

Kate turns on the camera app, and the living room glows black-and-white on her small, rectangular screen. The room is empty. Kate peeks her head out into the hallway. Mom's bedroom door is open, which was how she left it. Mom's snoring is muffled. She's likely in the exact same position as Kate left her.

Kate sneaks down the hallway to the living room. She watches herself on her phone. She starts out as a distant blip, progressing to the back of the couch, then walking around the front so that she stands a few feet from the camera. She likes this viewpoint, not because she wants to watch herself, but because she can see if anyone is sneaking up behind her. No one is there. Kate's eyes are fluorescent and her skin is washed out, almost green tinted. It's her but it's not her on the screen. Tommy would've joked that she was seeing the ghost-her. But ghosts aren't white or bright. Ghosts are shadows of someone or something gone wrong. Maybe she's the opposite, the film negative of a ghost, then, which is something that hasn't been given a name yet. This film-negative ghost-her isn't doing the haunting and is instead haunted by everyone (including herself) and everything.

Kate hits the Record button. She waves, and whispers, "In case you wake up and I'm gone. I'll be back. I promise." She wonders if Tommy was as confident that he would be coming back on the night that he and the boys snuck out to Borderland.

Kate is a little surprised that no one is outside waiting for her, although she isn't sure who it would be. She gathers her bike from out back and pedals down her street. Everyone is asleep. Nothing is awake. The quiet and stillness of the world at this time of night is both disconcerting and thrilling, like she's finally seeing the truth of things, of how they really are.

The night air is cool and dry, and despite the constant pedaling, goose bumps raise on her arms and legs. She should've brought a sweatshirt. Kate rides down Massapoag Avenue. Much of the road serves as a western border to Borderland. The woods to her right are dark, and there are marked and unmarked openings to trails, those mini-mouths into the forest, those invitations to come in, explore, and perhaps find someone waiting for her.

Kate keeps to the road and turns onto Josh's street. There's a police cruiser parked in front of Josh's house, silently flashing its blue lights. Kate jumps a curb, ditches into their neighbor's front yard, and takes cover behind a little grove of trees and shrubs at the edge of the two properties. She doesn't see any police waiting by the car, inside the car, or on the front doorstep. They must be in the house. Kate worms herself and her bike through the trees and bushes, forging a path that isn't there. Head down, the dried leaves and branches stick in her hair, scratch her arms and legs, grab at the handlebars, pluck the tire spokes. She makes too much noise but keeps going anyway. Once through, she runs with her bike across a small patch of grass to the side of the Griffins' house, out of view of the police car and underneath Josh's bedroom window. Kate balances the bike on her back hip and wipes madly at her face, arms, and legs as she passes through spider-webs somewhere along the way.

There's a light on in Josh's room. She's not quite tall enough to look inside his window. Even up on her tiptoes she'd need at least another half foot. She can reach the window frame, but there's nothing really substantial to grab on to to pull herself up. Nothing to stand on, either. She briefly considers leaning her bike against the house and standing on it, but that would end in disaster.

She texts Josh: *I'm here. Outside. Out your window. We need to talk.*

No response. Maybe he's not in his room. Maybe he's in the kitchen or somewhere else with his parents and the police. She didn't think the police would already be here. She doesn't want to think about what they will do if they find her skulking in the Griffins' side yard. Her plan was that Josh's parents would be asleep like her mom, and Josh would be lying awake or pacing his bedroom.

Kate is at the house, because talking to him on the phone would no longer cut it. She needs to see and watch and feel Josh say whatever it is he's going to say to her. It's that important. Only then will she know if he's lying.

She sends him a second swarm of texts, one separate text for each word of the message: *Josh. I. Am. Here. Open. Bedroom. Window. Now.*

He texts back: *????*

Kate: *Look outside.*

He carries his cell phone to the window; the glowing screen jostles like a fat and drunken firefly until he puts it down on the sill. He opens the window and whisper-hisses, "What are you doing here?"

"Come outside. Quick. We need to talk."

"There's two police in the kitchen, right now. I can't. Go home."

"Sneak out. Or I'll ring the doorbell." An empty threat. There's no way he'll try to sneak outside, but staying at the window and talking to her won't seem as ridiculous by comparison.

"Go ahead. Ring it." He starts to shut the window.

"No wait. Please. Josh. Stop."

"What."

"Just tell me one thing."

"You shouldn't be out here. It's not safe." Josh presses his forehead against the screen looking out, and left and right, as though he can see his front yard. He looks behind him, anywhere but Kate's face.

"What do you mean?" She says it fast, like it's all one word.

"Arnold. He comes here at night and stares into my window. I find tramped down grass out here every morning."

Kate looks down. The grass is wet; the sprinklers must've been on recently. She squirms her toes around inside her sneakers, as though searching for new footprints to step into. She can't tell if Josh is lying about seeing Arnold. He's agitated and twitchy but he's behind a screen, backlit, so she can't really see his face. And all of a sudden her coming here doesn't seem like such a great idea.

"I still don't understand why—"

"Go home, Kate. We're going to both get in real trouble, I can't—"

"Tell me why." Kate feels the cold again and starts feeling heavy, like it's all too much, and she wants to lie down on the grass, let things keep on growing around her. "Why'd you sneak out to Borderland?"

"It was Tommy's idea." Josh stops talking, holds up a stop hand against the screen, and looks behind him. He turns back and says, "I can't do this now. I have to go."

Kate considers threatening him again, telling him that she'll start yelling if he doesn't give her more. She says, "Wait. Don't go. Just tell me quick."

Josh whispers the next bit impossibly fast and Kate has a hard time processing what he says.

"We screwed up so bad we know we did and Tommy said we had to fix it we had to protect you guys and everybody we didn't know what to do and Tommy said we had to make it right had to make it right."

"Josh—"

"We didn't say anything because when we lost Tommy—" He sputters out at the end of the nonsentence.

"You *lost* Tommy?" Kate hates him for that phrase. *We lost Tommy*. Later, she'll replay Josh saying it in her head and fantasize throwing rocks through his window screen and yelling at him that Tommy wasn't theirs, he wasn't theirs to lose.

"No, I didn't mean that."

"What did you mean?"

"Kate. I don't, I mean, I didn't . . . We thought he was still out in the woods, you know."

"Yeah, so—"

"We thought he was still out there doing something about Arnold."

"Doing something?" She says it again, and twice more, each utterance taking on a new, deeper meaning. "Like what?"

Josh is a motionless shadow in his window, looking down at her, or maybe not at her, over her, through her, to somewhere else anywhere else. Maybe he's crying. It feels like he is, even if she can't see the tears on his face.

He looks behind him and then back out the window and says, "They're coming. I'm sorry." Josh shuts the window and disappears.

She says, "No, wait," loud. Too loud. The light in Josh's room doesn't wink out; its brightness changes, as though dimmed but then redirected at the same time. Do people displace light when they enter a room, like water in a bathtub? Kate thinks she hears canned, muffled voices from inside the house, inside Josh's room. She jumps on her bike, pumps the pedals once, twice, and veers left, away from the brush, toward the front yard and the street for a faster getaway. She cuts the wheel too hard, her back tire spins out in the higher gear, and the bike fishtails out from beneath her. Kate twists, lands knee first, foot folded up behind her, the various crooks and points of her leg chunking thick divots out of the grass, and then pitches forward onto her hands and elbows, sliding to a stop on her stomach. Wet, mud streaked, and shaking, she refuses to dignify how out in the open she is with any sort of glance back to the house or the police car. Back on the bike, she rides from the lawn toward the street, telling herself that if she can make tire contact with the pavement, she'll safely follow the black-top all the way to her house.

When Kate gets home she imagines her dead-of-night excursion is being played in reverse: she stashes her bike, waits on the front stoop for someone who isn't there or isn't coming, snakes around the front door, shuts it, locks it, listens for her mother, stands between the couch and the surveillance camera, deletes the video she recorded earlier, turns the camera back on, watches herself walk into the kitchen, drinks warm water from the tap, goes into the hallway, and Mom is in her bed, facedown and snoring, so Kate goes into her room, she studies the empty house on her phone, shuts off the camera, kicks off her socks and sneakers. She walks backward until the backs of her legs knock into the mattress. If only she could keep going in reverse long enough, far enough, to travel all the way back in time, to a week ago, and make Tommy stay home and then keep on going backward to the beginning of the summer and warn him about everything that will happen.

The next morning Kate is up with the sun and stumbles toward the bathroom with her heavy-with-sleep morning feet. There's dirt and mud on the floor in the hallway. She changes course and follows the dirt into the kitchen. It's a total mess. Her legs aren't that dirty so it all must've fallen in clumps from her socks and sneakers.

She gathers the broom and dustpan from the utility closet and gets a handful of sweeps in before Mom calls out from her bedroom, "What are you doing now?"

Allison Driving in Brockton with the Boys, He's Not Feeling Too Good, Three Horrors

A llison fights it, loses, and yawns into the back of her hand.

Officer Kimball asks, "Late night?"

Last night Allison was camped out in her father's room at the nursing home, sprawled in the recliner. The plan was to crash there. It was easier than going back to the house. She listened to her dad sleeping, his breathing alternating between deep and shallow, with sudden gasps and little moans, those personal night sounds, and Allison was almost finally asleep herself when Elizabeth called. Allison then rushed to the Sanderson house to read and retrieve the newest diary pages. Her hands were tremulous holding them and so was her voice, even when she was attempting to be stern in her interview of Kate. Part of her thought Kate had hidden these pages like the previous ones. The other part of Allison doubted herself; if Elizabeth and Kate were telling the truth about these last diary pages being in that large art book, how did she not find them during the room search? They showed her the book, and she vaguely remembered going through it, but did she go through it page by page and hold the book out so loose pages could fall out? Allison wasn't so sure, and she hasn't been back to sleep since Elizabeth's phone call.

Allison says, "Only every night this week."

Sergeant Charles Kimball says, "I hear you." He is a twenty-plus-year veteran of the Brockton Police force and a lifelong resident. He has a detailed map of the city in his head and claims it's as easily retrievable as his home phone number or his wife's middle name, which is why he is driving Allison, Josh, and Luis on their search through local neighborhoods. Charles is African American, shorter than Allison, and almost completely bald but for a patch of graying hair on the back of his head. He drives with his left hand on the wheel and the other in constant motion; adjusting the two-way radio, twisting and untwisting the cap of his bottled water in the cup holder, wiping some unseen speck of dust off the dashboard. He has a thick, platinum wedding band on his left hand and a giant class ring on his right.

After an hour of riding through and around the city, Charles is now headed toward Ames.

Allison says, "The neighborhood doesn't necessarily have to be close to Ames, Sergeant Kimball, remember? Is that correct, boys?" She knows the sergeant remembers but she wants to get the boys talking again. They haven't said anything in a while.

Luis and Josh are in the back seat of the unmarked sedan. They're dressed as though prepped for a school photo; just out of the shower, combed hair, brightly colored polo shirts, tan khaki shorts. Josh has his fingers in or near his mouth. Luis fiddles with the shirt collar that curls up at its points. They sit one at each window, scooted over against the doors, turned away from the middle and Officer Barbara. The officer is an impasse, a wall between the boys, comically large by comparison.

Josh says, "Yeah."

Allison turns around in her seat, looks at Luis, and says, "Anything to add?" Of the two boys, Luis has certainly been more willing to talk, and is more natural, easy with what he says and how he says it, as though he's relieved that others now know some version of the truth. Josh is more reticent, guarded, afraid of both consequence and the revelations sure to come, which actually makes Allison trust the both of them a little more now.

Luis: "We drove all over the place, for like a long time, before we got there. And then coming back was a blur."

Sergeant Kimball: "Tell me again how you know the house was in Brockton?"

Josh: "Arnold told us that's where he lived."

Luis: "I remember seeing that 'Entering Brockton' sign, too, on, uh, what is it, Washington Street?

357

Don't remember seeing any other entering-town signs."

First thing earlier this morning Luis and Josh returned to the Ames police station and formally submitted to a new round of interviews and statements. Both boys gave a much more detailed account of why they went to Borderland that night and what happened, and they admitted that everything Tommy wrote about in his diary was true. Initial checks of local hospitals for an elderly man being treated for the injuries described have turned up empty. The boys have not been placed under arrest but they (and their parents) were made fully aware that while the renewed cooperation and forthrightness is appreciated, they would, at a minimum, be processed for their admitted role in the brutal beating and stabbing of the as-of-yet unidentified elderly man.

Sergeant Kimball turns right onto yet another side street crowded with double- and triple-deckers in various states of disrepair. Their outer shells sag under the weight of time and neglect.

Allison leans toward Kimball and says, "Did we drive through here earlier?"

He says, "This was the first place we tried based on their description. I really thought it was the one. Now I'm thinking let's try coming up the other way." He points and stabs that impatient hand of his through the air. "Maybe they didn't recognize any of the houses because we didn't drive in the direction that they came from the first time."

Allison knows that even if the boys are being fully cooperative, they've only been to the place once, they were admittedly drunk, and there's no underestimating how trauma warps the lens of memory.

The cracked and potholed pavement has been recently patched and repatched, the street thick with rubbery tar lumps and looping and inter-secting black lines, like someone crossed out the street with a giant pen. They roll past houses with chipped paint and bent or missing panels of siding. Rusted chain-linked fencing sags and undulates between properties, more than one barnacled with red, askew BEWARE OF DOG signs.

Luis says, "Hey, this looks kinda familiar."

He said that once before. They pulled over in a similar neighborhood and they sat for a few minutes, no one getting out of the car. Luis and Josh had a quick grunt and monosyllabic exchange, ultimately deciding they had not found the house.

Luis scoots up to the edge of his seat, hands on the driver's headrest in front of him. He alternates looking out the windshield and the side window. He says, "Yeah. I think this is—it could be that gray one up ahead. There. Yeah. Right there on the left."

Allison: "The one with the broken trellis on the side?"

Luis: "What?"

Officer Kimball says, "That stuff on the side of the house that looks like, uh, a wall of picket fencing. A trellis."

"Oh, yeah. That's it. Definitely it."

Officer Kimball slows the car down to a roll. The gray triple-decker grows in height as they get closer.

Luis: "Is it all right—can you roll down my window? For a better look?"

"Yes."

Luis patiently waits for the glass to disappear. Hot, humid air rushes into the car along with the sickly sweet smell of the car's radiator working too hard. Luis sticks his head out the window.

Allison: "Josh. Talk to us. Tell us what you think."

Josh: "I don't know. It's hard to see from back here." He says that and moves his head around like he's trying to look around everything instead of directly at it. "I don't remember the trellis being there. But. Could be it, yeah."

They go quiet. The radio crackles static and bursts of conversation built in code words and numbers. The car inches forward and is now across the street from the house, parallel to the driveway.

Luis pulls himself up so the upper half of his

body is out the window. He yells, "Stop! Stop! That's his car! That's his car! See? The brown one? Holy shit! Um, sorry." Luis drops back inside the car. "Oh, wow." He isn't yelling anymore. He lowers into a whisper and crouches in his seat. "That's the house and the car. It totally is." He suddenly bounces back away from the car window and knocks into Officer Barbara. "Oh my God, I'm sorry. I'm so sorry. I didn't mean it, I didn't—"

Allison: "Luis. It's okay. We know you didn't mean it. But you need to calm down."

"Yeah, okay. I'm sorry. Okay."

Allison turns to Josh, who hasn't moved, isn't moving, but is slightly leaned forward, one finger at his lips, looking out the window. "Is that Arnold's car, Josh?"

Josh. "That's his car." He sits up straight, as tall as he can, pressing himself into the seat back, and closes his eyes, squeezing them shut, the lids crushing into asterisks.

Allison: "Josh? Are you okay? Talk to me, please."

Josh: "You promise there're police at our houses, right, to protect our parents in case Arnold comes for them? Tommy's house too? You have to promise. Are they there now? He could already be there. He—"

Allison: "Josh, yes. Yes. Like I said earlier, your homes are under surveillance."

"Okay. Okay." Josh bends in half, his head in his hands. "Oh my God, this is the place."

While waiting for backup (they don't have to wait long), they run the building address and car's plate through databases. Two men are listed as residing in the third-floor apartment: Martin Weeks, age sixty-eight, a retiree; Rooney Faherty, age twenty-three, no known employer, and he has an extensive criminal record with a list of breaking and entering and burglary arrests and six months served this most recent fall and winter. He's currently on parole. The car is registered under Weeks's name.

Two Brockton police officers are at the front door; their ringing of the third-floor apartment doorbell is going unanswered. Allison leads Sergeant Kimball and another officer down the driveway and they climb up the skeletal, zigzagging back stairs. There is more exposed wood than there is paint on the creaky stairs and railing. The deck is warped and sun bleached. A black, egg-shaped charcoal grill missing its cover and one of its legs leans against the railing and is propped up on a cinderblock. Full, untied garbage bags line the rear wall. Two of the three apartment windows are missing screens. All three have their shades pulled down.

The hinges groan and complain as Allison opens the back screen door. She knocks hard on the interior wooden door. Four, small, rectangular windows rattle and buzz in the frame.

"Hello, Mr. Weeks? Mr. Weeks, I'm Detective Allison Murtagh of the Ames Police Department, and we're here to make sure you're okay. We'd also like to ask you a few questions."

Inside, a thin, dingy lace curtain covers the door's windows like a cloud. Allison bends, cups her hands around her eyes, and hovers centimeters from the glass. She's looking into a kitchen. It's dark but there's light coming from another, unseen room to the left. On the floor there are empty boxes and more full untied garbage bags. Up against the far wall, a round table drips with newspapers, cereal boxes, and milk or orange juice cartons. The table is surrounded by three chairs, with the fourth having spun out of orbit, adrift in the kitchen.

She asks the officers behind her, "Can you hear that? A TV maybe?"

Kimball stays with Allison, but the other officer walks next to one of the apartment windows and says, "Yeah, I hear a TV."

"Hello, Mr. Weeks?" Allison pounds on the door again, this time with an open hand, and the door quakes and she's suddenly and absurdly aware of how high above the ground they are but continues hitting the door hard enough to send everyone and everything crashing down.

A male figure shuffles into the kitchen, medium

height and build, walking with a slight limp. He has something in his left hand, dangling down by his hip. As he gets closer to the door she recognizes it; a beer bottle. He places the bottle on the counter to his left and then unlocks the deadbolt.

Allison steps back, the door opens, only enough for the width of the young man's face.

"Hey. Sorry, I was, um, watching a movie." He swallows a half hiccup, half burp. His face is gaunt, as though he lost a lot of weight in a short time span. Cheeks are covered in thick stubble, and there are smudges of dirt on the bridge of his nose. Hair cut short, tight to his head, recently buzzed. The tide of his hairline is beginning to go out to sea, and his high forehead is dotted with acne and beads of sweat. He squints and his eyes are red, like he's been crying or drinking or both.

Allison shows her badge, introduces herself and her fellow policemen, and asks, "Are you Mr. Rooney Faherty?"

"Yeah. That's me."

"We've had officers ringing the front doorbell. How come you didn't answer?"

He shrugs. "Watching my movie." He scratches his face slowly, as though unsure of the need to scratch that itch. "We get a lot of ding-dong-ditch here. It's kind of funny, actually. It's not the best neighborhood in the world. Obviously, right? I mean, I know there are better, lots better places, just over in your town, right. Ames. Lots of nice houses in Ames. You probably live in a beautiful one. Right? I can see these things." He taps the fingers of his left hand against his temple.

Allison plays along, to keep him talking. She says, "Sure. It's nice, but it's seen better days."

"Most people who live in a nice house don't even get how nice it is. This place isn't so terrible, though. People aren't so bad here. They are who they are. I've been in worse, places that don't look worse but are, you know." He opens the door a little wider and peers around a corner, like he can see past Allison and the officers. His jeans and black T-shirt are baggy, two sizes too big, and filthy, like his face, colored with dirt, as though he came in from working a garden. "Tons of kids here, usually out running around in the street, which is great. Gotta let kids be kids. Can't worry about them all the time." Every few words a slurred one slips out. He's been drinking, but he doesn't break eye contact, doesn't seem uncomfortable or not in control. If anything, the more he talks, the more he animates and is energized, like he wants to keep on talking until someone makes him stop. This is a smart young man, one used to showing off with his mouth, talking his way both out of and into trouble. Allison unexpectedly feels bad for him, and is a little afraid of him, too.

He's still talking through the barely opened door, but leaning forward, out of the house, toward Allison, totally engaged, and with no end in sight. "My uncle complains about the kids, yells at them through the windows. I tell him to leave them alone but he doesn't listen. I tell him he's that old guy in the neighborhood now, yelling at kids to get off his lawn. Every neighborhood has one of those, right? He's a hard guy, had a hard life, I guess, lost everything, but tries his best, like we all do, that's all we can ask, but the kids drive him nuts. I tell him they're just kids doing what they do—"

Allison interrupts. "Is Mr. Martin Weeks your uncle?"

"Yes. Um, yes, he is." Hint of a smile. Wistful, drunk, cruel, secretive, remorseful? There are infinite smiles. A smiling face is often the hardest to read.

"Is your uncle home, Mr. Faherty? I'd like to talk to him. See how he's doing."

Rooney keeps to the long, tight rectangle between the door and the frame. "No," he says, then coughs. He opens the door a little more to snake out an arm and cover his mouth. His right forearm has a thick gauze pad taped around it. There's a hint of pink to it at the lower edges. "I think he went out with a friend or something, probably be back later this afternoon."

"Are you sure?"

Rooney nods. "Yeah, I'm sure. I'd call him but, you know, he doesn't do cell phones. Hates them.

A real Luddite's Luddite. Love that word. Isn't that a cool word?"

"Your uncle's car is still here."

He waves his injured arm, dismissing the comment. "His buddy picked him up. No idea when they'll be back."

"Is his name Arnold?"

"What?" He closes the door a little so that half of his face is visible, like a reflex, and opens it back up.

Allison can feel the officers behind her growing impatient. Maybe she's projecting her own impatience. She knows who she's talking to and the find-Tommy-clock continues to tick away, but she needs to slow-play this somewhat, get him to keep talking and not suddenly clam up. She asks, "Is your uncle's friend named Arnold?"

His face crinkles up like she asked the dumbest question in the world. "No. Joey G. picked him up. They like to go to Hooters or Doyle's. Look at the waitresses. Two dirty old men, you know."

"Is it all right if we come in and talk a little more, then?"

"I don't know." He smiles again and then looks back into the apartment and remains turned away from her.

"Rooney?"

"Hey, yeah, sorry."

"I'd really like to come in."

"I was just thinking I forgot to pause my movie.

It's a zombie movie. Classic. *Dawn of the Dead*, ever see it?"

"I don't think so. Rooney—"

"It's one my friends' favorite movies. They totally dig it." He sways in the doorway, his eyelids droop, and he pitches forward, then catches himself, pulls upright. He might be drunker than she thinks, or strung out, or maybe he's ill. The longer she looks at him, the more skinny and malnourished he's beginning to appear.

"Have you been drinking, Rooney?"

He says, "Hey, you guys are kind of like vampires, you know. I mean, I'm not trying to insult you, not at all, that's not what I'm saying. Really I know, shit, this doesn't sound right. Let me start over. Did you know a vampire can't come into a house unless you invite them in? That's why I said it. You're sort of like that. You can't come in unless I invite you in. It's kind of weird but makes sense, too. But I'm just messing with you."

"We're coming in now, Rooney, okay? I'd like you to back up, away from the door."

He scratches his face again, deflates a little, and for the first time during their conversation, looks at his feet. "Yeah, sure. Sorry. You can come in. Place is a total mess. It didn't used to be like this. Now it's kind of embarrassing and why I don't like to stay here. I didn't even stay here most of this week." He looks up at Allison and says, "I know you understand not wanting to stay in someone else's place, right, Detective?"

He says it like he knows she's temporarily living at her parents' house. Or he says it like he's a con man fishing for information. Allison is momentarily rattled but she settles on the latter and says, "It must be difficult."

"My uncle doesn't let me throw anything away, you know. He's like one of those hoarders or something. Should be on TV."

Rooney backs away from the slightly ajar door. Allison pushes it the rest of the way open and is overpowered by the stench of garbage, the sour tang of curdled milk, and the stuffy, humid air of the apartment. Sergeant Kimball and the other officer follow her in. One of them turns on a light and the other says, "Christ."

Rooney says, "Sorry. I know. It's not good in here. Not good. I'll get rid of all this as soon as you guys leave. I promise. I know, this is totally ridiculous." Rooney fusses with the garbage, slides one bag up against the wall, ties another bag closed, and goes on to the next one, pauses to wipe sweat off his forehead with his gauze-wrapped forearm. There's moaning and screaming coming from the TV in the other room.

Sergeant Kimball says, "You don't need to worry about that now, Rooney."

"I know, but it's disgusting. How can we live like this, right? You guys must live in such nice houses and this place is shit, total shit, you know. And it's our fault. I mean, we've had our share of bad luck too, not saying that we haven't, but this is, is unacceptable. This is bullshit. This is—"

Sergeant Kimball asks, "What happened to your arm?"

"Playing with some kids outside." He waves his arm again, rubs his face, his hands fluttering like dirty, injured pigeons. "I was chasing them and I tripped and took a digger into the rusty fence along the side out there. You saw that, yeah? Cut myself pretty good." He goes back to closing up the garbage bags and mutters to himself. He's breathing heavier, his voice going into a higher register.

Allison asks, "How much is left in your movie, Rooney?"

"It's almost at the end, I think. The zombies finally got in. So the heroes, or whoever—I guess they're not really heroes, just regular people. They're not going to survive, or make it. It's how all those movies end. I like them, but people need to be smarter, need to make better plans about that kind of stuff."

Allison: "Your friends who like that movie, did you invite them over to watch it with you?"

"No. I—I can't do that. Can't let them see the place like this."

"But you've had your friends over before, though. Right?"

He says, "Yeah," then shakes his head. "I guess. But it wasn't this bad. It wasn't like this." His eyes are big and he's clearly upset, on the verge of tears. He full-body slumps.

"Rooney, do you know anyone named Arnold? Who is Arnold?"

He looks around. Opens his mouth to speak then stops, wipes his face with both hands. The dirt and sweat mix and color his skin. He twice breathes out heavy.

"Rooney?"

"It's weird, but Arnold was my dad's name. I never met the fucker, but I found out that's what his name was."

Allison asks, "Do people call you Arnold?"

Rooney nods and stares past Allison and past the walls of the apartment. "Yeah. Some of my friends do." His voice goes baby-brother little and he sounds to be on the verge of tears.

"Is Tommy Sanderson your friend?"

He smiles, shakes his head, reanimates, or regroups. "Hey, I knew you were going to ask me that. I knew you were going to be here today, too. I see things before they happen sometimes. It's weird, I know. I even freak myself out. It's a talent that runs in the family. My uncle, the good ol' Rev, used to get all kinds of money from the true believers with his *talent*." He laughs. His hands open and close into tight fists.

Allison: "Is Tommy your friend, Rooney?"

"Yeah, he is. A real good one. I like Tommy a lot. Even if he's kind of a fuck-up and doing stuff to get me in trouble. You'll see. It was all him and the other guys. And all I ever wanted to do was help him out."

"Is Tommy here now?"

"He's not here."

"Where is he?"

Rooney doesn't say anything and looks into the other room, where everyone is screaming and running from zombies. Sergeant Kimball has a hand on his holster and walks into the TV room.

"Rooney, where is Tommy?"

"He's, uh, still at the park. He's still there at Borderland. He stays there now and won't leave." Rooney's affect goes cold, expressionless. "I haven't heard from him. He stopped talking to me." Rooney shuffles across the room, toward them or toward the kitchen door, she doesn't know.

Allison and the officer both pull their weapons from their holsters but keep them pointed at the floor. Allison says, "Stay away from the door, please, Rooney."

"Hey, I'm just going to finish my beer. That's all I want to do. I really want to finish it. I didn't think you're going let me finish it and I want to. I really want to, okay?" His voice is a whine, and there's a growl under there, too. He reaches for the bottle and watches Allison.

The police officer: "Leave it, sir. Step away from the counter. Slowly. Now."

For a moment Allison is convinced Rooney is going to try to grab the bottle anyway, or something else, anything. He's got that look she's seen hundreds of times before, the one that's so present in the present but at the same time running through the alternate universes of possibilities.

Allison says, "Please move away from the counter, Rooney."

Rooney backs away with his hands up. "Fine. I'm being helpful. I am. Right? You need to say it for me."

"You are being helpful, Rooney."

"I am. I know I am. And I'm going to tell you something because I want to help some more and I'm only trying to help—"

Sergeant Kimball storms back into the kitchen, talking into the radio strapped to his shoulder, then says, "Bedrooms are empty. But there's a door that's all sealed up with duct tape."

Rooney: "I told you I haven't been home all week. I only came back here late last night, and after I stopped by Tommy's place to look for the coin I gave him. I thought, I don't know, I could give it back to him or something. A peace offering, you know. Hey, the coin is his now and I wanted to make sure he had it, so I looked in his bedroom. But I couldn't find it."

Allison and Sergeant Kimball ask questions over each other and the radios on both officers are spewing static charged commands.

Allison: "You were in Tommy's house last night?"

Sergeant Kimball: "Why is the door taped? Is that the bathroom?"

Rooney steps forward, ignoring the other officers and goes to Allison, head turned, talking out of the side of his mouth, like he's telling a street-corner secret. He says, "My uncle's in the bathroom. Okay? He's not feeling too good, you know? But it wasn't my fault. My friends were here and things got so weird and out of hand, and then I didn't know what to do. I'll admit that my head got all messed up this week. I mean, all this crazy shit happened, and so, I left. I was outta here."

The duct tape covering the frame of the apartment's bathroom door is as thick as alligator skin. The forensic team has to use X-Acto knives to hack away at some of the tape before it finally gives in and peels off in tethered, serpent-like strips. The smell of rot and waste is the lumbering monster being kept inside, and it instantly rampages through the TV room. Allison can't help but think in monstrous terms. *That* smell: sulphur and methane and something else that can't be catalogued or accurately described but is ancient and sickly (and even sweetly) familiar. And how something so large and terrible can fit through the cracks between the door and the frame is the first horror.

Then they open the door. It swings inward about halfway, getting stuck or hitting up against something. Amorphous clouds of blowflies billow into the rest of the apartment. That monster smell goes atomic and they are all caught in the blast, the fallout. And there are groans and mouth breathing through their teeth and wet coughs. They turn away and cover their noses and mouths (and even the investigators wearing masks, they cover those, too), and they shoo flies and yell commands very few seem to follow or listen to.

Allison doesn't throw up but wishes she did. It would give her an excuse to look away. Inside the bathroom is pitch-dark. For a moment, Allison re-experiences her childlike fear of the dark, of the idea that there can be anything or anyone hiding inside. And there is a darker shape sitting on the floor, and in that initial snapshot, Allison thinks the shape is Tommy, the awkward teen she met once at a graduation party, the one with the moppy hair, pipe-cleaner arms and legs, skittish and friendly with an aw-shucks smile that would turn heads once he hit high school, and until now she's been able to separate the real Tommy from the one she's been searching for. Allison takes a step toward the dark bathroom, flies buzzing, people shouting, and Tommy is crouched on the floor, and then the slightest head-tilt up to look at her.

One of the other investigators flicks on the light switch. It's Martin Weeks's body on the bathroom floor (not Tommy's), and his body is the second horror: slumped, propped up against the side of the bathtub, sitting on the tiled floor, sitting in an ink blot, an oil spill of coagulated blood, peppered with spiders of black hair. The forensics team will later determine that Rooney shaved his head while standing over his dead uncle.

Weeks's legs span the width of the closet-small bathroom, feet jammed under the sink. Allison is no forensic expert, but she can tell that Weeks has been dead for more than a week, the putrefaction process well under way. Decomposition at the cellular level is called autolysis. With the cells no longer being active, the cytoplasm and mito-chondria swell, the various cellular processes shut down, including the nucleus, and lysosomes release their waste-digesting enzymes that dissolve and break down the individual and surrounding cells, turning muscle and tissue to liquid. Allison tells herself that there is nothing unique about what was happening to Martin Weeks's body. Nothing at all.

Fluids leak from his ears, eyes, nose, or from

those geographies anyway. His face has been bashed beyond recognition. One eye, his right, protrudes grotesquely from the socket and is cloudy and weepy. The other eye is hidden behind an eyelid swollen to the size of a softball. His yellow fingernails have fallen off, and teeth dot the pool of blood on the floor like bits of confetti. A black tongue balloons out of his mouth. His exposed skin is going purple and black. Giant blood blisters marble his exposed shoulders and the back of his bald head. His skin is loose enough that the top layer will peel or slough off if the forensic team isn't careful.

Weeks's gas-filled, bloated abdomen stretches and strains the sleeveless T-shirt that is indistinguishable from skin in places. The third horror is that even with the amount of decay present, Allison is able to identify small puncture and stab wounds in Weeks's stomach and chest, and the little starbursts of dark black-red that accompany them.

Elizabeth at Home and at the Station, Three Statements

Hours after the discovery of Martin Weeks's body, there are still investigators in Tommy Sanderson's room, finishing up their search for Rooney's fingerprints and for evidence of the late-night breaking and entering he admitted to earlier that afternoon. Rooney claimed he entered their home to look for the coin he'd given Tommy. It appears he was telling the truth as there are dirty footprints in Tommy's room, on the floor in front of his dresser and closet door.

Kate tells the police that she found dirt and footprints on the kitchen and hallway floors this morning when she got up. She assumed the mess was her fault, that it had come from her muddy sneakers, and so she cleaned it up before Mom woke up.

Elizabeth is sure there is something that Kate is holding back, not telling them, not telling her (again), but the what-and-why will have to wait. Elizabeth is on her way to the Ames police station for a full debriefing on everything they've discovered today, and that includes the opportunity for her to view the transcripts and videos of interviews with Josh, Luis, and this Rooney, or the man the boys called Arnold.

Janice, who arrived at the Sanderson home late morning, wants to go to the station, too, but Elizabeth insists she stay home with Kate. Earlier, Allison offered to send a car or to pick her up. Elizabeth declined, because she wants to be able to come and go from the station as she pleases, or stay as long as she deems necessary. And she wants to be alone. If she is to go to the station and learn how the horrible story of what happened to Tommy is also about how she failed him as a parent, then it will be a lesson she'll learn alone.

During the short ride to the Ames Police station, she keeps the windows cracked open and the radio off. Her phone buzzes with texts. She side-glances at her phone long enough to see they're from Kate. She still hopes to see Tommy's name come up on her screen. She still hopes to receive more messages, of any kind, from Tommy, and maybe see him again, even if it's in shadow, one last time.

She turns onto South Main Street and a flurry of lights and cars and movement are visible from almost a quarter mile away. Even though the investigation has expanded and splintered to state police headquarters and the FBI bureau in Boston, with Rooney himself being held at the Norfolk County Jail in Dedham awaiting arraignment, the tiny Ames Police station is a mob scene. Cars and news vans are parked on both sides of the road. There are cameras with cyclopean lights and well-dressed reporters holding outstretched microphones and fingers to their earpieces. Gawkers and locals mill about, some of them carrying signs she has no interest in reading, narrowing the street to less than one lane, and standing on the station's well-manicured grass and mulch frontage. Sagging yellow tape and impatient Ames officers stand at the amorphous boundaries of the crowd, ignoring shouted questions and recording cameras. Elizabeth's car stops in the middle of the road, people flittering through her headlights, like oblivious giant moths. She recognizes some of them, a lot of them, actually. The ones she knows by name look away, as if caught looking in her medicine cabinet.

The oafish Officer Stanton appears at her driver's-side window and knocks on the glass with his big flashlight. He talks rapidly, tone communicating he is angry with her, like this is all her fault. She looks at him and shouts, "I'm supposed to be here, you dick." She doesn't know if he hears her or not, and cameras and reporters converge on her car as do the shouted questions she can't possibly answer.

Police eventually herd the crowd far enough away from her car so that Elizabeth can pull into the station's blocked-off driveway. She parks out back, between two mammoth SUVs, shuts off her car, and reads her text messages from Kate; a collection of *let us know*s and *be strong*s and *we love you*s. Alone again and with the car's interior light on, she can't see anything outside her windows. A mosquito buzzes in her ear. She swats and swears at it. She writes back to Kate: *Ok. Going inside now.* She closes her eyes, exhales, and adds, *I love you too.*

Allison meets Elizabeth in the middle of the parking lot. They walk in the back entrance together. Elizabeth avoids making eye contact with the other Ames officers, all of whom she knows to varying degrees of well. There's no avoiding Officer Raymond Blanchard as they pass down a narrow hallway. He's a bowling ball of a man with kind, gray eyes and a mustache that takes up the rest of his face. He lives on the other side of Ames with his wife, Helen, who has been a science teacher at the middle school for more than a quarter century. Tommy hasn't had her for class yet. Is Tommy supposed to have her this coming fall? The fall, the school fall, is only a week away.

Allison finally leads Elizabeth inside and into a private, empty room with a flat-screen television on the wall. She gives Elizabeth a quick rundown of everything they learned today. She also tells her that a team of investigators, dogs, and divers are searching targeted areas of Borderland.

Divers. Elizabeth imagines Tommy at the bottom of an impossibly deep pond that is in a secret part of the park, one they'll never find, his hand outstretched in darkness, in blackness, beyond the light, beyond hope, beyond help, beyond rescuing, beyond finding . . . Elizabeth snaps out of her fugue when Allison presents a folder containing the transcribed statements/ interviews conducted with Luis, Josh, and Arnold. That his real name is Rooney and not Arnold makes her not want to hear anymore; she shouldn't be made to hear any of it or believe any of it is real.

Elizabeth sits at a table and dutifully watches the digital video recordings of Josh's and Luis's most recent statements. Each boy was in a room flanked by their newly hired legal representatives; neither lawyer said much during the interviews and were seemingly content to scribble notes onto their yellow pads. The boys were shown in profile via a camera mounted high up on a wall, or perhaps the ceiling. She wants to hug Josh and Luis and she wants to hurt them. It occurs to her that no one has told her where those boys are now. Are they in custody? Are they home, in their own rooms, sleeping in their own beds?

On the video, Josh seems like an imposter, usually so at ease and charming around adults, he is barely audible, speaks carefully in small complete sentences, at times sounding dull witted, and is asked to repeat an answer more than once. Luis was normally such a lovable wiseass, always willing to play that teen vs. adult obfuscation game, *you can ask but you won't get anything out of me,* but still make you smile and shake your head at the same time. In his interview, Luis is painfully polite and (unlike Josh) eloquent, expansive, and detailed in his responses.

At different times during the boys' interviews Elizabeth can no longer watch them speak. She instead itemizes their words within the printed transcripts, as though hoping that if she finds an error, their stories will unravel and the great lie will be exposed and her son will be found somewhere safe.

The third video is the interview with Rooney. Unlike the other videos, it starts with an empty interrogation room, the table in the middle, four chairs pushed in tight, a hiss of silence on the recording, white, digital time stamp inexorably ticking away in the lower right corner of the screen. Elizabeth says, "What—what happened here?" afraid she'll hear or see something within the digital nothingness, afraid the video will switch over to a recording from the camera in her living room, colored in that night vision, and Arnold (she will never think of him as Rooney) standing there, a shadow, *the* shadow, and instead of seeing Tommy in the dark spaces of the house and her head, Arnold will be there instead.

Allison apologizes and mumbles something about an editing time-stamp mistake. She fast-forwards. Allison and a man in a suit enter the room first, their bodies moving and twitching as quickly as insect wings, and then two correctional officers lead Rooney inside. Allison stops the fast-forwarding. Rooney wears handcuffs and a green jumpsuit. He waived the right to an attorney for the interview.

Elizabeth says, "I don't think I can watch. Not yet."

Allison: "Of course. Do you want to take a break? Do you need some water? We could go outside for fresh air, too."

Elizabeth sits with her hands over her eyes, but she isn't crying. Trying to quiet everything that is happening in her head, particularly the stubborn voice telling her that if she doesn't ever listen to or read what Arnold/Rooney says, then Tommy still has a chance. That is now the worst voice of them all.

"No. Can you tell me what he's like?"

"Rooney?"

Elizabeth says, "Arnold."

"I'm no psychologist but he's deeply disturbed. Lived with his uncle after—"

"No, I really don't care about that or him, at all. I'm asking what's he like? When you talked to him, what did you see and feel? Who is he then, when you're with him? I need to know why and how Tommy so desperately wanted to be his friend. How he could've fooled Tommy so easily."

Allison: "That's tough for me to answer, Elizabeth. I don't think I can answer that. I—I don't know who he is from just talking to him." Allison exhales and Elizabeth stares at her until she says something else. "He's broken. Badly broken. And I know that doesn't answer your question, but—"

Elizabeth interrupts with "Okay, okay" and sits up.

Allison stands from the table and walks toward the door, looking behind her, presumably expecting that Elizabeth will follow.

Elizabeth's *okay*s doesn't mean she's ready to leave this room, though. Not yet. She spreads out the three interview transcripts in front of her. She reads their first pages. She moves them around, shuffles their position, and reads the first pages again, in a different order. She turns to the second pages, and reads those. Then she turns back to the first pages and starts the process over again.

Elizabeth says, "I'm sorry but I want to spend some times with these. Is it all right if I do this by myself? I want to be alone with these transcripts. I think I need to be alone. I don't know if that makes sense." She pauses and looks up at Allison, who doesn't say anything, and Elizabeth imagines she probably wants to say that her being alone is a very bad idea. It probably is. But Elizabeth doesn't care.

"I can step out of the room, of course. As long as you're sure."

"I am. And I'll probably be in here awhile. I'm going to read these more than once. Is that okay?"

"Yes, of course. I'll keep an eye on the room and check in with you in a little bit. Or if you finish, hit this buzzer by the door and I'll come back in. Okay?"

"Yes. Thank you. For everything, Allison."

The detective leaves and it's now midnight. As if on cue, Kate barrages her with texts again: *Mom* and *U still there?* and *how long R u staying?*

Elizabeth: *don't know and don't wait up.*

Kate: *did they find Tommy yet?*

Elizabeth: *not yet.*

There are more texts. Elizabeth ignores them. Her phone stays facedown on the table, vibrating against the wood.

Elizabeth begins, finally, to read. She reads the statements one at a time. She reads them by pages and by pieces. She wishes she had Tommy's diary to include with these so that she could splice everything together, create a bible of what it was that happened.

Elizabeth rereads pages and passages. She reads them in order and out of order. She reads until she can pretend that the sentences and words are under her control. It's not so much a memorization as it is an anticipation and an ability to move the words to where and when she wants.

Despite the late hour and darkness, there are boats and divers searching the brackish ponds and isolated islands of Borderland State Park. They have not found Tommy yet, but Elizabeth is now sure, for the first time, that they will. Elizabeth refuses to go home and wait for that phone call, the call she's feared and knew would come ever since the night after he disappeared, the night she saw and smelled Tommy's presence in her bedroom.

So Elizabeth reads. And reads. And mixes and matches pages and sections and individual answers. And Tommy is there with her, not in the antiseptically bright, shadowless room, but trapped in the transcript pages, huddled between the lines.

Detective Murtagh: On the night of August 16th, Tommy Sanderson and Luis Fernandez slept over at your house, is that correct?

Josh Griffin: (inaudible)

Murtagh: Sorry, I couldn't hear you. Can you speak a little louder please?

Josh: I said yes. They slept over.

Police: Did you invite Arnold to meet you at Borderland State Park later that night?

Josh: Not me.

Murtagh: Who invited him?

Josh: Tommy.

Murtagh: Did you know that Tommy invited him?

Josh: (inaudible)

Murtagh: Could you repeat, please?

Josh: Yeah. He told us he was going to do it.

Murtagh: Why did he invite Arnold?

Josh: Tommy said that we had to fix it.

Murtagh: On August 13th, you drove Josh Griffin, Luis Fernandez, and Tommy Sanderson to the apartment you shared with your uncle, Martin Weeks, is that correct?

Rooney Faherty: I didn't know their last names. They sound kind of weird. Last names. Those names don't fit them. Yeah, the boys. We went for a drive. Just around. They were drinking too. I know I shouldn't have let them drink in my car, but I'm not their dad. But hey, I didn't give them nothing to drink. That's the truth. Not sure where they got the beers, wasn't me. Josh took them from his dad. Rich dude from what I heard, yeah? Luis might've taken some too. Whatever, it wasn't me. You should ask their parents why that was so easy, you know? I took them but they were all over me about wanting to see the place, see the hobo nickels I was working on. They wanted to see my uncle. I'd told them all about what a mess he was.

Murtagh: You're saying the boys suggested you take them to your apartment?

Rooney: That's exactly what I'm saying. Hey, I didn't know it then, if I did there's no way I would've taken them, right? But they wanted to cause some trouble, you know, like serious shit kind of trouble. And I had no idea what they wanted to do. No idea. I was really nervous about bringing them over, wasn't sure it'd be okay, but I thought they were good kids, you know, so I played along.

Murtagh: Was your uncle home when you got to the apartment?

Rooney: Yeah. He was home. Always home. On the couch. The Rev. Good old Uncle Rev. Drinking. Smelling. Sitting. Shitting. Just there. I can't lie and say that I loved the guy or had a great relationship with him, but don't get me wrong, he took me in when he didn't have to, especially after last winter. So he gets big respect from me for that.

Murtagh: What happened when you were all inside your apartment?

Rooney: It wasn't good. Nothing good happened. I don't think I really want to talk about what they did. It'll be hard.

Josh: How Tommy wrote about it, that's how it happened. All of it. I tried not to do anything. Arnold grabbed me first. Picked me first. Why did he pick me first? I wouldn't do it. I wouldn't hit him. I didn't. And then someone else did and Arnold kept making us hit his uncle.

Murtagh: We found Arnold's uncle, Mr. Martin Weeks, dead in the apartment today.

Josh: Oh my God.

Luis Fernandez: No, I do understand, ma'am. I was pretty drunk, we all were, and I don't know how to explain it. It was like we were living in a shared bad dream or something, and you want to move but can't, everything's stuck in slow motion and can't escape. It was like that. We didn't want to move. I don't know, I can't explain it well. We knew his uncle was hurt real bad, especially after Arnold kicked him in the head right before we left. Tommy was the last one in the bathroom with his uncle, and told us after that he was breathing. We never thought . . . we didn't think . . . we didn't want to think . . .

Murtagh: Didn't want to think what?

Luis: That he could die. Could be dead, ma'am.

Murtagh: If you were so upset by what happened, why not help the uncle by calling an ambulance or the police? Did you ever consider calling for help?

Luis: Yes. Yes we did, ma'am. We did. But. But we were afraid to.

Murtagh: Were you afraid of getting arrested?

Luis: No, ma'am. I mean, I can't say that we didn't know we were in like the biggest trouble. But we were like so more scared of Arnold. I swear. I swear on a thousand Bibles. Like I said, Arnold threatened to kill us and our families if we ever said anything to anyone about his uncle. We really thought he would kill us or hurt us. He would've, too. He definitely would've. He was legit threatening us the whole ride home. How he looked and sounded, it was real. Driving us back he sped his car right at trees and telephone poles and swerved out of the way at the last

391

minute. The last tree was on Massapoag, near where we'd dumped our bikes. I thought for sure he wasn't going to stop that time. He was screaming, "This is it," and we were all screaming, and the car bounced up, off something, a curb maybe, and he didn't actually stop the car in time. The front of the car skidded past the tree. It was right up against my door and I was sitting in the back. He really tried to hit the tree and missed it because of the curb or something. He tried to kill us right then. He did. I know he did. After he told us to get out of the car and he sat there and we rode away on our bikes.

Murtagh: Did you talk about what happened when you got home?

Luis: No, ma'am. We left each other. Went home. Later that night we were on our Minecraft server and talking and we were ready to call the police. I swear. We were scared but we were going to do it in the morning, but then in the morning we went to Josh's house and Josh was all upset because in the middle of the night he saw Arnold standing outside his window, staring into his bedroom and watching him. And so we knew Arnold would do something awful to us, or to our families, if we said anything about his uncle.

Murtagh: When did you decide to meet Arnold at Borderland?

Luis: The next day, ma'am. We spent that whole day after talking about Arnold. What we should do. And we didn't know what to do. It started off mostly me and Josh talking but not saying much more than like what are we going to do? Tommy was throwing up he was so nervous and scared, and everything. Then after a little while Tommy started saying that we had to take care of Arnold ourselves. Make things right. He said we had to fix this. He said that a lot. He said everything that happened was our fault and that we had to make it right. Then Tommy said he had like a plan.

Murtagh: Did you hit your uncle first?

Rooney: Are we going to talk about Tommy? I'd really like to talk about Tommy. I still don't understand why he tried to hurt me.

Murtagh: What was his plan?

Luis: Have a sleepover at Josh's house because it was like the closest to Borderland. His backyard is right up against it. Then we sneak out and meet Arnold at Devil's Rock late at night when no one is around. And then kind of trick him into having an accident. Like fall off the rock or something. Tommy talked about how whenever we were at the rock Arnold would always jump back and forth over the split and if we got him drunk enough maybe he'd fall in on his own.

Murtagh: And what were you going to do if he didn't fall on his own?

Luis: Tommy said that we would push him, ma'am. Into the split. Or if he got close enough to an edge, he'd push him off. Me and Josh were going crazy when he first said it, you know? We were like no way, there was no way we could do it, we couldn't push him off. We just couldn't do something like that. And it would never work. But then Tommy said that he would do it. He would push him. He even said it should be him to do it.

Murtagh: So you planned to kill Arnold?

Josh: No. Not like that. I mean, I guess we did. But we weren't thinking of what we were going to do like that.

Murtagh: How were you thinking of it?

Josh: Tommy never said we were going to kill him. We just wanted to stop him. Stop him.

Murtagh: Stop him from doing what?

Josh: You don't understand! He went to my house that night! He knew where I lived. I never told him that. He found my house on his own. He was standing there and looking in my window and he's been there, outside my window, like at least three more times since Tommy disappeared and he's probably been to Tommy's house and Luis's house.

Luis: Tommy kept saying this is how it has to be. That we had no choice that Arnold was going to hurt us or someone we loved and it wasn't like if it happens but when it happens. I said something stupid and kind of mean to him about being a seer, and Josh was a mess and kept asking Tommy what he meant by the not-if-when stuff, asking if he knew something he wasn't telling us. Tommy was the only one of us who Snapchatted with Arnold, right? And I don't know, it felt like Tommy was hiding something. That he knew something else we didn't but he didn't say anything more, asked us to trust him, that this is how it had to be. And even through all that, me and Josh still said no. We did. We told him no and it wouldn't work. But it was too late.

Murtagh: Why was it too late?

Luis: Tommy said he'd already told Arnold we'd meet him at the rock the next night.

Rooney: I'm not going to talk about this too much because you're not going to understand. You've already made up your minds anyway. I can tell. I can see it. Didn't the boys tell you I'm a seer? Future teller? Mind reader? Runs in the family, you know.

Murtagh: We haven't made up our minds, Rooney. We want to know the truth.

Rooney: Let me tell you a secret. We are all seers. We just can't see everything all the time. Or maybe we can and we're like purposefully blind to it. We don't want to see it. We couldn't live without going totally batshit crazy if we could see the connections to everything, so you have to screen stuff out, ignore some of it. You see what you want to see. That's it, there. You have to want to see it. Simple as fucking pie. Tommy knew that better than anyone else. He wanted to see.

Murtagh: Rooney, please tell us what happened when you and the boys entered your apartment.

Rooney: I'm going to say this quick. Get it over with. And this is the God's-honest truth, right? I swear on the pus-covered soul of my mother and if she's not dead, she should be. Sorry. I'm kidding, bad joke, I know. Sorry. I'm sorry, I'm nervous because I'm not sure you'll believe me.

Murtagh: We're here to listen to what you have to say, Rooney.

Rooney: The boys were so drunk and I should've taken them home then. They stumbled up the back stairs and I stayed behind them, the caboose, in case one of them fell, you know. I was worried and even then I was like this is a bad idea. My uncle's probably sleeping. But they went on ahead, let themselves in, and ran into the apartment. They went into the living room and my uncle was there, drunk, kind of half asleep in front of the TV like he always was. I told them I kept the coin stuff in my bedroom but we had to be quiet and the boys were hooting and hollering and didn't listen to me. They took some of my uncle's beers and started pounding those down and spilling everywhere. My uncle finally woke up a little and he growled at them. He's a growler, always was. He gave him a little dose of the Rev's voice, you know? Told them to get out of there, leave his beer, dropped a few f-bombs on them. And then the boys went crazy laughing and started yelling fuck off and then, Josh, he was the first one, he slapped my uncle with an open hand. Just crack! Like that, and then he hit him again real quick, then bounced back behind his friends, hiding or something. Typical Josh shit, you know? And then it started blurring, the three of them were all over him, like a, like a pack of, what, jackals, or something. Hitting, punching, kicking, and they wouldn't stop.

Murtagh: Why didn't you stop them?

Rooney: This is why I don't want to talk about it. You're not going to believe me. I know it looks bad, real bad that I didn't do anything to stop them, especially after how you found him today. But I did. I froze up, shut down. Have you ever seen a beating? Not a fight or one punch. Have you ever been right there for a total beatdown? It's awful. Makes you sick. Changes you. It does. It changes you just seeing it. And I've seen and taken my fair share of beatings in my life, some really bad ones, awful ones. You have no idea how awful, how awful it can be. And I don't know, there in the TV room, I did what I always did. I stayed silent. Didn't move. I just took it. I watched.

Josh: We filled my backpack with a bunch of my dad's beer. We had to take enough and get Arnold to drink a lot of it. We watched superhero movies until my parents were asleep and snuck out.

Murtagh: Was Arnold at the rock waiting for you?

Josh: No. We were there by ourselves, the whole time.

Murtagh: By yourselves?

Josh: We never saw Arnold that night. We weren't lying about not knowing what happened to Tommy. I never saw Arnold there that night. He was there outside my window the next night and the night after that, and again after that. But I didn't see Arnold in the park.

Luis: Tommy said he chatted up Arnold to make it seem like we were still his friends and everything was normal. Said he told Arnold that we were solid, wouldn't ever tell on him, and you know, said we still wanted to hang out with him and stuff. Tommy said Arnold was totally into coming out to the rock. Excited about it.

Murtagh: Did you see the texts? Why did Tommy think Arnold was excited?

Luis: No, ma'am. They weren't texts. Snapchats, and they like disappear right after you look at them. Tommy said that Arnold was excited to meet us out there.

Murtagh: If you were so afraid of Arnold, why would you meet him out in the woods in the middle of the night?

Luis: We were totally scared, but because Tommy went ahead and told Arnold we'd be there we were more scared to not show up. If we didn't show up, then Arnold would think we were like setting him up or something, and then he'd come after us for sure. I was so scared, ma'am. And . . .

Murtagh: What is it, Luis?

Luis: I was scared of Arnold and mad at Tommy. He put us in that spot. We had no choice. We had to go. Walking out into those woods was the scariest thing I've ever done in my life.

Rooney: I stood there even when they started smashing beer bottles over his head. And then, then, they jabbed pieces of glass right into him. Just fucking stabbing him, right there in front of me. It wasn't real. It wasn't happening. My uncle, he was passed out, knocked out, and didn't do anything. I couldn't believe he wasn't doing anything. I wasn't doing anything. I backed up into a corner, crouched down into nothing, I was nothing, and watched. I watched. That's all I do, I watch. Those times I've been arrested. I never take anything or do anything in their houses, I just watch. I'm not a bad guy and I don't do those terrible things. I want to see what it's like to be in those other places, you know, the nice houses I broke into. I just watch. It's all in my record, right? You know this. It's all there. I haven't ever done what they did.

Murtagh: Can you repeat that please, Josh?

Josh: Tommy. Tommy said we had to drink some of the beers. I didn't want to. I never even liked drinking ever.

Murtagh: Why did you have to drink?

Josh: He said that when Arnold showed up we had to make sure everything seemed normal. I only took a couple of sips. I stood on the rock and poured the rest of mine out right in front of them.

Luis: I did drink a beer, ma'am. Only one. Tommy drank a couple, I think. Josh poured his out. And I was scared because I knew this wasn't going to work, and I was going to tell Tommy we should go home and come up with something else. Then Tommy told Josh that pouring out the beer was fine, that it was good, because it would make the rock smell like beer, like we'd been there waiting for him for a while. He said that Arnold would be there any minute.

Murtagh: Josh had the backpack of beer. What did you bring with you?

Luis: I didn't bring anything, ma'am. I'd grabbed a walking stick in the woods, before we got to the rock. I wasn't planning on doing anything with it. Nothing planned. Maybe protection. Just in case.

Murtagh: Did anyone bring a flashlight or a lighter?

Luis: We used our phones as flashlights, totally drained our batteries so fast. But we could still see okay. It was surprisingly bright out. Especially on top of the rock. Clear sky, big moon.

Murtagh: Did Tommy have anything with him?

Murtagh: Did you ever hit or stab your uncle, Rooney?

Rooney: No. I didn't do anything. He was dead, right there on the couch.

Murtagh: Are you're saying the boys killed your uncle?

Rooney: I don't think they meant to, but they couldn't stop hitting and jabbing him once they got started. The boys finally quit when they were totally exhausted. Wore themselves out on my uncle. They finished and kind of wandered out of the room into the kitchen and one of them called out to me, said let's go. So I did. I drove them home in a state of shock. I don't even remember the ride or where I dropped them, and I don't remember the ride back to the apartment. Total autopilot, you know? When I got back, my uncle was sitting on the bathroom floor, sitting in his own blood and everything, and I tried to get him up, to help him, but there was nothing I could do. He was gone.

Murtagh: Didn't you say that your uncle

was dead on the couch? How did he get to the bathroom?

Rooney: Yeah, he was dead before he got to the bathroom. He still got there somehow. Maybe he didn't know any better. I'm sorry, I'm so nervous telling you all this, because there are more parts that don't make sense like that part. Yes, yes, he was dead on the couch. But when I got back he was in the bathroom.

Murtagh: There wasn't a lot of blood on the couch or living room rug, Rooney. Very little. A few drops. But there was a lot of blood in the bathroom. Do you—

Rooney: (interrupts) I want to go back. Can I go back now? I want to go back.

Police: Go back?

Rooney: To my cave. I should've stayed there.

Josh: It was in the pocket of his cargo shorts. He showed it to us. It was dumb and scary. That's when I poured out my beer. After he showed us that.

Luis: It was a jackknife, ma'am.

Murtagh: How big was it?

Luis: I didn't get a long look at it. I remember that he finished his beer before I did and put the empty back in Josh's pack. Then he didn't say anything about it or what he was going to do with the knife. He took it out of his pocket, opened it up real quick. It looked small to me. Then he folded it up and put it back in his pocket. I didn't see him take it out again.

Murtagh: Did you know he was bringing it?

Luis: No, ma'am.

Murtagh: Had he ever previously shown you the knife?

Luis: No, ma'am.

Murtagh: You named it Devil's Rock, is that correct, Rooney?

Rooney: No, I told the boys that is what it's called, should be called. I can't name stuff. I'm not that important. Never was.

Murtagh: Tommy contacted you via Snapchat and invited you to meet them at Devil's Rock on the night of August 16th. Is that correct?

Rooney: It is. It is indeed. Indubitably. Sorry. Okay, sorry.

Murtagh: That's okay, Rooney. We thank you for talking with us and helping us. You still want to help us, right?

Rooney: Yes, I do. I want to help.

Murtagh: Did you go to Borderland on the 16th?

Rooney: I did. Yes, I did.

Murtagh: Why did you meet them there? After everything you said they'd done to your uncle, why would you go?

Rooney: I wanted to talk to them. Convince them to turn themselves in and get my uncle the help he needed.

Murtagh: Why didn't you call for help yourself?

Rooney: Right after it happened I was helping him. I was watching him, making sure he was comfortable. I couldn't call the police or anything because you wouldn't have believed me that it was them, all them. So they had to call and tell the truth and then my uncle could get more help.

Murtagh: Who taped up the bathroom door, Rooney?

Rooney: I don't know. I'm having a hard time figuring that out myself, you know? I don't remember. Really, I don't. Seeing them attack the Rev like that, it messed me up pretty good. Knocked me loose for like a whole week. I mean, why would my friends do that to my uncle? And how did they tape the bathroom, you know? It wasn't me. I wouldn't do that. I wouldn't. I wouldn't do that!

Murtagh: You don't have to shout, Rooney. We're sitting across from you and listening.

Rooney: Yeah, okay. I know. Thank you. I know. Hey, but, yeah, I left. I wasn't even home for a long time, until today. When you found me there. I was gone before that. For a long time. For as long as Tommy was gone. So maybe they came back to my apartment and taped up the bathroom door. Ask Josh and Luis about that. About the tape. It wasn't me. I was gone.

Murtagh: Where were you?

Rooney: I was at Borderland.

Murtagh: Where in Borderland?

Rooney: Over in the way north end of the park. No one ever uses those trails, especially over by the old Moyles quarry. Tough hiking and climbing there. Did you know they built that old viaduct in Canton from those stones? It's true. Look it up. And Tommy's dad crashed into those rocks. Same rocks. Weird, huh? Coincidence, yeah? There's no fucking coincidences. You know that. You have to. Your job is about finding how all the coincidences fit together. I know you know everything already and the only reason you're here and I'm here is to mess with me.

Murtagh: Rooney, that's not true.

Rooney: After Tommy tried to hurt me I walked around, walked around, tried to figure things out, get my head on straight, and I walked to the other end of the park where there were all those rocks everywhere and I stopped, and this is something you're not going to believe me about either, and maybe I don't believe it now, like I said, seeing them kill the Rev totally fried my brain and then Tommy trying to hurt me didn't exactly help . . . Anyway, so I wandered over to the quarry and there were all these rocks everywhere, and then rocks, they kind of opened up, like, like a flower, and they took me in.

Josh: It was so hard sitting there waiting and waiting for Arnold. Watching the woods, listening, jumping at every stupid bird or squirrel or whatever in the bushes. Tommy called out to Arnold like every two minutes. It echoed and the noises we heard would always stop after he called out and it would be quiet again and then we would think we heard something so we didn't say anything for a long time. Tommy said we should talk and sound like we're having fun so Arnold wouldn't suspect anything. I told him this was stupid and Luis told me to shut up. I said okay let's talk about the jackknife then. Tommy said he was sorry he didn't tell us about the knife. He said it was a contingency plan, like in case there was zombies out here too. He said that was a joke. Luis and Tommy started talking and laughing a little, but I didn't listen to them. I . . . I don't know.

Murtagh: Go on, Josh. Were you going to add something?

Josh: I think maybe Tommy and Luis talked to each other about the plan, the Arnold plan, without me. It felt like I was there because I lived next to the park and I could get the beer. It felt like they were a lot more comfortable with the plan and that night in general, so, I don't know, maybe they talked about it before without me.

Murtagh: Do you think they were hiding something from you or not telling you something?

Josh: No, I don't know. I don't think so. I mean, I don't think Luis knows anything more than I do about what happened to Tommy. I'm not saying that at all. All summer, I was kind of on the outs. It didn't used to be like that.

Murtagh: What were Luis and Tommy talking about that night on the rock?

Josh: They talked about zombies. I wasn't really listening. I was in my own head. I wanted to go home. I was going to call my parents. Even with Arnold knowing where I lived and like stalking my house the night before I really was going to call my parents and have them come get us or call the police. I made up my mind that this was stupid and we were going to get hurt, but before I could call them Tommy was standing over the split and they stopped talking. Luis was saying what is it? What is it? And Tommy. Tommy . . .

Murtagh: It's okay, Josh. You can take a moment.

Murtagh: Had you and Tommy discussed the plan to meet Arnold in Borderland by yourselves, without Josh?

Luis: No, ma'am. Definitely not. After we got back from Arnold's apartment I tried calling Tommy that night and then the next morning but he didn't want to talk about anything. I was thinking that he and Josh were talking about it because they've been friends since kindergarten.

Murtagh: The night you were all in the park, what were you and Tommy talking to each other about right before he ran off into the woods?

Luis: He was trying to be normal, you know? He told us about a new Minecraft house he built. He asked me and Josh if we were working on anything. We said no. Then I think he made some kind of joke about zombies when Josh asked about the jackknife again. Then he started talking more about zombies. He said what if there are different kinds of zombies. And I said like fast or slow? Tommy said no, and said he was thinking more like no two zombies were the same. I made a joke about zombie snowflakes. Tommy said what if every zombie was different based on the personality of who you were. I said something about nice people being nice zombies, and vegetarian zombies would eat like lettuce heads. I was going to ask Tommy if we should just go home and then Tommy started in on zombies again. And all this I remember because I thought he was trying to tell us something.

Murtagh: What do you think he was trying to tell you?

Luis: I'm not sure, ma'am. Like maybe he knew then he was going to run off by himself, without us, that it was his real plan all along.

Murtagh: What else did he say?

Luis: He said maybe it was more like zombie-you would be totally opposite your personality, or the secret side of who you were, the you you kept in your head and the worst part was that you were still in there and watching the zombie-you doing all the terrible things and you couldn't stop it from happening, like at Arnold's apartment. He said that. And I didn't know what to say. I think that was our last chance. Maybe. I think I blew it right there, ma'am. If I said let's leave, Josh totally would've said yeah and maybe Tommy would've left too, and as scared as we were, call the police. Or maybe he would've stayed there by himself anyway and told us to leave. So, I don't know. We just kept going. Seems so crazy now, even to me, especially to me, like it wasn't us, wasn't ever us, but we just kept going. Like Tommy said about those zombie-yous. We were the zombie-yous.

Rooney: Tommy sent me some messages asking me to meet them out at Devil's Rock in the middle of the night. Nothing good happens in the middle of the night, right? I didn't know what was what. I was so confused about my uncle. I didn't want to be home anymore. I couldn't help my uncle. What they did to him, it broke something inside me. And I wasn't thinking too straight. Seeing what they did brought everything back that had happened to me when I was younger with Mom and then with the Rev. All that awful shit came back, you know? I'm not telling you so you feel sorry for me, I'm telling you because it's the truth. Okay? So I went for a walk. That's what I did. A long one. I like to walk. Only thing that clears out my head when it's all messy. Gets me in trouble some-times too, I know. A bunch of my bull-shit trumped-up home invasion arrests were me walking around in neighbor-hoods a guy like me wasn't supposed to be in, that's all it was, walking, cutting through some yards and stuff. I was just walking, walking, and then I walked all the way to the park. It's not as far as you think. Blinked my eyes, took a couple steps, and poof I was there. Maybe I stepped into one of them wormholes. Me taking a walk and then finding myself at Borderland, right? I was there anyway, so I decided that yeah I would go meet them at Devil's Rock. That's what we called it. Our rock. I knew it might be dangerous with the three of them and only me, but I was going to try to talk some sense into them, tell them what they did was wrong, so wrong, and that they had to fix it, make it better. I was going to follow them home if I had to, and make them call for police, for help.

Josh: Tommy called out Arnold's name one more time and asked if we saw something. He pointed like crazy out into the middle of the woods and not along the trail. I don't think Luis could see anything.

Murtagh: But you did see something?

Josh: (inaudible)

Murtagh: Josh? Did you see something?

Josh: No. Maybe. I'm not sure. It's weird. I think I did. A little later.

Luis: He looked at us and said, "You guys don't see that?" Then he scrambled down off the rock so fast. Like he fell off and slid down the side. He must've scraped up his arms and legs but he landed hard and didn't stop, and he ran off the trail and into the woods. I climbed down and called after him. I couldn't see him but heard all kinds of like shaking crashing branches, and it was darker down at the bottom of the rock, couldn't really see into the woods, and Tommy wasn't saying anything. I shouted out Tommy's name. I didn't know what was happening. Then Tommy, I don't know, started moaning. It was so low and lasted so long and then started rising and it . . . it was . . . It was the worst sound I ever heard.

Murtagh: It's okay, Luis. You can continue when you're ready.

Luis: And then he was screaming. Full on screaming. And he called out to me and Josh. We were yelling at him to come back and I tried to get my phone out, turn on the flashlight so he could see me better but my phone was already dead. I stayed on the path and shouted for Tommy and the sounds came toward me, and Josh was somewhere behind me, I think. Then Tommy came stumbling out of the woods and fell | onto his knees. He was looking all around and he said, "Did you see it? It came through here, didn't it? You had to see it." But I didn't see anything.

Josh: I saw it. Right before Tommy came crashing out of the woods I saw someone else come out first and go down the path, running away from us and the rock, toward our right.

Murtagh: So you saw Arnold come out of the woods first and then Tommy came out after him? Are you saying that Tommy was chasing Arnold?

Josh: No, no. I didn't see Arnold. I told you I never saw him. Not in the park that night, anyway. I know it's weird and confusing, but right before Tommy fell out onto the path, I thought I saw Tommy come out. So I'm saying that first person I saw come out of the woods, or thought I saw, was Tommy.

Murtagh: Why did you think it was Tommy and not Arnold?

Josh: It looked like Tommy, running away. It was so dark and I didn't see a face or features or anything like that, but it had Tommy's shape. Tall, skinny, and it moved like him. It's hard to describe how Tommy moves, but I know him when I see him. So when Tommy fell out onto the path after, I was expecting Arnold because I'd already seen Tommy running away. I figured Tommy was running away because Arnold was chasing him. I'd even picked up a rock and was ready to throw it at Arnold. But it was Tommy, and I didn't know what happened, how it could be him right there in front of me when I already saw him running away. When I looked back down the path what I saw was gone.

Murtagh: Did you tell Tommy what you saw?

Josh: Yeah. Tommy wanted to know what we saw and Luis was yelling that he didn't see anything. I ran over and helped Tommy get up. Then I told him that I saw something and I thought it was him. I actually said that. Tommy made like a groaning sound and started shaking his head no and talking real fast to himself, under his breath. Couldn't really make anything out at first.

Luis: I asked him over and over what he saw, was it Arnold? He said it wasn't Arnold, that it definitely wasn't Arnold, but Tommy was sure that he was there, in the park. He said, "I know he's here," more than a couple times. That's exactly what he said, I swear. Swear to God that's what he said. He said it wasn't Arnold but he's here. And then he was saying oh my God a lot and looking around everywhere.

Josh: Tommy looked at Luis and then at me. Luis went to pick up his walking stick, I think, and then Tommy stood and got real close, his face right in my face, and he whispered to me, "You saw me come out?" And I said, "I saw you," because that's what I thought I saw. And then he said real fast, so fast, "I saw me too. It was me, it was me. God, it was me it was me" and he stopped. I remember him stopping there and then saying, "You saw it, too? It looked dead. Did you see the eyes? There was something over its fucking eyes." I was getting upset and whispering back that he couldn't have seen himself, and then Tommy started groaning and crying.

Luis: Josh was helping Tommy up and I went to find my walking stick, just in case I needed to use it like, I don't know, a bat or something, if Arnold came by. So I don't know. I didn't hear Tommy say, like words. Why, did Josh say he heard Tommy say something?

Rooney: There was a whole bunch of yelling echoing through the park, like the woods was alive and dangerous, ready to attack, then it stopped. I have to tell you it was kind of scary, being out there all alone with those three somewhere waiting for me, or more than those three, maybe, I didn't know, sounded like more than three kids yelling, like an army, but I didn't stop and didn't go away. I had to keep going. I knew what they were going to try to do to me. I knew it but I didn't want to believe it. I thought I could get to them, convince them what was right, you know. So I kept going, kept walking, and I was on the main trail. When the yelling stopped I turned onto, what is it, the Northwest Trail, I think, and got up over the first hill, it was hard to see, just outlines, and darks that got darker, and that's when Tommy came running at me. He was by himself. I could see him. And he had a knife in his hand.

Luis: I was trying to calm Tommy down and tell him that it was okay and he only thought he saw something and scared himself. Tommy did calm down and stopped crying and yelling, and he said, "Don't follow me." He said it real quiet.

Josh: "Don't follow me. No matter what. I don't want you guys to get hurt."

Luis: I don't know what Tommy saw or what he thought he saw in the woods. And I don't know how or why he knew Arnold was there, if Arnold was even there at all, right, because I never saw Arnold that night. I didn't. I know Josh never saw him either. When we're done, done talking, will you tell me if Arnold was actually there and what happened to Tommy?

Murtagh: Tommy had told you not to follow him, is that correct?

Luis: Yes, ma'am. I was totally freaked out and kept saying, "Let's go, let's go home, come on, let's go." We tried to stop him. I swear we did. We were ready to drag him out of there. We were telling him to come home with us. He told us, and he was like so calm now, to stay at the rock or we could go back and wait for him at Josh's house and he promised us that he would come back. He did. He promised us he'd be back but only after taking care of everything. Then he laughed a little. I swear he did, and then he said something really crazy about him being a real seer now and that it had to happen this way. I told him to shut up and stop it and swore at him, called him a hardo and everything, trying to get him to listen and leave with us.

Murtagh: Did he say anything else?

Josh: He kept backing up. Told us not to tell anyone anything until after he came back, and then he said something quiet like he was embarrassed. I couldn't hear what he said. I'm sorry I didn't hear him. I'm so sorry.

Luis: No, ma'am. He did not have his knife out. He turned and sprinted down the path away from us and I tried to grab him but I knocked into Josh and he fell and I tripped over him, on top of him. We got up and ran after but he was way too fast for us, even if he didn't have that head start, Tommy's too fast. We weren't going to catch him. We lost him.

Rooney: Once he saw me, Tommy came charging right down the path with that knife raised over his head like he was a warrior or something. Never seen anyone look like that, totally possessed. It wasn't Tommy. It was and it wasn't. Not the Tommy I knew or thought I knew. And after what he and his friends did to the Rev I was scared so I turned and ran away. There was nothing I could do, no talking to him. And I could hear Luis and Josh somewhere behind him yelling too, so I ran. Just put my head down and ran.

Murtagh: Josh?

Josh: I said me and Luis stayed together. We didn't split up. We went down the path a little bit. We called for Tommy. It was so dark away from the rock and under the trees. I used my phone as a flashlight until the battery died. Luis's was already dead. Couldn't see much more than the path. We couldn't see Tommy. Couldn't even hear him or anything. We kept calling out to him.

Murtagh: You mean the Pond Walk?
Luis: Yes, ma'am. We didn't get very far. We didn't know what to do. We called out to Tommy and we stood there and listened, heard nothing.

Rooney: Like I said, seeing what they did to the Rev and everything else had my head all a mess. But it was like we ran all night, all night, and we were in this great and terrible story or legend, a really old one, you know? We kept running. We were, like what, like a stream or a river through the woods, carving out our own path, and it was epic. We would always be running. We would never stop and that was the story, and it's so hard to remember how it happened but it flipped, you know, it flipped, me and Tommy switching spots. Tommy wasn't chasing me anymore. I was chasing him. We never said anything. No names. We were both seers. We knew it had to be how it had to be. Just the running and it was beautiful, you know, and then we were off the trails and he ran into one of the ponds.
Murtagh: Which one?
Rooney: Doesn't matter. We were deep in

the park. He ran into one of them, he ran into all of them. I followed him in. The muck grabbed my shoes and lily pads wrapped around my legs and arms like they were alive, and I thought that was part of his plan, to suck me into a trap. None of the weeds seemed to bother Tommy, he weaved through all that shit into deeper water. It was so easy for him I thought he was a ghost, and it all passed through him. And he swam out and away. The kid's a great swimmer, swimming in the moonlight, and I thought it was going to be the last thing I'd ever see, but the muck and weeds let me go, and you know, it was a test, a goddamn test, and I passed. I'd done nothing wrong, I wasn't wrong. I was a good person, and I was allowed to keep going.

Josh: After waiting for a long time on that stupid path we walked back to Devil's Rock. We thought we heard someone walking in the woods around us and hoped that maybe Tommy calmed down and doubled back to the rock. I ran ahead of Luis and got there first. I looked inside the split. I looked inside.

Murtagh: Josh? What did you see?

Josh: Tommy wasn't there. I know he

wasn't. I looked too quick. I thought I saw him sitting there all hunched up, like he was hiding. But he wasn't there. I went inside the split to make sure.

Luis: Josh was kind of freaking out crying and talking out loud to Tommy, like he was there and he kept asking why would you leave us, then don't leave, don't leave and we're still here. I made Josh climb up the rock with me so maybe, I don't know, we could see him or see whatever from up there. Josh sat up against the tree still saying that stuff over and over and I told him to be quiet because I couldn't hear anything but it didn't matter. There was nothing we could do there anymore. Our phones were dead and we'd been there for hours, it had to be hours.

Rooney: Tommy swam all the way to this island and I don't know if it was there when we first started swimming, and I mean that like I didn't see it there when we hit the water and then boom it was huge, fucking looming, you know, but even though I didn't see it there at first I knew it would be there so it was there. You get me? Tommy climbed up onto the shore, wormed through bushes, and I climbed up after him, got all scratched up and out of breath but it didn't matter, I knew this was the end. I was going to tell Tommy that I knew it was the end and that I knew that he knew it too. It's why we led each other there. Away from the shore there was a clearing and some paths, paths that have always been there, they were there for us, to lead us where we needed to go, and I couldn't see Tommy but I started following the path, believing in it, and he jumped out at me with his knife and I twisted away at the last second, but he got me good on my arm, quick little slash, and I rolled away from him and I was trying to protect myself. I never wanted to ever hurt anyone, even my bastard uncle. That's not me, never been me. I don't hurt people. I don't, but I could hear him behind me and Tommy was laughing like they were all laughing when they killed the Rev, and laughing at me like they always did. I had a rock in my head and then I had a rock in my hand. I'd fallen right next to it. There was no plan. I picked up the rock, and I only wanted to stop him, get him to listen, and I hit him in the head with it. I swung wild, not aiming for a spot, not even seeing where I would hit, more just trying to get him to back off, trying to protect myself, and I hit him in the head and he dropped his knife and stumbled backward and fell, landed sitting up. He looked at me. I told him I was sorry and I was sorry. Tommy's like a brother, a real brother to me, the only one who understands me and what I could see, and I would never do anything on purpose to hurt him. I told him too, right there, and it was true. I said you're my brother. We were alone on an island and I told him that. I was crying it felt so good to say it to him. But Tommy, I think Tommy was real mad at me because he wouldn't talk to me. Didn't say anything.

Luis: We were there awhile, ma'am. I'm not sure how long but I told Josh that we should go back to his house and maybe Tommy would be there. Tommy had told us to go home and he promised he would meet us there. So that's what we did. We went back to the house and, you know, he wasn't there. Josh's mom was out on the porch waiting for us.

Rooney: Tommy got up, holding his head, and I told him I was sorry again and again. He got up and slowly walked away. I reached out and grabbed his shoulder. He shook me off, didn't try to do anything to me again, and I begged him to say something to me but he didn't, didn't even look at me. He kept walking and followed the paths to the middle of the island. There was this tiny clearing and there's a small boulder formation there, three boulders almost pushed together, and he sat between them and closed his eyes. I kept trying to talk and he wouldn't say anything back. He wasn't being fair to me. I got mad, I'm sorry, I did, even though he's my brother, brothers get mad and fight sometimes, I said stuff I wish I didn't say and I left him. I left him there and I swam back to shore and started walking again thinking I would never stop walking, walk the earth, right, we were those brothers in the Bible the Rev made me read all the time and memorize when I was little and I walked and would always walk, and I ended up on those granite trails toward the quarry and the rocks opened up for me because I was in the right place and I crawled inside a deep cave, down in the dark, and at first I thought it was a terrible place like all the other terrible places people make me live in and that I belonged there. But you know what? It wasn't terrible. It was quiet and so dark I couldn't see myself and that was okay and I stayed there for days and days and days and that's how it was supposed to be.

Josh: Mom didn't even wait for us to get inside before yelling at me that I was grounded. She'd tried to text me and I pulled my phone out to show her it was out of battery. She yelled some more and even yelled at Luis too. Then she stopped yelling and asked where was Tommy.

Luis: We had no real plan at that point, ma'am. Really we didn't. We walked back to his house, and we didn't talk about what we were going to do or say when we got back. We were hoping that Tommy would be there waiting for us. That's all I could think about because he'd run off and neither of us had seen Arnold. I know I was thinking and hoping that Arnold wasn't there and Tommy had freaked out, and that he'd go back to Josh's house once he didn't find Arnold. Then we got to the house and Josh's mom was yelling at us, and she asked where Tommy was. Josh said, "I don't know. He ran off into the woods."

Murtagh: Can you repeat what you said to your mom?

Josh: Yes. "I don't know, Mom. He just ran into the woods." I answered her question and I answered it truthfully. I didn't know what else to say or do. So that's all I said and it was the truth. Everything started happening from there. Then the next night after Tommy ran off, Arnold was outside my bedroom window again. I told Luis about it. Right away. That was enough for me and him right there.

Murtagh: What do you mean by "enough for me and him"?

Rooney: I told you I did not go back to the apartment and that I was at the park, in the quarry caves. My caves. I was hungry and thirsty but I didn't care, because the caves were mine and beautiful and I didn't have to look at myself or anything else inside them. I slept during the day and no one ever came by and bothered me. I walked around the park at night and sometimes I walked to other places too. I won't deny that. In the caves I was all right, but outside? I wasn't right. I was all messed up. I wasn't myself.

Luis: Josh's mom made him call Tommy's mother to ask if Tommy went home. I wanted to believe that he went home on his own, too, but he wasn't there. We weren't lying then. Tommy had got up and run into the woods all by himself. That's what happened. And I didn't know what to think. Maybe Tommy's mom would call the police and they would find Tommy was okay and hopefully find him without Arnold in the park. That night I couldn't help but think what if Tommy found Arnold and killed him or something and then ran away himself, and I didn't want Tommy to get in trouble. I knew it wasn't likely, but I was so afraid of everything. I can't say it any better than I didn't know what to do so I did nothing. Then later, when Josh said Arnold was standing outside his window at night I knew nothing was okay, but the longer Tommy was gone and the longer we went without saying more it was like we couldn't say anything.

Josh: I know I'm not explaining this well. We didn't know Arnold's uncle was dead, and we didn't know if Arnold was actually in the park that night, and I still don't. You haven't told me. We were hoping that Tommy would come back eventually. And when they didn't find him in the park we thought there was a chance he couldn't handle what we'd done at Arnold's place and ran away. Tommy is a different kind of kid and is always thinking in his own Tommy way, you know, so we thought anything was possible. And we were afraid. That's really it. We were both afraid. Me and Luis spent all this time after together and it was like we were waiting for our turn to go away and disappear.

Rooney: Isn't it so silly? The park was like a shared bedroom, and me and Tommy had made an imaginary line. You stay on your side and I'll stay on my side. I wanted to talk to him, to make up, to go back to how we were all summer long, but I didn't know how to do that. I'm not very good at stuff like that, never have been, and that's not my fault. I didn't have brothers, real brothers, and I walked around at night trying to figure out what to do and say but I stayed away from his island, made sure he had his space, and then I figured out what I needed to do. I'd get him his coin back. I gave him a hobo nickel, a special one, one that I made just for him. I used to practice making them when I ran away as a kid, stayed in shelters, awful places. Terrible places. So sick of terrible places, you know, no one deserves to live in terrible places, they don't and I know I've done bad stuff but no one deserves terrible places. It's not fair and it's not our fault sometimes, and that was it right there, that was what I was going to tell Tommy, and that's why I went to his house to find the coin. His house isn't a huge McMansion. It's a regular kind of house and I loved that about it. Been there a few times, yeah. I watched the house for a little while and his sister walked out the front door, went out back, got on her bike and took off. I wasn't expecting that, but then I knew she'd be gone for a bit and that's when I went inside. I didn't go inside before because I didn't want to make Tommy even more mad, but it was good. It was okay. I went into his room and it was like he was in there. All his stuff, I wanted to go through it, but I had to focus. That wouldn't have been right. I looked for the coin I gave him but couldn't find it. I did find a few old pennies on his bureau and took those thinking that it's the thought that counts, right? That's what people say about giving gifts, and this was a gift, a peace offering, and I made my way back to his island in the park and it took me forever to find it because it's not easy to find, not obvious. I had to be patient, but I found it and swam out there. It wasn't like the first time we were there. It was harder to see, cloudy, and the water level had gone down because it hadn't rained in a while. He must've heard me struggling to get out there, because he was sitting where I'd left him and was still giving me the silent treatment. He wasn't going to forgive me, and that, that was the worst feeling right there. I knew it was over and that we weren't brothers anymore.

Murtagh: What did you do next, Rooney?

Rooney: I gave him the pennies and then I left his island. I left. That's where he wants to be so I left him there and walked back to the apartment that night. I wanted to stay in the caves but I was feeling guilty about my uncle, figured I should check in on him, yeah, and, of course be there for when you guys showed up so I could explain everything. I told you I knew you were going to be there, right? I did. Tommy had the right idea, I think, to go away, disappear. I know I told you all this and everything, but maybe you're better off leaving him alone. Tommy will come back when he wants to come back.

A light knock. "Hello, Elizabeth?"

Allison enters the room, sidestepping the door, letting it swing gently shut behind her. She is dressed in clothes she was not wearing earlier that evening; her tan suit is now a blue blazer and jeans. Allison must be able to read the look of confusion on Elizabeth's face and says, "Yeah, I changed. You've been here for a while, and you've been busy."

Elizabeth separated the three transcribed statements and spread them out into neat rows and columns covering the entire table. The pages are out of order, or not in their original order. Elizabeth spent the night cataloguing, mapping, and piecing together the pages to where she thought they fit. The table is a matrix that can be read horizontally or vertically and in any order a reader may choose, and the end is always the same. Elizabeth is not done with her rearranging, however, as she hopes to find a reading with a different ending. She is not ready to hear whatever it is Allison has to say.

Elizabeth says, "I can put everything back the way it was, if you need me to. It's not so hopelessly out of order. Here, let me do that. I hope it's okay that I, uh, did this." She stands up and her leg and back muscles rebel against unbending. She picks up her cell phone off the table. Maybe now's the time to check and respond to all of Kate's messages.

"That's not necessary, Elizabeth. We can take care of that." Allison walks into the room, her flats clack on the linoleum. She stands across the table from Elizabeth, buttons her blazer, the one gold button, folds her hands in front, then lets them hang. "I'm so sorry, Elizabeth. We found your son's body at Borderland. We found him on one of the pond islands."

Elizabeth spent so much time during of her previous days and nights imagining the worst, imagining this moment—being told Tommy was dead. She constructed countless permutations in settings: she sat at the kitchen table with Kate and Janice when the phone rang; she was in her living room serving police officers coffee; Allison brought her to Josh's house or to a stranger's house in a suburb or a farm or in a big city or to a ditch on a lonely country road; or she was left at a podium at a press conference. Within the framework of those settings and scenarios she imagined all manner of delivery in which they inform her Tommy was dead: confident, uncaring, empathic, awkward, stuttering, commiserative, cold and quick. Her imaginary response was always the same. There would be crying followed by unhinged screaming and the destroying of everything within her reach. She smashed dishes and mugs and coffeepots and windows and windshields and microphones and snapped chair legs and punched holes in plaster and punched faces, so many faces, and they would deserve it even if they didn't. She imagined a fire inside of her heroically immolating all and everything and, even if for one feckless moment, the world would be made to feel the unfairness, meaning-lessness, horror, and impenetrable sadness.

Now that it's been said, finally and definitively declared that Tommy is dead, there is no flame inside of her, not anymore. Elizabeth does not wipe the tabletop clear of its pages, flip the table, throw a chair at the Plexiglas windows. She sits down and stacks the statement pages in a neat pile as though gathering ancient and brittle documents. "Is Tommy here?" she asks.

"No. He's on his way to the state coroner's."

Elizabeth waits for Allison to say more but she doesn't. She wants to ask who will be there with Tommy, will they stay with him until she can see him.

Allison: "Can I get you—"

Elizabeth interrupts and asks, "What do you think Tommy and Josh saw in the woods?" She points at the statement pages. "Tommy saw something and ran into the woods, and then Josh said he thought he saw Tommy running away down the path. What did they see?"

"I can't really speculate—"

"Allison. I'm asking you. I need you to tell me what you think."

"Tommy probably saw Rooney hiding in the woods and Josh saw Rooney running away. It's possible they didn't see anything, too. Their eyes might have been playing tricks on them, as it was so dark and they'd been drinking a little, and how on edge they must've been, with everything going on, with what they were planning."

Elizabeth considers arm-swiping the table clear of pages after all, to see if it makes her feel better, feel anything. Instead she gathers a few more pages and adds them to the stacked pile. She says, "Tommy said he saw himself. Josh says that here. On this page." Elizabeth plucks the page off the table and holds it up. "He says that Tommy saw himself. I believe Josh and Tommy."

Allison doesn't say anything.

"Tommy's body—" Elizabeth pauses for a deep breath. "I don't know if I want to know."

"We don't have to do this now, Elizabeth. Let me take you home, so you can be with Kate and your mom, and—"

"No, not yet. First tell me. You have to tell me. What happened to Tommy's eyes? They had pennies over them or in them, right? Did you find him with pennies over his eyes?" Elizabeth fights back tears and shuffles through pages roughly, holding up the last part of Rooney's statement/confession. "Those pennies, those fucking gifts Arnold wanted to give Tommy. He did give them to him, right?" Elizabeth screams and does finally give in to the urge and swipes the table clean, the pages curl and drift to the floor.

Allison looks at Elizabeth almost comically wide-eyed and her mouth open. "Yes—Jesus. How'd you . . . Did you figure that out from the statements?"

Elizabeth says, "This is going to sound—" She stops and shakes her head. She doesn't care how it sounds. She's going to say it and say it all without stopping. "The night after Tommy didn't come back home, and it was late, real late, and dark, and

I couldn't sleep, and I came out of the bathroom, and I saw Tommy between the chair and end table in my bedroom. He was crouched there like he was hiding. It was Tommy but it wasn't. It was like his living shadow or something. I couldn't see his face, not at first, but it was him. I saw him, felt him, could even smell him. That's the part I still can't get over. I could smell him, Allison. Then I went over to him, tried to touch him, but he was gone. But right before he disappeared, I saw his face. Or *a* face. And it was like a flash, so quick, I wasn't sure what I saw initially, or I knew and I didn't want to accept what I saw. Still I was so desperate to see him again, I spent the next days and nights walking around the house always looking for him and thinking sometimes I almost did. I got the camera because I was trying to see him again, see if he was really there. And I did see him again, or I did see what I saw in my bedroom when we found that diary page with the drawing. That awful goddamn picture he drew that fucking got passed around online and everywhere. That was the face I saw in my bedroom. It was Tommy's face all swollen and beat up. It was his dead face with those pennies on his eyes. That's what I saw in my bedroom. And I think Tommy saw it too. He fucking saw his own dead self there out in the woods and then he ran away, and oh, God, he must've been so scared, Allison. My poor baby . . ."

Allison walks around the table and puts an arm around Elizabeth's shoulders.

Elizabeth is crying now, the kind of tears that debilitate the rest of your body. Movement is impossible, as there's only the crying and pieces of yourself leaking away, never to be retrieved. She says, "My Tommy's been alone on that island all this time and he'll be alone forever."

Elizabeth texts Kate and Janice: *Sorry I've been here so long. I'm on my way home.*

On the walk out of the station, to the parking lot, and during the ride to her house they don't talk. Tomorrow will be for discussion and the official identification of Tommy's body, and Elizabeth will insist upon seeing his actual body and not just photographs, and she will look at those too, and as one of her final and most important acts as his mother she will bear witness to what happened. She won't flinch from the smell of his rotting body and she won't turn away from his bloated and destroyed face, a face with two pennies for eyes, a face she once saw late at night in her bedroom and then again on a piece of paper. Elizabeth will be told that Rooney pressed the pennies into Tommy's eyes postmortem, as though that makes it better. She will ask Allison if she thinks the picture Tommy drew looks like his body and she will ask three times before Allison finally answers with "It does." There will be days ahead where Elizabeth will be able to remember Tommy for the beautiful boy he was and not what happened to him. But there will be days where she can't think of anything else but his body and his ruined face and life, and then spiral into a blow-by-blow reimagining of how he got to be that way, and the uncanny picture he drew, and what it was Tommy saw that night in Borderland.

Allison pulls into Elizabeth's driveway, as far up as she can go, and parks next to Janice's car. The headlights flood her backyard. Busy moths and gnats float in the electric light above the tall and sagging grass. She shuts the car off, the spotlight disappears, and the secret nocturnal life of the backyard retreats into darkness again.

Elizabeth opens her door, careful not to ding Janice's car. There are two news vans parked at the edge of the front lawn. Allison puts herself between Elizabeth and the news crews as they walk to the front door. Shouted questions echo in the emptiness of the sleeping neighborhood.

"Don't listen to them. Keep on walking. You're doing fine. You're a strong, amazing person, Elizabeth, truly, and Kate is lucky to have you. . . ." Allison drones on in a low, tremulous voice that reflects a lack of confidence, anger, or discomfort, Elizabeth isn't sure which. How Allison sounds registers with her, though, and she is grateful.

On the darkened front stoop Elizabeth takes Allison's hand, squeezes it, says, "Thank you," and then opens the door. It's unlocked.

Inside. All of the lights are on in the kitchen and the living room and the main hallway and Elizabeth will later find the bathroom and bedroom lights, desk and reading lamps included, are all on, too. The house is as bright as it can be and everything is still.

Janice and Kate stand together in the living room, in front of the couch but not so close that they can sit down without having to take a few steps backward. Neither is in her pajamas or nightclothes. They both are wearing jeans and a sweatshirt; Kate's is thin and green, the hood missing its drawstring, and Janice's is a faded navy blue, hoodless, and too long in the sleeve. They are holding hands and they are already crying.

Elizabeth and Kate and the House and the Notes

June 20, 7 p.m. of the day before the longest day of the year.

The slowly setting sun hovers over the treetops across the street. Elizabeth sits on the front stairs, drinking a bottle of warm water (she'd left it in the car this afternoon), and talking to her mother on her cell phone. It's almost ten full months after the discovery of Tommy's body.

Elizabeth: "It was hard to listen to. It's all hard to listen to."

Janice: "I'm sorry I couldn't be there. It'll only get harder."

"Yeah. It will. Anyway, they started late, went through some procedural BS, and then it was lunch, and after a long lunch the defense interviewed expert witnesses and they talked about Rooney's childhood and what happened to him when he was a teen and that kind of stuff."

"Waste of time and money. He's a monster."

"Mom . . ."

"What? He's not a monster?"

The prosecution spent the previous week plus presenting the case that Rooney was indeed a monster, a sane monster—a manipulative, highly intelligent sociopath of sound mind who understood what he was doing and understood the consequences of his actions.

Elizabeth: "No, no, he is. But, I don't know, at the same time, he's not."

"Okay, Elizabeth, but—"

"Can I give you the quick recap, Mom?"

"Yes, of course."

Eight days into Rooney's trial and sharing the recap is her way of trying to understand why Tommy was drawn to him, would become friends with him, and try to see what it was he saw.

Elizabeth: "They talked about his criminal record and all those break-ins but he never took anything, or never took anything of big value. He even broke into the mayor's house in North Adams. He didn't take anything but just stood there, watching the mayor and his wife sleeping."

"Jesus."

"I know. They talked about how those break-ins, or they called them home invasions because people were home, should've been a big warning sign that even though he hadn't done anything violent yet, he was capable of it and was on that path. The last expert witness was a child psychiatrist, and she said that Rooney claimed he was sexually abused by strangers who would come and go in his mom's apartment. He'd tell his meth-head mom about it, and she would then send him to the church youth group his uncle led, the kind of group that paints the abused as tempters and sinners."

"She said that?"

"No, I'm saying that. But that's what she was implying. They showed the court some of the hellfire-and-brimstone kind of literature from those youth groups. Just awful stuff. And Rooney was part of those groups for years, and they would travel around to other churches and carnivals. Rooney tried to commit suicide twice before he was even fifteen, and his mom was arrested and the court took him away from his mother. His uncle took him then, but that was short-lived. His uncle was forced out of his parish—well, not his parish; his uncle's evangelical, not Catholic or whatever—but you get the idea. He was taking money from people he claimed he could heal or tell their future. Kind of like how Rooney told the boys he was a seer. Anyway, he got booted. Rooney was on his own for a little bit, bounced around foster homes for a few years, and that's when he started breaking into places, and he eventually went back to live with his uncle, who had relocated to Brockton. And I don't know. I don't know why I need to tell you any of this. It doesn't change anything."

"You don't have to go and listen to all that."

"Yes I do. I want to be there and hear it all. I do. Everything they have to say and show. But then after, I can't keep it all inside. I need to get it all out of me."

"I understand, totally, dear. You can tell me anything."

"I'm calling it psychological bulimia. That's the name of my band."

Janice laughs politely, as did Elizabeth's therapist when she made the same joke earlier in the week.

Elizabeth says, "I sat in the back today. As far back as I could go. Wore my sunglasses, too, which made it a little better. Spent most of the time looking at the back of Rooney's head, waiting for him to turn around and look at me, but not wanting him to. He's just a kid, Mom. It's all so fucked. Or I look at the back of Josh's and Luis's heads, their parents, sitting there in suits. It's all fucked. Totally fucked. And, I don't know. I should go. I think I heard Kate shut the vacuum off."

"I'm sorry you were there by yourself today, but I'll be there tomorrow, I promise, and we can talk more if you like."

"Mom, you really don't need to be down here until after the closing, which is at 2 p.m. The trial is taking the next two days off, making a long weekend of it, apparently."

"Okay. Text me the address of the new place, I'm sorry I misplaced it already, and I'll meet you over there after the closing."

"Great. Will do. Thanks. I love you, Mom."

"I love you, too. Tell Kate I love her."

"I will."

Elizabeth walks into the empty house. Half of their stuff is packed on a moving truck and the other half thrown out or donated. Kate didn't want to throw out anything. She even wanted to keep the nasty rug from the living room. Elizabeth was ruthless in her packing efficiency and mandates of what was tossed and what would be saved. It was the only way she could get through this move without screaming. When they cleared out Tommy's room Elizabeth stoically fought to remain on task while Kate picked at the piles of stuff, said, "I'm keeping this," and flittered in and out of the room like a bird gathering random scraps for a nest.

The Sandersons are downsizing to a two-bedroom condo in a newly built complex on the southwest side of Ames, close to the Mansfield border. There are ten units in total, and the association has a pool, a duck pond, and a tennis court. Against Elizabeth's better judgment, she acquiesced to Kate and agreed to stay in Ames. Kate made it clear that she did not want to move to a different town and that she wanted to continue to go to the Ames middle school and be with her friends. Given the impossible circumstances, sixth grade for Kate was a miraculous success both academically and socially. But at that school the sixth graders are kept separate, secret, and safe from the seventh and eighth graders. In September, she's to be thrown in the deep end of that water. There will be sharks. Elizabeth hopes that the familiar faces will continue to rally and support her.

She fears the emotional baggage of what has become the town tragedy, the town scandal, the town lore, and she fears the rumors and whispers will continue to grow in volume and power, adding yet another ring to the hell that is middle school. Kate has already told her some of the rumors she's heard, including the most popular one: Tommy was a human sacrifice (some say a willing sacrifice) in a satanic ceremony and that the shadowman still walks the park at night. There's a shadowman Twitter hashtag that gets multiple entries per day, spiking during weekend parties. The high school kids drink and then swim out to the island with spray paint and permanent markers and they write notes and draw symbols on the rock pile where Tommy's body was found and they post their pictures of them standing next to the rocks or crouching down between them to Instagram and there was one kid who had a picture of him writing "Satins Rock" go viral and result in his arrest. Kate reports it all to Elizabeth.

Elizabeth asks, "How's it going in here?"

Kate sweeps the empty living room floor. To

start this summer, she's gone all blue with her hair and makes noises about keeping it for the fall, too. Her last baby tooth fell out in February. She'll need braces at some point with her upper jaw canines poking out higher in her gumline than the rest of the crowd of teeth. She can smile this thin, tight smile that shows off the whites of those canines. She calls it her vampire smile. In the last ten months her weight has fluctuated wildly and she has grown an inch and a half, getting her to five foot one. She's very proud of the one.

Kate says, "Just about done."

"Don't go too crazy. Doesn't have to be spotless. They're going to gut the place anyway. I heard them talking about knocking down walls, new floor in the kitchen, new paint, the works."

"I really want to see what it looks like when they're done. Do you think they'll let us come see the place when they're done?"

"I don't know. That might be kind of weird for them, don't you think?"

"Why? We didn't do anything wrong."

Kate's therapist made it clear to Elizabeth that while she should of course continue to parent, set limitations, and say no to Kate as she sees fit, she does need to validate Kate's emotions and thoughts throughout the grieving process. Kate has really connected with Dr. Jennifer Levesque, often quoting her advice and aphorisms. Kate has not shut down, gone near catatonic, as Elizabeth had feared she would, and as Elizabeth did herself for the first month after Tommy's death. Kate has instead become an open book, unfiltered and raw in saying what she's thinking, feeling. While Janice gamely struggles with Kate's emotional honesty, the newly unfettered, unedited version of Kate has saved Elizabeth. Someday, maybe soon, she will tell Kate that she has saved her. Elizabeth's own therapist doesn't want her to put that kind of pressure on Kate; Kate shouldn't have the burden of being her mother's strength in addition to everything else she's dealing with. So maybe she won't tell her. But, selfishly, Elizabeth wants to, because she doesn't know how long this sometimes painfully open level of communication with her daughter will last. She irrationally hopes that it will last forever.

Elizabeth: "I will ask them tomorrow at the closing."

"I think they'll say yes. The wife likes me."

"What about the husband?"

"He thinks we're creepy and sad."

Elizabeth laughs. "You know this how?"

"Because we are creepy and sad?" Kate smiles and rolls her eyes, so clearly sarcastic, commiserative, and directed at the couple buying their house, Elizabeth guffaws and snorts.

Elizabeth says, "I'm only creepy when I snort-laugh."

Her amazing daughter seems so confident and adult now, but she's still only twelve and won't be thirteen for another four months. Elizabeth's new worry on the ever-expanding list of worries is that Kate has bypassed teendom altogether and she'll be doomed to be an outcast for the next six years of school. How can kids her age possibly relate to her now?

Kate says, "The wife. What's her name again?"

"Carrie."

"She saw my lax stick on their last walkthrough and asked me about it. The husband stood there with a lame lets-go smile."

They carry the vacuum, broom, and dustpan out to the rental truck and deposit them in the back of the cab. None of the neighbors are out to say goodbye. Which is fine by Elizabeth.

Elizabeth: "One last look?"

"Definitely."

"Will you hold my hand?"

"Only when we're inside."

"Deal."

Kate says, "And we have to talk. We have to say what we're thinking."

Elizabeth doesn't respond. She doesn't want to make any promises that she can't keep.

They walk back into the house. It is so quiet and empty, and with the light fading and filling the house with soft shadows, Elizabeth isn't sure she will make it through this. She lets Kate lead her, pull her along from room to room. In each room Kate details some memories and what she'll miss.

Living room: "I'll miss sleepovers on the couch, watching *Pacific Rim* with Sam. And spying on the boys playing video games."

Kitchen: "I'll miss being the first one up and eating cereal, the cold floor on my feet, and Tommy always spilling his orange juice, you standing at the counter asking him if he needs a sippy cup."

Hallway: "I'll miss hallway dodgeball. And turtle races. I still have like this little scar on my knee from them."

Her bedroom: "I am going to miss my room. All of it." Kate doesn't say anything more.

Elizabeth's room: "I'll miss running in and jumping on the bed to wake you up on Sunday mornings."

Elizabeth looks at Kate. Elizabeth is crying. Kate is not. She is resolute. Has the look of a person with a plan, determined to see it finished.

Elizabeth says, "I will miss that, too, but you can do that and wake me up in the new place." She will not miss this room, not at all. It's become a box of sleepless nights and endless nightmares, both waking and not. The night she and William moved in, they didn't even sleep in this bedroom. They were spooked by how quiet it was and dragged a mattress out into the living room and slept with the curtains open. Leaving the rest of the house behind is difficult. Leaving behind the memories created in this bedroom is necessary, a matter of survival: the shattering arguments with William; the late-night phone calls, one for her ex-husband, one for her son; the past year's worth of secret tears, hidden from Kate; the interminable hours hoping that because they'd found Tommy, he'd come back to see her one last time; staring at the empty space between the chair and the end table, which she never moved or rearranged despite promising herself that the next morning she would move the furniture, and that promise, that lie to herself, was the only way her body would allow her to fall asleep.

The chair and end table are not coming with them to the condo. Elizabeth donated them. She would light this bedroom on fire if she could.

The last stop of the last tour is Tommy's room. His room is completely empty. They stand crowded together in the doorway. They both exhale at the same time and share a nervous smile. Kate is crying now, silently, and wipes at her eyes with her free hand.

Kate says, "You need to say something, Mom."

The memories and emotions swell, and in the shadow of this world-destroying, two-thousand-foot-tall monster wave, there is horror and awe, and privilege, and a sweet, aching melancholy of wonder, of *I was here when he was here,* as the wave breaks over her and will continue to break over her.

She says, "This room is still his, isn't it? Even empty."

"Yeah."

Elizabeth says, "We will spend the rest of our lives saying something about how much we love and miss Tommy. And how much of him is us. And how it all sucks. Sucks hard."

That last part makes Kate laugh a little, and the laugh turns into a shared cry.

Still holding hands as they walk through the hallway toward the front door, Kate lets go, pulls up, and says, "Oh my God. I almost forgot. There's one more thing we have to do, Mom. Is it okay? Just one more?" Kate sounds nervous, and like a kid fighting to not go to bed.

"Okay, yeah. What is it?"

"I left it in the truck. I'll go get it. It'll take me two seconds." Kate doesn't wait for permission and runs out the door, leaving it open.

Elizabeth walks out onto the front stoop and watches her daughter sprint to the truck and then back again, holding something against her chest.

Kate stomps past Elizabeth and into the house, out of breath. "Come on. Back in. Just for a minute. I know this is going to seem weird, but

I talked about it with Dr. Jennifer and when I explained it to her she thought it was okay, and I hope you do too because like I really want to do this. It'll mean a lot to me." She has two pieces of folded paper in her hands. The paper is yellow tinted.

"Where did you get the paper?"

"They're from one of Tommy's sketchbooks."

"What's written on them?"

"Nothing."

Kate hands Elizabeth a page, unfolds it, and it is indeed blank.

"What are we going to do with these?"

"We're going to drop them on the floor and leave them here."

"What?"

"We're not leaving Tommy behind, just like you said in his room, he's us, and that's why there's none of his drawings on the pages because it means we're taking him with us. And it means no more secrets. That's what we're leaving behind us. The secrets."

Despite the new levels of honesty between Kate and Elizabeth, they've spent the last ten months not talking about notes or Tommy's diary pages. They have not discussed the last notes they found, the crumpled ones, and how it was they got to be pinned underneath the avalanche of Tommy's comic art book.

Elizabeth is both proud and terrified of what

her daughter said and of what she's proposing they do with the empty pages. This doesn't feel like a good idea.

Kate grabs Elizabeth's hand and squeezes it. "We'll do it together, at the same time. Please, Mom?"

Elizabeth's hands are sweating. The paper sticks to her pinched fingers. "Okay. Slow down, give me a second. Okay, um, do we need to count down or anything?"

"No, let's drop them when we're ready."

Leaving these two empty sketchbook pages feels wrong, feels sadder than leaving behind an empty house, but it doesn't matter what she thinks, because if it's important to Kate, if Kate needs to do this to be able to go on, then that's what they're doing.

Elizabeth says, "No secrets. I'm not ready. Um, okay, jeeze, I think I need a countdown."

Kate counts to three and they drop their empty pages to the floor. There's a slight rustling sound as they land.

"Thank you, Mom."

Already she regrets the act. It's all she can do to not reach out after the pages, scoop them up and clutch them. Instead, she wraps up Kate in a hug, and then Elizabeth kisses the crown of her head. She should say something but she can't, and the thought of more words—spoken or written—makes her dizzy.

They walk out of the front door arm in arm, and it's too bright outside. She closes her eyes but light fills her head anyway, and it's too much, there can be too much light, and suddenly her need to go back into the house, her house, *their* house, to hide and hunker down at least until it's not so bright out anymore, is a compulsion.

Elizabeth lets Kate go ahead a few steps toward the rental truck as she stops walking altogether. She regrets having to tell a lie, and she hopes it's one that Kate won't catch her in. It could ruin everything between them again, but she has to go back into the house and she has to do it alone.

"Kate. I'll be right out. I have to go pee. Like wicked bad."

"Seriously?"

"Yes. I had two iced coffees. I'll be right out."

Elizabeth is afraid that Kate will follow her back inside the house, so she runs inside and closes the door behind her. Everything is quiet. There's nothing more melancholy than a lived-in, hollowed-out, empty house. She sidesteps the pieces of blank paper they dropped on the floor moments ago and then jogs down the hallway.

Tommy's empty room is a rectangle, half as wide as it is long. The windows have no curtains. Dust floats lazily in the fat sunbeams. The blue walls have nicks and scars and stray pen and pencil marks. Elizabeth is aware of the closet to her left, open just a crack, and aware of the darkness inside it. If she opened the closet door, would the darkness all spill out and cover up the two folded pages in the middle of Tommy's bedroom floor?

The pages are yellow but not an old yellow. The paper is thick, or matted; not regular paper on which you'd scribble lists and reminders. This is serious paper. Special paper.

Elizabeth drifts into the room, so slowly she could get caught in the amber of the sunlight, in the amber of time. Did she hear Kate shutting the truck door? Does that mean she's now sitting in the truck cab, or did she climb out to come back into the house? Either way, Elizabeth knows she can't linger here for as long as she wants to, which is the rest of her life.

She picks up the pages with shaking hands. Their folds feel as thick and formidable as book spines. There is writing on the pages, not much, but it's there, the dark ink bleeding through the backs of the pages. Maybe there's only one line, one small sentence on each page. She's afraid to read the pages, because she thinks she already knows what they have written on them.

She could keep the pages like this, folded and unread, and keep them hidden, and then bring them to the new condo, their new home, the one that isn't a home yet and might not ever feel like one, and then late one night she could drop the pages on her bedroom floor, pretend that Tommy followed them there and would always follow them and would always be with them.

She could open these pages later, sometime later, when she needs to. When she has to.

Elizabeth unfolds the pages and starts to read.

Acknowledgments

Thank you to my family for their love, patience, and understanding.

Thank you to my editor, Jennifer Brehl. She is simply the best. I leaned on her heavily with this book. Or, more accurate, she carried me through the edits of this one. I cannot thank her enough for her support, her levelheadedness, her guidance, and her uncannily keen insight.

Thank you to the whole team of amazing folks at William Morrow. Go team!

Thank you, as always, to my friend and agent, Stephen Barbara, who has been by my literary side for ten years now.

Thank you to writers and friends John Mantooth and John Harvey for being beta readers. Beta reading is not easy, and their input was invaluable. It's not the first time they've helped me, and hope-fully not the last, and no, I am not sharing them with anyone else.

Thank you to all my friends and colleagues who've supported and helped in large ways and/or didn't tell me to shut up when all I was doing was blabbing and stressing out about this book. Laird Barron, Edward Baker, JoAnn Cox, the Dixons, Jack Haringa, the Ferrandizes,

Stephen Graham Jones, Andy Falkous, the Gagnons, Nick "The Hat" Gucker, Sandra Kasturi, John Langan, Sarah Langan, Jennifer Levesque, Stewart O'Nan, the Purcells, John Ryan, Dave Stengel, the Stones, Brett Savory, and Dave Zeltserman.

About the Author

Paul Tremblay is a multiple Bram Stoker Award finalist and the author of *A Head Full of Ghosts*, *The Little Sleep*, and *No Sleep Till Wonderland*. He is a member of the board of directors of the Shirley Jackson Awards, and his essays and short fiction have appeared in the *Los Angeles Times* and numerous year's-best anthologies. He has a master's degree in mathematics and lives in Massachusetts with his wife and two children.

Center Point Large Print
600 Brooks Road / PO Box 1
Thorndike, ME 04986-0001 USA

(207) 568-3717

US & Canada:
1 800 929-9108
www.centerpointlargeprint.com